Insurance

FOR

DUMMIES®

2ND EDITION

Insurance FOR DUMMIES® 2ND EDITION

by Jack Hungelmann

Wiley Publishing, Inc.

Insurance For Dummies®, 2nd Edition

Published by
Wiley Publishing, Inc.
111 River St.
Hoboken, NJ 07030-5774

www.wiley.com

Copyright © 2009 by Jack Hungelmann

Published by Wiley Publishing, Inc., Indianapolis, Indiana

Published simultaneously in Canada

For general information on our other products and services, please contact our Customer Care Department within the U.S. at 877-762-2974, outside the U.S. at 317-572-3993, or fax 317-572-4002.

For technical support, please visit www.wiley.com/techsupport.

Wiley also publishes its books in a variety of electronic formats. Some content that appears in print may not be available in electronic books.

Library of Congress Control Number: 2009926381

ISBN: 978-0-470-46468-7

Manufactured in the United States of America

10 9 8 7 6 5 4

WILEY

About the Author

Jack Hungelmann's policy knowledge, problem-solving expertise, and coverage analysis skills were gained through more than 2,000 hours of education and 35 years in the insurance business as a claims adjuster, agent, and consultant. He has advised individuals and commercial enterprises on their insurance needs and has earned several distinguished designations. Among these are the Certified Insurance Counselor (CIC), the Chartered Property and Casualty Underwriter (CPCU), and the Associate in Reinsurance (ARe).

Jack graduated from the University of Minnesota in 1969 and has taught professional continuing education classes for the CPCU Society and the National Alliance for Insurance Education & Research. He has been published numerous times in *American Agent & Broker* magazine. More recently, he has written and continues to write quarterly articles on personal risk management and insurance for the Web site of the International Risk Management Institute (www.irmi.com).

Jack has personally written newsletters for his clients three times a year for more than 20 years. You can check out back issues of the newsletter, as well as subscribe to future electronic versions, at Jack's Web site (www.jack hungelmann.com). The site also contains Jack's contact information and links to most of his articles from the past several years.

Jack lives in Chaska, Minnesota, with his bride, Judy.

Dedication

To Jewels, the love of my life for 40 years, for her support of the original year-long project, for sacrificing much of our time together, and for her being quiet as a mouse so I could concentrate on the updates needed for this second edition (not easy to do for a flaming extrovert!).

And to the One from whom all inspiration flows, who gave me the vision for this book, the passion for the subject, and the help along the way that made it all possible.

Author's Acknowledgments

Both the original and second edition of this book would never have been possible without the help of many people. In addition to those people who were so helpful in assisting me with the first edition, there are some others I would like to acknowledge for their help with this second edition. I'd like to especially thank my wonderful insurance agent and account manager, Carol Bechay, who was able to handle the majority of the needs of my clients during the writing process. Thanks again to the multitalented Shaun Kuffel for taking such good care of my business clients and helping me solve all kinds of computer dilemmas. Thanks, Brett Erickson, for saving the day and my sanity when my printer kept crashing. Thanks again to Linda Peterson for her continued administrative assistance with the updates to several chapters. Thanks again to Jeanne Hansen, my agent, for all the effort in first believing my book had potential, for all the effort in finding a publisher, and for her help in negotiating the deal. Thanks to the customer-service agents at Corporate 4 Insurance Agency in Edina, Minnesota, where I office, for covering for me and servicing my clients: Randy Macey, Sharon Anderson, Dawn Nelson, Margaret Woolery, and Mary Page.

Thanks to these insurance folks for their technical assistance: Michael Sir (long-term disability), Sonia Kieffer (flood), Rob Olson of IRMI (auto, home, and umbrella), Debra Newman (long-term care), and Ivey Jackson (medical evacuation). Thanks to Maxine Coldren for again allowing use of her calligraphy talents on the Perils of the Sea artwork in Chapter 1.

Thanks to all the folks at John Wiley & Sons for their efforts on this second edition, especially my editor, Elizabeth Kuball. Her regular challenges to me to clarify passages definitely make this second edition easier for readers to understand.

A special thanks to those many clients who have believed enough in my efforts to offer value-added agent services to support the concept financially. I am still in business today, almost 30 years later because of them. Thanks to those of you whose stories I have anonymously shared in this book to help make for better understanding by readers.

And finally, thanks to a fine gentleman, Mr. E. W. Blanch, Sr., a staunch supporter of insurance education and professionalism, who provided me with my first job in the insurance business 30 years ago and who, unknowingly, became a source of inspiration and resolve on my part to pursue those same ideals.

Publisher's Acknowledgments

We're proud of this book; please send us your comments through our Dummies online registration form located at `http://dummies.custhelp.com`. For other comments, please contact our Customer Care Department within the U.S. at 877-762-2974, outside the U.S. at 317-572-3993, or fax 317-572-4002.

Some of the people who helped bring this book to market include the following:

Acquisitions, Editorial, and Media Development

Project Editor: Elizabeth Kuball
(Previous Edition: Keith Peterson)

Acquisitions Editor: Lindsay Lefevere

Copy Editor: Elizabeth Kuball

Assistant Editor: Erin Calligan Mooney

Editorial Program Coordinator: Joe Niesen

Technical Editor: Bruce Payne

Senior Editorial Manager: Jennifer Ehrlich

Editorial Supervisor and Reprint Editor: Carmen Krikorian

Editorial Assistants: Jennette ElNaggar, David Lutton

Cover Photos: Brand X Pictures

Cartoons: Rich Tennant
(`www.the5thwave.com`)

Composition Services

Project Coordinator: Katie Key

Layout and Graphics: Samantha K. Allen, Carl Byers, Reuben W. Davis

Special Art: Maxine Coldren

Proofreaders: Evelyn W. Gibson

Indexer: Becky Hornyak

Publishing and Editorial for Consumer Dummies

Diane Graves Steele, Vice President and Publisher, Consumer Dummies

Kristin Ferguson-Wagstaffe, Product Development Director, Consumer Dummies

Ensley Eikenburg, Associate Publisher, Travel

Kelly Regan, Editorial Director, Travel

Publishing for Technology Dummies

Andy Cummings, Vice President and Publisher, Dummies Technology/General User

Composition Services

Debbie Stailey, Director of Composition Services

Contents at a Glance

Table of Contents

Part V: Managing Life, Health, and Disability Risks... 239

Introduction

"*I*t takes rough seas to make good captains." So says a plaque on my desk, given to me by a good friend who knows that I love to sail.

Storms *do* come up, in all shapes, sizes, and colors: fires, tornadoes, hurricanes, earthquakes, floods, premature death, disability, catastrophic health problems, lawsuits . . . the list goes on and on. You can't always prevent these storms from occurring. But you can take many constructive actions before the storms occur that greatly reduce the damage they cause in your life.

You're already familiar with many of these actions, such as controlling your diet, exercising, wearing your seatbelt, driving a car with an airbag, and installing a home alarm system. And you're at least a little familiar with the device that allows you to share the impact of any losses you have with others — insurance.

Insurance. A dreaded word for most people. Its cringe factor ranks right up there with such joys as filling out your income-tax return, or balancing your checkbook when the bank says you're $500 overdrawn, or shopping for your own cemetery plot. My beloved wife, Judy, has a favorite saying when she has to deal with such dreaded tasks: "I'd rather eat glass!"

If you're a cringer when it comes to insurance, I wrote *Insurance For Dummies* for you. In this book, not only do I demystify the complexity of insurance policies, but I also point out the traps and pitfalls and tell you how you can best protect yourself from getting hurt by them. I wrote this book so that when you need help understanding any insurance topic, you can pull the book down from the shelf and quickly find what you need to know to protect yourself properly.

About This Book

Insurance For Dummies is a reference. You don't need to read the chapters in order from beginning to end — instead, dip into the book to find the information you need today, and pull it down off the shelf when you have questions next week, next month, or next year. I don't expect you to remember anything in this book, either — there won't be a test on it. You can always return to the book when you have questions.

This book is different from other insurance books in several important ways:

- This book is written by someone who has actually worked in the trenches, directly with consumers (people like you!), helping them creatively manage and insure the risks in their lives. So I've filled this book with practical, hands-on advice that really works — not academic stuff.

- This book emphasizes solutions to problems other than just buying insurance. In fact, I include a whole chapter on creative non-insurance strategies that not only help prevent or reduce the chances of a loss happening, but can also lower your insurance costs — strategies like putting jewelry you don't wear in a safe-deposit box rather than insuring it, or carrying higher deductibles than normal on your health insurance if you're fit and healthy.

- This book includes two full chapters on getting what you deserve at claim time — for both claims for damage to your car as well as to your home and belongings. These chapters contain tips I've gathered from my experience as a claims adjuster and an agent, helping clients get what they deserve for 30 years, including

  - How to get paid top dollar for your car when it's stolen or totaled in a collision

  - How to be in the driver's seat and minimize hassles when dealing with insurance adjusters

  - How to create an inventory of your belongings, after they're stolen, so that you can collect the full value of what you lost

- This book addresses *all* areas of personal insurance. Most insurance books are more limited — for example, covering only life insurance, only health insurance, or maybe auto and homeowner's insurance together. But this book covers just about every type of insurance you could ever need help with.

Conventions Used in This Book

I don't use many special conventions in this book, but there are a few you should be aware of:

- When I introduce a new term, I put it in *italics,* followed by a definition of the term (often in parentheses).

- I list Web addresses and e-mail addresses in `monofont`, so they stand out from the surrounding text.

Note: When this book was printed, some Web addresses may have needed to break across two lines of text. If that happened, rest assured that we haven't put in any extra characters (such as hyphens) to indicate the break. So, when using one of these Web addresses, just type in exactly what you see in this book, pretending as though the line break doesn't exist.

What You're Not to Read

You don't have to read any text preceded by a Technical Stuff icon (see the "Icons Used in This Book" section, later, for more on icons) in order to understand the subject at hand. And you can safely skip *sidebars* (text in gray boxes), too — read them if you want the full picture, but know that you can skip them without missing anything critical.

Foolish Assumptions

I don't make many assumptions about you, but I do assume that you're a consumer looking to buy insurance for the first time, or adjust your insurance based on life changes. You may even be an insurance agent (new or seasoned), who's looking for an easy way to explain insurance to your clients.

How This Book Is Organized

Insurance For Dummies is divided into six parts. Here's a thumbnail sketch of what each part contains.

Part 1: Getting Started

In your lifetime, you will face hundreds of insurance decisions. How much is enough coverage for lawsuits? How big a deductible should you choose? Should you buy earthquake insurance if you live in Nebraska?

In this part, I fill you in on seven principles that help you make good insurance decisions — principles like "Don't risk more than you can afford to lose" or "Consider the odds." I also give you non-insurance strategies for reducing the chances of a loss in your life — strategies that can help lower your insurance costs. Finally, I show you the smart way to buy insurance so you'll have all the right coverage when you need it most — at claim time.

Part II: Cars, Boats, RVs, and More: Insuring the Things You Drive

Cars. Boats. Trailers. Recreational vehicles. Whether you own, borrow, or rent, in this part, I give you answers to questions like:

- How much coverage should you buy for lawsuit protection?
- How large a deductible makes good sense for you?
- How do you properly insure your 1965 Mustang, fully restored, so you get paid top dollar for it if it's stolen?
- How can you avoid being uninsured when you rent cars?

Plus, I offer strategies that you can use to get paid what you deserve for your auto insurance claims.

Part III: Home Sweet Home: Understanding Homeowner's Insurance

In this part, I show you how to insure your home and your belongings. I explain what kinds of personal property *aren't* covered by a typical homeowner's policy and tell you how you can get them covered. I introduce you to the most common homeowner's policy exclusions and show you how you can avoid being hurt by them. I cover the special needs of renters and condominium owners. I tell you how to cover yourself against personal lawsuits. And I even show you some of the basics when it comes to insuring a home business. Finally, I teach you some strategies to avoid problems and collect what you deserve for homeowner's property claims.

Part IV: Singin' in the Rain: Umbrella Policies and More

Many people don't realize that, despite their best intentions, they're still at risk of being sued. In this part, I introduce you to umbrella policies, and explain how they protect you from catastrophic lawsuits. I show you how to choose an umbrella policy that covers you for lawsuits not covered by your other policies.

In this part, I also fill you in on the changes you should make to your insurance program when you experience changes in your life, such as getting married, having a baby, hiring a nanny, and losing a loved one.

Part V: Managing Life, Health, and Disability Risks

In this part, I show you how to calculate how much life insurance to buy and what type is best. I offer tips on buying individual health insurance. And I introduce you to Medicare, including prescription drug coverage, and show you what makes a good Medicare supplement policy. I also give advice on buying long-term disability and long-term-care insurance.

Part VI: The Part of Tens

This wouldn't be a *For Dummies* book without The Part of Tens. In this part, I describe the ten ingredients of a watertight insurance program, outline ten government insurance programs and explain how they work, and show you ten ways to save big bucks on car insurance.

Icons Used in This Book

Throughout this book, I use *icons* (little pictures in the margins) to draw your attention to certain kinds of information. Here are the icons I use and a key to what they mean:

This icon reminds you of information so important that you should read it more than once, just to make sure it stays with you.

Maybe you want to know a little more on *why* some insurance strategies work better than others. Maybe you're dying to know the mathematical model I recommend for choosing the most cost-effective deductibles for you. This icon is the place to look for that sort of information. On the other hand, if you just want to catch the basic concepts, give this icon a pass.

This icon flags things that are especially useful for making the most of your insurance program.

This icon alerts you to areas of potential danger. Read any paragraphs that are flagged with this icon and take a close look at your life and your insurance situation.

Where to Go from Here

You've got your copy of *Insurance For Dummies*. Now what? You can dive into this book wherever you want! If you're a new homeowner looking to insure your humble abode, head to Part III. If you have a sneaking suspicion that you don't have the best car insurance, turn to Part II. Use the index and table of contents to locate the topics you're most interested in today.

My wish for you is that your sail through life be a mostly peaceful one, full of gentle breezes. But if storms do come up, I hope the information and the tips I share with you in this book help you buy just the right insurance so that you're fully covered and get paid promptly and fairly.

Part I
Getting Started

The 5th Wave   By Rich Tennant

"Let's see if we can determine your capacity for assuming risk. Now, how familiar are you with snake handling?"

In this part . . .

*B*eing well insured gives you peace of mind. Many people think that they're well insured, only to find out otherwise at claim time. The chapters in this part start the process of fixing that problem by introducing you to principles that will help you make good insurance decisions while at the same time helping to minimize your insurance bill. Then your coverage gaps will be plugged and the peace of mind you feel will be real.

Chapter 1

Building a Great Insurance Program

In This Chapter

▶ Identifying the two keys to a great insurance program

▶ Seeing each type of insurance policy as a component in your overall plan

▶ Dealing effectively with all five major risk areas in your life

Most people buy insurance policies from all over the place. Car insurance here. Home insurance there. Two or three different life insurance policies bought at different times. Some group life insurance at work. Health insurance through an employer. They buy one type of insurance from their travel agency, another from their credit card company.

The first time I meet with a new client, this situation is fairly typical. A virtual hodgepodge of insurance, with several different agents, and no one overseeing the big picture. They're wasting money on overpriced coverages full of gaps and exclusions, and completely missing major coverages like long-term disability.

Does this sound familiar? If so, this book is for you!

Protecting against rovers and assailing thieves

My favorite insurance clause, Perils Clause 12 (see below), comes from the ocean marine cargo policy, crafted by members of the original Lloyd's coffee house in the 1600s, insuring cargo on its way to the new world — and it's still in use today! Metaphorically, you're on a sailboat navigating through life. On your journey, you'll experience rough seas from time to time. Rovers and assailing thieves will appear. But if you've taken the time to build a solid insurance program one policy at a time, your boat will weather the storms.

Perils Clause 12

The adventures and perils which the said Company is content to bear and does take upon itself, are:
of the Seas,
Fire,
Rovers,
Assailing Thieves,
Jettisons,
Criminal Barratry of the
Master and Mariners,
and of all other like perils, losses and misfortunes, that have or shall come to the hurt, detriment, or damage of the aforesaid subject matter of this insurance or any part thereof except as may be otherwise provided for herein or endorsed hereon.

Excerpted from the General Provisions of an Open Cargo Policy

Arming Yourself with the Basics

What makes a great insurance program? Two things:

- **Balance:** A solid insurance program covers all five major risk areas:
  - Major damage to or destruction of your residence
  - Major lawsuits
  - Premature death
  - Long-term disability
  - Major medical bills
- **Customized coverage:** every policy covering these five major risk areas has been custom-designed with high limits and the proper endorsements to cover the unique risks in your life that otherwise would not be covered by off-the-shelf policies.

Throughout this book, I refer to seven guiding principles that can help you make good choices on what to insure and what not to insure. For example, one of the principles is, "Don't risk more than you can afford to lose." If you can't afford to lose your income, you need to buy long-term disability insurance, in case you're ever disabled. Chapter 2 gives you all the guiding principles.

Believe it or not, insurance isn't always the answer. In Chapter 3, I introduce four non-insurance strategies for managing the risks in your life. Implementing these strategies (for example, pay extra for added airbags and antilock brakes to reduce your risk of injury) can help lower your insurance bill.

What's the best way to buy insurance: Here's a hint: It's not by calling around for quotes, making sure the coverage is "apples to apples" and then buying insurance from whoever has the lowest bid. The best way to buy insurance is to select a highly skilled agent who can help you build the best possible insurance program. In Chapter 4, I tell you how to find the best agent for you.

Insuring the Things You Drive

Several of the major risks you face in your life are associated with driving your own vehicles — whether it's your car, a rental car, a boat, an RV, or some other type of vehicle.

In Chapter 5, I walk you through each of the coverages of a personal auto policy. I help you figure out how much liability insurance is enough, tell you how to save money by eliminating overlapping medical coverage or opting for higher deductibles, give you advice on when to drop collision and comprehensive coverage from your older car, and more.

In Chapter 6, I tell you about specific risks that you take on when renting a vehicle and how you can protect yourself from each of them without spending the enormous amount of money that rental agencies charge. I also explain the coverage pitfalls of the free company car your employer provides you for work and how to sidestep them. I also give you tips on covering special vehicles, such as motorcycles and antique and collectible cars.

Chapter 7 deals with the risk of boats, RVs, snowmobiles, golf carts, and more — including both liability and physical damage issues whether you own, borrow, or rent them. I show you the most economical way to buy the coverage that you need. In Chapter 7, I also address all different types of trailer risks — for example, the liability risk when you tow an owned or non-owned trailer behind your vehicle, when you park your trailer at home or, if you have a camping trailer, when you park it for the summer on a rented trailer lot.

In Chapter 8, I show you how to get paid what you deserve at claim time for all different types of automobile claims — when the accident is your fault, when it's the other guy's fault, when your vehicle is stolen. I give you tips for collecting more than blue-book value for your better-than-average car. I also show you how the appraisal clause works when you and the insurance company can't agree on a price.

Finding Your Way Home with Homeowner's Insurance

Your home is likely the biggest asset you'll ever own. Insuring your home adequately is essential. Every homeowner's policy is divided into six parts, each with its own coverage limits (see Chapter 9). I introduce you to six different homeowner's forms as well — four forms designed for homeowners, one form for renters, and one form for condominium or town house owners. I show you how to choose the proper coverages for your building, contents and personal liability.

But homeowner's insurance isn't just about insuring the house itself — it's also about insuring your property inside the house. Many different exclusions and limitations apply to personal property. For example, jewelry has a dollar limit for theft, as well as the exclusion for loss of the stone from the setting. Jewelry is also very difficult to value after the loss. Scheduling jewelry specifically by having it appraised and added to the policy is the insurance industry recommendation for this type of risk — but it's not the best solution for an antique piece with huge sentimental value, which you have no intention of replacing. If cash won't make you whole, I don't recommend scheduling these kinds of jewelry. In this case, you're far better off putting your special item in a safe deposit box and preventing the loss from happening in the first place. In Chapter 10, I give you the information you need to prevent this type of exclusion and others from hurting you.

Chapter 11 is all about many of the exclusions and limitations in a homeowner's policy and ways to work around them. For example, a homeowner's policy contains an absolute business exclusion, which means that if you frequently work from home and occasionally have UPS deliver a business-related package to your home, and if that delivery person slips on your icy driveway, is injured, and sues you, your homeowner's policy will not defend you, nor will it pay any judgment against you. Why? Because the injury was business-related. But you don't have to live with this gap: The solution to this particular problem is to add a $20-per-year endorsement to the policy that covers that type of claim.

Chapter 11 also covers flood insurance and whether you're a candidate for it. Here's a hint: You probably are — even if you don't live anywhere near a body of water; but you're probably not if your lower-level floor is below ground level on all four sides.

Condominium and town house owners have special insurance needs and have a homeowner's policy form created just for those needs. If you buy the standard condominium unit owner policy off the shelf with no customization and no special endorsements, odds are, if you have any kind of claim, you'll be sorely disappointed. In Chapter 12, I alert you to what the pitfalls are and give you my recommendations on how to circumvent each of them so you don't get hurt. If you own a town house or condominium — or even a vacation timeshare — you'll benefit greatly from Chapter 12.

If you have a home-based business, you need to deal with many risks — both property and liability risks. In Chapter 13, I fill you in on these risks and tell you how to get the insurance you need as a business owner. (**Hint:** It's generally not to buy an endorsement to your homeowner's policy. Even the best of these business endorsements are too restrictive, particularly when it comes to liability off premises.)

I wrap up the part on homeowner's insurance with tips on collecting what you deserve for homeowner's claims. I give you the steps to take to get a great structural claim settlement. And if you have a personal property loss, you'll benefit from my tips for getting paid top dollar for your claim.

Preparing for a Rainy Day with an Umbrella Policy

One of the most important personal policies you can own is the personal umbrella policy, which has three basic advantages:

- A million dollars or more of catastrophic liability protection
- Extra defense coverage in case you're sued
- Coverage for some of the exposures not covered by auto and home-owner's insurance policies

Chapter 15 covers the basics of umbrella policies, and in Chapter 16, I detail the many different gaps that an umbrella policy can cover and show you how to choose a policy that covers the gaps in your life not otherwise covered by your auto or homeowner's policy.

In Chapter 17, we switch gears a bit. Here I cover many of the changes you face in your adult life (everything from getting married to having a baby to building a house to hiring a nanny and more), tell you what some of the added exposures are during those changes, and explain the changes you should make to your program so these new exposures are covered properly.

Life, Health, and Disability: Protecting Yourself and Those You Love

Health insurance consists of several important ingredients, and in Chapter 18 I tell you what those are and how to get them right. If individual health insurance is what you're after (because you don't have insurance through a job, for example), you'll appreciate the money-saving tips in Chapter 18, too. I show you how you can pay for medical costs with pretax dollars and intro-duce health savings accounts and how they work. Plus, I offer tips on dealing with various types of health insurance problems (from finding health insur-ance when you can't qualify medically on your own to deciding whether to continue to cover your college-age kid on your policy or take her off and rely on just the coverage available from the college).

Just because you have health insurance through your job doesn't mean you're off the hook. In Chapter 19, on group health insurance, I show you how to make a good decision when your employer offers you two or more different plans. I also help you evaluate whether to cover your dependents on the group policy or get them individual policies. And I explain your rights when you're leaving a job. Finally, I explain how a new program guarantees you the right to get individual or group coverage without facing any limitations on any pre-existing medical conditions you or your family members might have.

Chapter 20 is a brand-new chapter to this edition of *Insurance For Dummies* — it's on Medicare and Medicare supplements. Volumes of books have been written about this subject, but if you're like most people, you're overwhelmed. So, I start out the chapter by outlining the steps that I recommend my own clients take when they qualify for Medicare. In other words, I cut to the chase. And yes, the chapter does include information and tips to help you make good choices around the complicated and confusing Medicare Part D prescription drug coverage.

Chapter 21, also new to this edition of the book, covers the basics of long-term care insurance and helps you evaluate your own need for coverage. I explain the new Medicaid partnership program and how it makes it easy for most people to determine how much coverage to buy.

Long-term disability is the subject of Chapter 22. I help you determine how much coverage to buy and evaluate possible sources of coverage. I also show you the shortcomings in group long-term disability programs and how to get supplemental insurance to protect yourself.

Last, but not least, is Chapter 23 on buying life insurance. In this chapter, I help you determine how much life insurance to buy; plus, I introduce you to the different types of life insurance and explain which ones make the most sense for your situation. I close the chapter introducing several different myths and misconceptions about life insurance (for example, that life insurance is cheaper when you're young — it's not!) and provide accurate information.

Chapter 2

Introducing Seven Guiding Principles of Insurance

I'm writing this book to help you take responsibility for your life. I'm writing for people who don't want to be victims — people who want the tools and information to be empowered when they make decisions. If that sounds like you, you're in the right place!

Throughout this book, I regularly refer to seven guiding principles, all of which I cover in greater detail in this chapter. Follow these seven principles when making decisions about your insurance program, and your decisions will be good ones.

Keep It Simple

Managing *risk* (the chance of a loss happening) and buying insurance is tough enough without making it any more complicated than it has to be. For every risk I show you, generally more than one strategy exists that effectively minimizes that risk. Using the keep it simple principle, you take the simple path. *Simple* means easier and more likely to be implemented — simple is not less effective.

Here's an example of how this principle can be used: Following a major fire or burglary, one of the requirements in a homeowner's policy is to create an inventory of what was lost or destroyed, including, if possible, any receipts and canceled checks. Does that sound like a nightmare to you? It is! Even harder than *documenting* what you had is *remembering* what you had! Imagine coming home from a hard day at the office and finding either charred remains of what was once your dream home or finding your front door broken and your home torn apart by a burglar. The emotional trauma is bad enough. But, in addition, you have to remember what's missing, because you only get paid for what you can remember.

A *policy* is the legal contract between you and an insurance company in which the company agrees to pay covered claims when you have them in exchange for a monthly (or some other periodic) payment from you. Any given policy contains many coverages.

Conventional insurance wisdom has always held that the solution to this dilemma is to fill out a household inventory booklet prior to any loss, listing descriptions and values for every piece of personal property you own in every room of the house. Talk about a fun way to spend an evening — or, more realistically, your two-week vacation.

A written inventory isn't such a bad idea, but it violates the keep it simple principle because it's complex, and it takes far too much time. As a result, it's rarely accomplished.

A far simpler strategy for handling this documentation is a video or photographic inventory. This approach is easy, fast (you can film the whole house in an hour or two), and even fun — especially when you add a verbal description: "This vase here that looks like a garage sale reject is really an antique from the Ming Dynasty worth $2.5 million."

I particularly like the video strategy because everything you own can be on one tape or DVD, it's easily stored, and, best of all, you can easily add to it when you acquire new things. If you don't own a video camera, you can easily rent or borrow one. An extra benefit of having filmed documentation at claim time is a reduced need for receipts: Most adjusters will waive that requirement if they can see the item in your home prior to the loss, in some kind of photographic format. All in all, the video strategy is superior in every way to the written inventory strategy. Of course, if the house burns down, so will all your records, so be sure to store the photos or DVD safely off-premises (for example, in a safe-deposit box at your bank).

Don't Risk More than You Can Afford to Lose

I'm all for taking risks if it makes economic sense. Carrying large *deductibles* (the amount of a loss that you pay out of your own pocket before insurance kicks in) to lower insurance costs is a smart gamble if you save enough on your *premiums* (the price you pay for the insurance policy covering a defined time period — for example, six months or a year). Not buying collision insurance on older cars that you could afford to replace is another smart gamble. But be sure to insure any risk that is a part of your life if the risk could cause you major financial loss — if it's more than you can afford to lose.

For example, the financial hardship of your paycheck stopping as a result of a long-term illness or injury is substantial. About one-third of all workers, at some point in their career, have a long-term disability. Yet, many people who totally depend on their paycheck don't have disability insurance. Big mistake — it's a clear violation of the principle to only risk what you can afford to lose. Disability insurance is the most under-purchased major insurance coverage in this country. (*Coverage* is a promise to pay a certain type of claim if it occurs; other examples include automobile liability coverage, theft coverage, and so on.) If the loss of your income would cause major financial problems in your household, and your employer doesn't provide disability insurance for you, make sure you carry a good disability policy. (I explain what makes a good disability policy in Chapter 22.)

Don't Risk a Lot for a Little

Spending a little now (for coverage) makes more sense than spending a lot of your own money later when something happens that you're not covered for.

Most people who buy insurance can't afford to buy unlimited quantities; you probably don't have millions of dollars of liability coverage, for example. So you tend to buy a limit that feels comfortable and doesn't blow your budget. But too many people are considerably under-insured, and, tragically, they're seldom aware that better insurance would cost them very little.

Liability is your financial obligation to another person (or persons) for injuries or property damage you cause. Liability coverage is a promise in an insurance policy to defend you in court and pay what you owe another person (or persons) for injuries or property damage you cause, up to the liability limits you chose.

Using car insurance as an example, the most commonly purchased liability insurance limit in the United States today is $100,000 per person for injuries you cause to others. Is that enough to pay for a seriously injured person's medical bills and lost wages, as well as compensation for that person's pain and suffering? Just the medical bills alone could easily use up the entire coverage limit, leaving you to personally pay all other costs, plus some of your own defense costs. Your personal, uninsured financial loss could easily reach several hundred thousand dollars. Table 2-1 shows some typical annual costs for additional liability coverage for two cars in a metropolitan area.

Table 2-1	Typical Annual Liability Costs for Two Cars	
Liability Limit	Additional Annual Costs beyond the Cost for $100,000	The Amount of Additional Coverage beyond $100,000
$300,000	$50	$200,000
$500,000	$80	$400,000
$1.5 million	$150	$1.4 million
$2.5 million	$225	$2.4 million

Following the rule to not risk a lot for a little means that you shouldn't buy only $100,000 of coverage when each additional $100,000 of coverage costs so little. In fact, you can usually pay for the extra cost simply by boosting your policy deductibles to the next level. Increasing your deductible by $250 to $500 often saves you enough on your insurance bill to pay for most or all of the added cost of additional liability coverage.

Consider the Odds

This rule says that when the odds of a claim happening are virtually zero, and the insurance costs are inappropriately high, you shouldn't buy the insurance. Considering the odds also means buying insurance when the possibility exists that a serious claim could occur.

Homeowner's policies exclude earthquake losses. But they do offer an option to buy the coverage for an additional charge. Here are two examples of how the principle of considering the odds applies: It's estimated that only about 20 percent of California homeowners had earthquake coverage to protect themselves against the devastating California earthquake of 1989, despite the high odds of an earthquake occurring. The 80 percent who were uninsured were in clear violation of both this rule (to consider the odds) and the rule not to risk more than you can afford to lose. As a result, many homeowners suffered ruinous, uninsured earthquake losses that easily could have been avoided with the purchase of insurance.

But, if you live in an area that has no prior history of earthquakes and is located nowhere near any known fault lines, the probability of an earthquake may be near zero. In this instance, considering the odds means maybe not buying earthquake insurance if it costs more than a few dollars a year.

Like earthquake damage, flood and surface-water losses are excluded under the traditional homeowner's policy. Considering the odds means that if your home is located high on the pinnacle of a hill overlooking a valley and your basement is unfinished, you probably don't need to spend your money on flood insurance. On the other hand, if your home is located in a low-lying flood plain or near a river, you probably should consider buying flood insurance, because the odds of a large loss are good. (Flood insurance is available from the federal government — more on that in Chapter 11.)

Risk a Little for a Lot

This principle encourages you to avoid insurance when the risk is small in relation to the amount of the premium. Say, for example, you own a 1996 Honda worth $1,000. You were just hit with a DUI, and you're facing premiums of two to three times what you had been paying — not just this year, but for each of the next three to five years. Your collision insurance premium with a $500 deductible has just increased from $100 to $300 a year. If you keep this coverage, the maximum risk to the insurance company is the value of the car ($1,000) minus your deductible ($500) minus the salvage value of the car ($50), which totals $450. This rule advises you not to buy what turns out to be $450 of insurance for a $300 annual premium. Under these circumstances, the smart move is to drop the collision coverage.

Avoid Las Vegas Insurance

Avoid any insurance that transfers only part of the risk to the insurance company, leaving you unprotected for the rest. Accidental-death insurance purchased from an airport vending machine is a good example. It often only pays if you die in a plane crash in the next few days! What you really may need is more life insurance, protecting you all the time and from any cause.

With Las Vegas insurance, you are, in effect, betting that if the claim occurs, it will be the result of a limited cause of loss you bet on. Not smart. Table 2-2 shows some examples of Las Vegas insurance and a better alternative that gets rid of the gamble.

Table 2-2	Types of Insurance and the Associated Risks	
Type of Insurance	*The Pitfalls*	*Better Solution*
Accidental death	Pays only if you die accidentally	Life insurance
Travel accident	Pays medical bills only if incurred on a trip	Major medical health insurance
Cancer or dread disease coverage	Pays only medical bills caused by a specific calamity	Major medical health insurance
Rush-hour liability insurance	Doubles your lawsuit protection if the accident occurs between 7 a.m. and 8:30 a.m. or between 4:30 p.m. and 6 p.m.	Adequately high auto liability limits

Yes, the last item in Table 2-2 is tongue in cheek — no insurance company has come out with rush-hour insurance yet — but I hope it makes the point. The bottom line? If you buy any insurance that transfers only part of the risk — as these examples of Las Vegas coverage do — you leave yourself vulnerable. Spend a little more money, and get much better insurance.

Buy Insurance Only as a Last Resort

This principle advises you to buy insurance only when it's the best and most cost-effective solution. You have many options in treating any given risk; insurance is only one. Treat your risks with non-insurance strategies first. (See Chapter 3 for all kinds of information on how to do that.)

Here's one example of how this principle works: Say you've inherited Grandma's heirloom sterling silver. It's precious to you, so, naturally, you want the best coverage possible. Your agent has you get an appraisal that costs you $100. You buy a special rider to your homeowner's policy covering the silver's appraised value of $10,000 at a premium of $90 a year. One year later, burglars break into your home and steal your precious heirloom. In the meantime, the silver has increased in value to $15,000. You collect the $10,000 insurance proceeds from the policy, but you've suffered three disappointments:

- ✔ The $5,000 difference between the value of the stolen silver and the amount that insurance covered.

- ✔ Grandma's pattern has been discontinued and it's difficult to find an identical match.

- ✔ Even if you find the same pattern, it doesn't have the sentimental value that Grandma's *exact* set had.

Insurance is not the best solution for managing this risk — not only because cash is a poor substitute for treasures, but also because of the hassle and cost of the appraisal, as well as the insurance premium that's due every year.

A better, non-insurance, method for handling Grandma's silver risk (and at the same time following the keep it simple strategy) is to store the silver in an off-premises safe-deposit box, thus preventing the loss almost entirely. Or, if that isn't practical because you want to use the silver for special occasions, hide it well, reducing by about 90 percent the chance of a loss through theft. You can further reduce the risk by adding a central burglar alarm.

When it comes to irreplaceable treasures, preventing the loss altogether is a far better strategy than insurance, without the costs or the pitfalls of insurance coverage.

Chapter 3

Managing Your Risk without Buying Insurance

In This Chapter

▶ Using non-insurance strategies to manage the risks in your life

▶ Watching out for contracts that give you all the liability

▶ Applying insurance and non-insurance strategies to everyday problems

My goal with this book is to provide you with the tools you need to effectively manage the personal risks in your life. Insurance is an effective way of managing risk, but it's not the only way. You can identify risks and treat them with creative, non-insurance strategies — and you should do so whenever possible, instead of limiting yourself to buying insurance. Non-insurance strategies reduce your insurance costs and are often more effective than their insurance counterparts.

Many people throw insurance at every problem. Their kid turns 16, and they rush out to buy insurance. They inherit a stamp collection worth $50,000, and they buy more insurance. They rent a car on vacation and buy insurance for that car.

In this chapter, I fill you in on a different and better way of doing things: risk management. The essence of risk management is to treat risks with non-insurance methods first and to buy insurance second. I start this chapter by giving you four non-insurance strategies for reducing risk. Then I put those strategies into action with a real-life case study.

Practicing the ARRT of Risk Management

When it comes to risk management, there are four non-insurance strategies you can put to work in your life. To make it easier for you to remember them, just think of the acronym *ARRT*:

A = Avoid

R = Reduce

R = Retain

T = Transfer

In the following sections, I get into greater detail on each of these.

Avoiding risk

Avoiding risk means exactly what it says: When none of the other strategies for treating a risk seems suitable, sometimes the wisest decision is to simply avoid the risk. I avoid risks like skydiving, hang gliding, and auto racing. I'm sure I would enjoy those activities if I ever took them up. It's just that, for me, the rewards aren't worth the risks.

Here are some other examples where avoiding the risk may be the best strategy:

- Not licensing a teenage driver who is clearly still immature and irresponsible
- Not buying an expensive sports car while your driving record is poor and insurance costs are sky high
- Canceling your vacation plans to a war-ravaged part of the world
- Not buying a backyard trampoline for your kids because you can't prevent unsupervised use by other neighborhood children

Reducing risk

Reducing risk means taking actions that lower the probability of the loss happening at all or, if it does occur, lowering the loss's possible severity. If you've inherited Grandma's sterling silver, you can reduce the theft risk by installing a central home alarm and/or by hiding the silver well. If you have a valuable baseball-card collection, you can greatly reduce the water damage risk by mounting and sealing the cards in waterproof plastic album pages (as my son, JP, did with my card collection for Father's Day one year).

Here are some other examples of ways you can reduce your risks:

✔ Regularly checking prongs on a valuable diamond ring to reduce the risk of loss of the stone

✔ Eating healthy foods and working out regularly, not smoking, and getting plenty of rest

✔ Not drinking and driving

✔ Buying cars with safety features like air bags and antilock brakes and that test well in crash tests

Reducing risk has the advantage of being the one treatment strategy you can do the most with and have the most personal control over. It has other advantages, too. If you significantly reduce a risk:

✔ The risk may be small enough that you feel safe avoiding insurance altogether. For example, if you've stored your valuables in a safe-deposit box, you may not feel the need to insure them.

✔ You may feel comfortable carrying higher deductibles. For example, you may be able to save 50 percent on your health insurance costs by buying a $2,000 deductible, and know that a high deductible is a smart choice because your healthy lifestyle results in few claims.

✔ You may be able to get insurance at a better cost.

Throughout this book, I talk a lot about reducing risk — and I recommend it as at least a part of the solution to managing many of the risks in your life.

Retaining risk

Retaining risk refers to the strategy of paying losses out of your own pocket. Retaining risk can be *voluntary* (such as carrying higher deductibles in order to lower your premiums). Retaining may mean choosing to take the entire risk on less valuable items; for example, you may forgo insurance on a $300 canoe. Retaining may mean not carrying insurance to cover low-frequency catastrophic losses that have almost no chance of happening where you live; for example, you probably won't buy earthquake insurance if you live in Minnesota.

Retaining risk can also be *involuntary* — bad news. In this category are the surprises you get at claim time, the risks you take every day without even knowing it, such as:

- ✔ Not having any coverage to protect against an injury lawsuit from the person who delivers a package to your home-based business and falls and is injured on your icy sidewalk

- ✔ Not being protected against the lawsuit from your co-worker who was injured while riding with you in your company car

- ✔ Receiving only $30,000 for your $50,000 kitchen fire because of depreciation deductions under your homeowner's policy

- ✔ Being sued by a car-rental company for $10,000 in damages to a rental car — damages caused by a friend or co-worker — for which you naively agreed to be responsible when you scribbled your signature on the rental agreement

Much of the focus of this book is on uncovering these involuntary retentions — the many pitfalls of personal policies. Throughout this book, I expose these hidden risks and show you steps you can take to protect yourself.

Transferring risk

Transferring risk refers to shifting the risk in whole or in part from yourself to another party. The most common form of transfer is the insurance mechanism whereby, in exchange for a predetermined premium payment, an insurance company will assume losses that you would've otherwise had to absorb yourself.

Here's an example: You transfer the risk of fire damage to your home to an insurer for $800 a year. Your home is destroyed by fire. The insurance company pays the entire cost to rebuild, the cost to replace all your destroyed belongings, and even the additional costs you incur to live elsewhere while your new home is being rebuilt.

The other type of transfer (the bad kind) occurs in just about every contract you sign in your daily life. "But I *never* sign contracts," you're thinking. Really? I bet you do — we all do. In any given year, you likely sign contracts for an apartment lease, a boat rental, a vacation condo, a rental car, a credit card, a real estate purchase, or a home-repair proposal. These are just some examples of the contracts you sign in your daily life. I could give you many more. It's almost impossible to be alive and not sign contracts in today's busy world. In just about every one of these contracts, someone is trying to transfer some kind of risk to you, often without your knowledge. If there's a problem, you're simply out of luck. Courts don't accept failure to read what you've signed as an excuse.

Take a closer look at two types of everyday contracts in which you assume responsibility unknowingly, and the surprises that can be waiting for you.

- **Renting a chainsaw from a hardware store:** You assume absolute liability for damage to the saw, even if it's not your fault, as well as all liability for injuries to another person (for example, a friend using the saw), even if the injury was caused by a defect in the saw. You also release the store from responsibility for your injuries, even if they're caused by a defect in the saw.

- **Wedding reception catering:** You assume all liability for injuries to guests, even when they're caused by the negligence of the restaurant (for example, food poisoning). You agree to pay all defense costs of the restaurant in such injury lawsuits and to pay any judgment against the restaurant out of your own pocket.

Can you imagine how upset you'd be if some dear friends at your daughter's wedding reception suffered serious illness or even death from contaminated food, and you were forced to pay to defend the restaurant? Plus, you had to pay all judgments against the restaurant, just because you innocently signed a contract to do so?

Does this scare you? I hope so. Fear is a good thing when it keeps you from hurting yourself. And if you don't start paying attention to the routine contracts of your daily life, you could easily assume a risk that can ruin you financially.

Putting ARRT into Action: A Case Study

The four risk treatment strategies of avoid, reduce, retain, and transfer work together. In fact, you're more likely to combine the strategies instead of using them individually.

Here's a case study that's just one example of how you can put ARRT into action in your daily life: Let's say your son is about to turn 16, and he wants to get his driver's license.

You can obviously **avoid** the risks associated with a 16-year-old driver by not allowing him to get a driver's license. Other methods of avoiding this risk include chaining your teenager in the cellar or giving him up for adoption — but I'm guessing that, no matter how annoying his attitude can be at times, you're not quite ready to get rid of him.

Avoiding is the strategy to take when none of the other strategies for treating a risk seems suitable. Odds are, when it comes to your teen, you'll be able to manage the risk through a combination of the other three strategies and allow him to drive. (And no, he didn't put me up to this.)

You can **reduce** the risks of injuries, property damage, and lawsuits by:

- ✔ Requiring your teenager to spend 30 or 40 hours of practice behind the wheel, alongside you, while facing all different driving scenarios and weather conditions

- ✔ Buying him a structurally solid and mechanically safe car, with working seat belts and air bags, to minimize injuries

- ✔ Asking your teen to sign a contract such as the Students Against Destructive Decisions (SADD) Contract for Life (available at www.sadd. org/contract.htm), where he agrees not to drive after using drugs or alcohol, and you agree to pick him up anytime, anyplace, without giving him a hard time

You can **retain** some or all of the risk of damage to the car itself (collision, fire, theft) by either not buying damage insurance on the car at all or, if the car is worth too much, at least choosing large deductibles. This strategy will save you a bundle on your insurance costs.

You can **transfer** the ownership risk of personal lawsuits related to vehicle maintenance by transferring the vehicle title and maintenance responsibility to your teenager. This strategy won't absolve you of responsibility for your teen's behavior, but it can avoid lawsuits against you related to not maintaining the vehicle in a reasonable manner. Your teen has considerably fewer assets and income than you do and is much less a target for lawsuits than you are, so he'll need far less liability insurance coverage. (See my tips on insuring your teenage driver in Chapter 6.)

Be sure to check your state law to find the minimum age at which your teen can legally own a vehicle; you can find this information by contacting your state's Department of Motor Vehicles.

Managing super risks

In 1992, the Super Bowl was held in Minneapolis, which created an unexpected windfall for a few of my clients with nice homes. The hoopla of the Super Bowl attracts many more people than will ever attend the game itself, and there's a severe shortage of hotel rooms and other types of housing. About a month before the game, I started getting calls from clients who were being offered incredible sums of money ($10,000 for two weeks) to rent their homes to wealthy groups of international visitors wanting a nice environment for sleeping and entertaining. Understandably, the offers were incredibly tempting. But they were dangerous too, because the standard homeowner's insurance policy is normally suspended during such a significant increase in exposure, which means my clients would have been totally uninsured for fires, injury lawsuits, and many other claims occurring during the rental.

The safest strategy was obviously to **avoid** the risk altogether and not rent out their homes. But for those who succumbed to the lure of the large cash offer, I suggested the following strategies:

✔ We **reduced** the risk by collecting sizable damage deposits and checking references.

✔ We **transferred** risks contractually to the renters through a short-term rental contract making them absolutely liable for all damages to building and contents, as well as all injuries, regardless of fault. And we required them to provide proof, prior to occupancy, of both property and liability insurance, which named each of my clients as an additional insured for the duration of the rental.

✔ Just in case the contractual transfer didn't hold up, we **transferred** property and liability risks to insurance by successfully negotiating with my clients' home and umbrella liability insurers to waive any coverage suspensions on grounds of the short duration of the rental. *Note:* The only time this negotiation is possible is *before* the loss. All the insurers reluctantly agreed. To make certain that there would be no misunderstandings with the insurance companies, we got written confirmation.

By paying close attention to all the risks and applying creative insurance and non-insurance strategies, the potential financial ruin was averted, and my clients were $10,000 richer. I wish I'd been working on a percentage!

Chapter 4

Buying Insurance

· ·

In This Chapter

▶ Looking at the dangers of buying insurance on price alone

▶ Identifying the two components of a great insurance program

▶ Finding a top insurance advisor at no extra cost

· ·

great insurance program has two key components:

✔ Your program is in balance in all major risk areas.

✔ Each policy that you buy is well-designed with high limits for major loss coverages and with all the right endorsements that customize your policy to cover the risks in your life that would not otherwise be covered.

You'll have a better chance of accomplishing both goals if you take time to locate a highly skilled insurance agent who's an expert on every type of personal insurance that you need.

Yes, the cost of insurance is important. You want your costs to be competitive and manageable. But the true cost of your insurance program is not only what you pay upfront in premiums but more importantly what you have to pay out-of-pocket at claim time. Most people who shop for insurance put all the emphasis on the front end costs — the premiums — and then may end up having to pay thousands or hundreds of thousands of dollars in uncovered claims later.

When it comes to insurance costs, it's far better to pay a little too much in premiums than to pay for an uncovered major claim later.

Understanding What Makes a Balanced Insurance Program

There are several major risks that you face regularly throughout your lifetime that, if they occur, can cause your financial ruin: major medical bills, major damage to or destruction of your residence, major lawsuits and the cost of defending them, long-term disability, premature death, and — especially for those over age 40 — the risk of extended long-term care.

Your insurance program is in balance if each of these major risk areas are equally well covered and you're not spending too much on one area and too little on another.

Many people have major-loss coverage that's out of balance. They may have a good medical plan with high limits, but no coverage for long-term disabilities. They may have $1 million of life insurance on the breadwinner, but none on the homemaker. Their home may be fully insured, but they have only $100,000 of coverage for lawsuits and no umbrella liability policy.

A highly-skilled agent can help you identify imbalances in your insurance program and suggest the corrective action needed, which is why taking the time to find the right agent is so important. Most people who buy insurance don't take the time to find the right agent for them. They let whoever answered the phone and gave them the quote be their agent, without any knowledge of that person's skill level. And, in the end, they get a less-skilled agent than they could have had for the same price.

For more information on finding the right insurance agent, turn to "Choosing Your Professional Advisor," later in this chapter.

Customizing Each Policy to Meet Your Unique Needs

The ideal insurance policy is a single page that simply says, "If you have a loss — no matter what the cause and no matter how high the cost — we will cover it in full." No exclusions. No 20-page policies. Wouldn't that be wonderful?

Because that policy isn't going to be available anytime soon, you want to get as close as possible to that ideal using a combination of several policies. In this book, I introduce you to the basics of each kind of personal policy and how to choose limits for each coverage. I show you what optional coverages everyone should buy and what optional endorsements are available to cover those risks unique to you that would not otherwise be covered under the basic policy.

One of the key guiding principles from Chapter 2 says, "Don't risk more than you can afford to lose." That means having all major risk areas in your life well covered. In order to accomplish that objective, you should work with a highly skilled professional agent.

Choosing Your Professional Advisor

Automobile, home, boat, umbrella, and other personal policies, as they're sold off the shelf, rarely, if ever, cover all your major property and liability risks. But they will cover most, if not all, of those major risks if they're customized to your needs with proper coverage limits and appropriate coverage endorsements. Customizing a policy requires a great deal of coverage expertise and care. And that's why, for most people, locating and hiring the best possible advisor has to be the very highest priority when it comes to buying insurance.

Bargain-basement brain surgery

Suppose you've been told you need brain surgery. If you shop for it the way many people shop for insurance, here's what you do: You start by calling around town, getting quotes over the phone. You probably aren't exactly sure what kind of brain surgery you need, so you decide to get a price for the type that you think you *probably* need. You get quotes from all over — from surgeons, clinics, hospitals, and even medical-school interns. You're not concerned about skill — just price. After all, it's only brain surgery.

You find a clinic that will do the surgery you think you need for the lowest price. You sign up for the brain surgery. The intern who answered the phone when you called does the surgery, even though one of the top brain surgeons in the area works for the clinic and would do the surgery for the same price as the intern. The intern, lacking the expertise to diagnose the exact type of surgery you need, performs the surgery you asked for in the quote. The top brain surgeon would have known enough to recognize that what you requested was the wrong procedure for you and would put you at risk for serious brain damage. She would have recommended a different, more expensive, but much more helpful surgery instead.

Insurance isn't brain surgery. But it isn't a commodity either. The moral of the story is that if you shop for insurance like this, you'll probably end up with the wrong diagnosis, with possible serious side effects, and with a less skilled advisor than you need and could have had for the same price.

Understanding how agents get paid

In almost all states, agents selling personal insurance get paid the same commission as every other agent representing that particular insurance company — usually about 10 percent to 15 percent — regardless of the agent's experience, the agent's skill level, or the quality of the insurance plan that the agent designs. This payment structure is both good news and bad news for you.

The good news: Getting an expert for the price of a novice

Although the flat commission compensation system is anti-consumer (rewarding quantity of sales rather than quality), you can really benefit from the system in one way: You can buy the very best talent for not a penny more than you would pay for the worst possible agent! Can you see how ridiculous it is to select your agent based on the warm body who gives you the quote? The vast majority of the time, the person you talk with the first time you call a company will not be one of that insurance company's most skilled agents.

Almost all insurance buyers see an insurance premium as buying them one thing — an insurance policy. In reality, the premium pays for much more than that. The policy, the coverage, and the insurance company make up about 85 percent of the premium. Professional advice, policy service, and help from a professional agent when there is a problem make up the other 15 percent. Spend that 15 percent wisely! Get the best agent that you can find.

The more complex your lifestyle and the more of a lawsuit target you are, the more important it is to take the time to find an agent with the most expertise that you can.

The bad news: Finding a needle in a haystack

The "everybody gets paid the same" rule for agent compensation has one big drawback: The marketplace pushes agents with greater skills away from smaller, personal insurance policies and their small commissions into business insurance, where the premiums and commissions more appropriately compensate the best agents' greater expertise. The current compensation arrangement makes finding agents with great personal insurance skills a difficult task.

Knowing what you want in an advisor

Okay, so you're sold on the idea of finding the best advisor that you can for the commission dollars that you're spending. Where do you look for candidates? And when you find two or more candidates, how can you select the one that's best for you?

I suggest you build a checklist of what you want in your agent. Ask yourself the following questions:

> ✔ **Do I want my life, health, disability, long-term-care, and other coverages with the same agent?** You'll have the best-designed program if you can find one agent with the expertise to oversee your whole program — expertise in every kind of personal policy. At the very least, it's wise not to have more than two agents that you work with.
>
> ✔ **Is a regular, yearly review important to me?** If so, add this to your shopping list. I recommend regular reviews. A well-designed insurance plan starts to rust with coverage gaps if it's not polished up every year or two.
>
> ✔ **Do I have a home business?** If so, you must find someone with small-business insurance expertise. Add that to your list.
>
> ✔ **Are top claim skills important to me?** Do you want the best possible claims coaching, to maximize your claim when you file it? Do you want an agent skilled enough to fight, successfully, for your rights if your claim is unjustly denied or underpaid?

Then use the answers to these questions to screen potential candidates.

Searching for candidates

You're looking for an agent to probe your needs, identify coverage gaps, solve problems, help you resolve claim disputes, do annual reviews, and, in short, provide greater expertise. Here are some possible sources for candidates. Try to get at least two to three prospects.

Word of mouth

Word of mouth is always one of the best sources when seeking a professional of any kind. But be careful not to fall into the price trap. Because so many people buy their insurance solely on price, when you ask for a referral for a good agent, you might get: "Call Bob. He's a good guy. He saved me $200 a year. And he always remembers my birthday." So you call Bob, get his quote, save your $200 or more, and end up with a good price for the wrong coverage (and an annual birthday card). And you've done nothing about your uninsured coverage gaps.

To avoid the price trap, be specific when asking for a referral. You don't necessarily want the best salesman or the one you'd most like to go to a ballgame with. You want the person who will give you the best professional advice.

Professional societies

An insurance agent can earn a number of advanced insurance designations by completing a series of courses and passing the exams. Here are just a few:

- Chartered Property Casualty Underwriter (CPCU)
- Certified Insurance Counselor (CIC)
- Certified Life Underwriter (CLU)
- Accredited Advisor in Insurance (AAI)

Many others designations exist as well. Anyone earning any insurance designation has to spend 100 hours to 1,000 hours (for the CPCU) in the classroom and studying on her own, as well as pass national exams. These are people who have gained additional expertise in certain areas and who have a commitment to professionalism and ethical behavior. Don't choose an agent based *solely* on her professional designations, but weigh these designations (or the lack thereof) heavily in your decision.

Managing risk with a personal risk manager

When it comes right down to it, buying a bunch of insurance policies, even from very knowledgeable agents who customize all the coverages to your particular needs, still leaves you wanting. For example, you may need help sorting through your group health insurance options at work to pick the plan that offers your family the best all-around coverage for the least cost. If you're married and both you and your spouse have group options from your respective employers, you may need help determining which plan is best to insure your children. What about your group options for additional life insurance? Should you apply for that if you have diabetes or other health issues? How much do you need? If you're 65 and still working, should you apply for full Medicare now or stay on your employer's group plan? The list of questions is endless. . . .

Personal risk managers are insurance agents who are highly skilled in every type of personal insurance policy. They help consumers identify and manage the risks in their lives — not just those covered by policies the agents handle — in exchange for a value-added, annual, risk-management fee in addition to any commission earned by the agents.

There is no society of personal risk managers — at least not yet. You find one by first finding an agent highly skilled in every type of personal policy and then offering them the job. Offer to pay them an annual fee in exchange for helping you manage all the risks in your life — not just those covered by those policies that the agent handles for you. I know it's possible because I've been practicing that way for my clients for over 20 years.

If you want some good leads to an agent prospect with expertise in personal property and liability policies — auto, home, umbrella, and so on — contact

- ✔ **CPCU Society** (phone: 800-932-2728, ext. 4; e-mail: membercenter@ cpcusociety.org; Web: www.cpcusociety.org): From the home page, click on Agent & Broker Locator to find an agent in your area.

- ✔ **The Society of Certified Insurance Counselors** (phone: 800-633-2165; e-mail: alliance@scic.com; Web: www.scic.com): Call and request a list of CIC agents who share your zip code.

Whatever names you get from these two societies will be good prospects for your agent search. (CPCU agents are more scarce, so you may need to request a state listing rather than asking for agents in your zip code.)

Insurance companies

If you already know you want to be insured with a particular company, go directly to that company for agent referrals. You can also go to the insurance company for agent leads if you've shopped ahead for a certain type of insurance and found one or two insurers that are the lowest priced. (***Remember:*** All you know at this point is that they're the lowest priced for the coverage you shopped but not necessarily the coverage you need!)

What you need to find out from the insurer is who the company's best, most knowledgeable agents are. The insurance company knows who these agents are, but the company is unlikely, for legal and other reasons, to give you their names. So here's what I recommend: Call the local company office and ask them to fax or e-mail you a list of all their agents in your state who have a CPCU or CIC designation. They may not have a list at their fingertips, but they can get it for you. Whichever method you use, it should yield a small supply of quality prospects.

Making the choice

At this point, you've narrowed down your choice to one or two candidates for your "job opening" for an agent/advisor. You're probably thinking, "How do I, with limited knowledge, make this choice? I don't even know what to ask."

Start by requesting a face-to-face meeting for the purpose of doing an insurance review for every policy that you have including your group coverage at work. You'll be able to tell by your gut feel whether this is the person for you.

If you've narrowed your field to two candidates, I recommend that you have both of them do the insurance review for you. The agent with the greater expertise and greater care for your well-being will stand out.

The insurance audit

Suppose you're pretty content with your agent and even your insurance company. But you've got a lot to lose and you'd like a second opinion. You're a little nervous about whether all your bases are covered, especially considering that you have an older home, a lot of artwork and antiques, a vacation condo in the mountains, and a small business you run from home. The question is: How can you get a second opinion from an expert? How much will it cost? And what results can you ask for?

If your state allows agents to charge fees for added services, approach an agent with good expertise and request an audit of your entire insurance program. Agree on an hourly rate or flat fee for the service. Here's the format I use that works well: First, I meet with the clients for about 1½ to 2 hours and probe to identify the property and liability risks in their lives. If they want, I also include life and health risks. I particularly focus on the risks not covered by standard insurance policies. I make sure that their program is balanced, that all the major risk areas — large lawsuits, major damage to residence, major medical bills, death and long-term disability — are well covered, that no one major risk area has excessive coverage at the expense of another major risk area being grossly under-insured.

Next, I try to measure the size of the risks I've identified. I briefly review the prospective clients' income and assets to assess how likely they are to be sued, and I help them determine an appropriate liability insurance limit. I gather information on their home to double- and triple-check the adequacy of their home structural coverage. I help them determine how much life insurance to carry. I make sure that they have solid long-term disability coverage.

I review their contracts and leases, such as condominium association agreements or home business contracts to see what risks they have assumed in those agreements.

Then, I gather and review all their personal insurance policies, including group insurance — life, health, disability — with the purpose of discovering where the holes are, or where the program is out of balance.

Finally, I prepare a written report listing the problem areas and my recommended solution for each. The reports are usually two to three pages long and identify 8 to 20 problems.

The clients pay me for the report and can then use the information to buy insurance from any company or any agent. Or they can simply use the information to have their current agents make whatever policy changes are needed to plug their coverage gaps.

I've done scores of insurance audits. I've never had a client not benefit immensely. Any advisor you select can do the same for you for a fair price, if your state permits it.

The job of protecting you from financial ruin caused by property or liability claims is an important one. Approach it as seriously as you'd approach choosing a doctor, lawyer, or accountant.

Don't get quotes at this stage yet. If you're comfortable and she has the exper-tise you're looking for, ask her to design a program for you with all the right coverages. Then have her quote what she recommends and meet with her a second time to review the quotes and get her help making choices. Once all those changes are implemented, you should have satisfied both the compo-nents of a great insurance program! How about that!

When you've completed the reviews, ask about the agent's background, his educational and practical experience, and the kind of ongoing help you can expect — both in terms of regular fine-tuning of your program and in terms of the kind of assistance you'll get in a serious claim or dispute. I wouldn't con-sider any candidate who doesn't offer you the big three:

✔ The expertise to help you design a great protection plan with the least possible gaps

✔ Ongoing reviews and regular contact about new developments so your plan stays current

✔ Outstanding assistance at claim time, both coaching you and being a strong advocate for your rights in a dispute

Choosing an Insurance Company

A good agent can advise you on both the financial strength and the quality of claim service of any insurance company that you're considering. If, however, you're buying direct without advice or you just want more information on a particular company, go to www.ambest.com.

A. M. Best analyzes and rates insurance companies based on their overall quality and financial strength. It gives insurers grades, much like school — A++, A+, A, A–, B+, B, and so on. (For more details on each of the grades, go to www.ambest.com, click Ratings & Analysis, and select Ratings Definitions.) The higher the rating, generally, the safer you are from the risk of the insur-ance company closing its doors and not being able to pay your claim.

Don't buy insurance from any insurance company with an A. M. Best policy-holder rating of less than A unless you have no other choice.

The larger your exposures and the greater your coverage limits, the stronger the insurance company rating you should seek. For example, if your income and/or assets make you a target for lawsuits, you'll probably buy an umbrella policy (see Chapter 15). The A. M. Best rating for that umbrella policy should, ideally, be an A+ or A++. Picking an insurance company can be a gamble. Fortunately, organizations like A. M. Best help improve your odds.

Part II

Cars, Boats, RVs, and More: Insuring the Things You Drive

"Frankly sir, issuing you reasonably priced auto insurance isn't going to be easy given the number of crashes you've been involved in."

In this part . . .

1 drive, therefore I am. For most people, a vehicle is as indispensable as oxygen. When you drive, you careen about at amazing speeds in a multi-ton container of metal, glass, and explosive liquid. You expose yourself (and others) to incredible liability simply by driving. Insurance on your vehicle is as indispensable as the vehicle itself. Without insurance, you could lose everything.

In this part, I show you how to protect yourself and others from all the different driving risks you face each day, whether you're driving a car, a boat, an RV, a snowmobile, or something else. I also give you some sound advice on collecting what you're owed at claim time.

Chapter 5

Managing Your Personal Automobile Risks

In This Chapter

▶ Reducing the risks of automobile ownership

▶ Determining the amount of lawsuit protection you need

▶ Protecting yourself from those who don't have enough insurance

▶ Deciding which deductible is right for you

Americans have a love affair with their cars, and because Americans own more cars per capita than any country in the world, a good place to begin examining insurance risks is to look at those associated with the ownership, maintenance, and use of our beloved cars. Unless you walk around with a loaded gun, an automobile is the most dangerous device you own. In one split second, driving a car can result in lawsuits, death, long-term disability, major medical expenses, and major property damage.

That's why it's so important to spend time setting up a solid car insurance program that will keep you from suffering heavy financial losses following a serious car accident. In this chapter, I show you how to create a solid car insurance program.

Protecting Against Lawsuits

Your personal automobile is the single largest possible source of catastrophic lawsuits and legal judgments against you for major injuries, death, and property damage. In this section, I fill you in on some specific strategies you can follow to protect yourself against this risk — first, by reducing your risk in the first place, and second, by buying liability coverage.

Reducing your lawsuit risks

You can reduce your risk of being sued by taking some non-insurance steps — steps that not only lower your risk but often lower your insurance costs as well:

✔ **Obey traffic laws, including the speed limit.** People who speed have many more accidents. A California study indicated that, with one speeding ticket in the last two years, your probability of having an at-fault accident increased 95 percent. With two tickets, your probability increased 170 percent. If you received three speeding tickets, you were 254 percent more likely to have an accident. If you have four speeding tickets, you're almost 300 percent more likely to have an accident. This should help you understand why insurance companies bump your rate up when you get speeding tickets.

✔ **Don't drink and drive.** Always use a designated driver. Period.

✔ **Perform regular safety maintenance on your vehicle.** Have your brakes, tires, steering, and lights checked by a mechanic.

✔ **When you're shopping for a car, buy a vehicle that's highly rated for low damageability and passenger safety.** Check out the Insurance Institute for Highway Safety Web site (www.iihs.org/ratings) for crash test results on various makes and models.

✔ **Opt for added safety features like air bags or antilock brakes.** They cost more, but they'll save you money on your insurance premium and reduce your risk of injury.

✔ **Always wear your seat belt and insist that your passengers do, too.**

✔ **Buy child safety seats and always use them.** Look for a seat rated by the National Highway Traffic Safety Administration (NHTSA). For tips on child safety seats, go to www.nhtsa.gov and click on the Child Safety Seats link.

✔ **Take a behind-the-wheel defensive driving class.** Even if you don't get a premium credit, you'll be a better driver and have less chance of being involved in a serious accident — either one that is not your fault or one that you cause. And fewer accidents means better rates (and maybe longer lives).

✔ **Require your teenager to have at least 30 hours of practice behind the wheel on his permit under all sorts of driving conditions before allowing him to get a driver's license.** No one can ever develop the skills needed to be a safe driver in just a few hours of mandatory driver's education.

✔ **Allow your teen to drive based upon your determination of her ability to responsibly operate a car — *regardless* of when your state says she can legally drive.** A teen who behaves immaturely and irresponsibly out of a vehicle usually behaves immaturely and irresponsibly *in* a vehicle.

Buying liability coverage

Liability insurance provides for your defense and pays legal judgments on your behalf. People who buy liability insurance frequently make two mistakes:

- ✔ **They buy far too little coverage.** "How much is enough liability insurance?" you may be asking. It depends on who the victim is. It also depends on how suable you are. I call this your *suability factor* (see the "Your suability factor" section, later in this chapter).

- ✔ **They buy inconsistent limits.** For example, they have a $100,000 limit on their car, $300,000 on their home, and $50,000 on their boat. Suppose these are your limits and you injure someone seriously with your car. You have only $100,000 of coverage, yet had the same injury occurred at home, you would have $300,000 of coverage. See how illogical that is? Your only hope for enough coverage in this scenario is to drag the victim's bleeding, unconscious body home, throw him down the stairs, and hope he doesn't remember the car accident!

I cover how to fix both of these common mistakes in the following sections.

Your suability factor

I define *suability factor* as the probability of an injured party suing you for large sums — often for more than the amount of liability insurance you're carrying. In order for that to happen, you must be worth something, either currently or in the future. Why? Because if there's nothing to go after — no pot of gold at the end of the rainbow — many attorneys won't take the case and help an injured party sue you.

Your suability factor is influenced by several elements:

- ✔ **Your current income:** The more you make, the higher your suability factor.

- ✔ **Your current assets:** If you have expensive cars and homes, lots of investments and savings, and other assets, your suability factor is higher.

- ✔ **Your future income:** If you're a medical intern, a law-school student, or an MBA student, your suability factor is higher, even if you're currently living in a studio apartment and eating ramen noodles every night.

- ✔ **Your future assets:** If your parents are wealthy and you stand to inherit a good chunk of change, your suability factor is higher.

People with high current incomes or assets usually are aware of their suability. But people with little current income or assets often overlook their future income or asset potential and the effect it has on their current suability.

Why who you hit matters

You're on your way to work. You're running behind schedule. You decide to run a yellow light. But just before the intersection, the light turns red. You slam on your brakes, but it's too late. You broadside another vehicle. The driver is taken to the emergency room, undergoes surgery, and spends a month in the hospital. Following his release, he spends two years in rehabilitation, in and out of physical therapy, missing two years of work. His medical bills come to $100,000, but your potential liability depends a lot on what his occupation and income is. Here are a few examples. Note that awards for pain and suffering are also influenced by a person's income loss. The total award for each example includes the $100,000 in medical expenses each incur.

- If he's a teacher, his lost wages for 2 years might be $120,000, his pain and suffering might be $300,000, and his total claim (including the $100,000 of medical expenses) might be $520,000.

- If he's a banker, his lost wages might be $240,000, his pain and suffering might be $400,000, and his total claim might be $740,000.

- If she's a doctor, her lost wages might be $600,000, her pain and suffering might be $500,000, and her total claim might be $1,200,000.

- And if he's a professional baseball player, his lost wages might be $12 million, his pain and suffering might be $10 million, and his total claim might be $22,100,000!

Pretty eye-opening, isn't it? Can you imagine what the numbers would be if the driver were killed, or had a permanent disability with a lifetime loss of income? The most common liability limit I see when I review a prospective client's insurance is $100,000! As these examples illustrate, that's ridiculously low.

I'm not suggesting that you rush out and buy $22 million or more in liability insurance in case you happen to hit a professional athlete. (You probably won't even be able to find liability insurance with limits more than $5 million to 10 million.) I *am* suggesting that you reevaluate your coverage limit based on a combination of this new awareness, the cost and availability of higher insurance limits, and how suable you are. To help pay for the increased cost of higher liability coverage, shift premium dollars away from less important coverages, like higher deductibles on coverage for damage to your own vehicle.

If you have one or more of these four elements contributing to a high suability factor, you're more apt to be sued for amounts greater than your insurance coverage, and you need higher liability limits on *all* your insurance policies. An added advantage of higher liability limits is that the closer your liability limit comes to the economic value of the injury you cause, the greater the likelihood that the injured party will settle for your insurance policy limit and not pursue you — personally — beyond that.

For some people, another variable in choosing a liability limit is their sense of moral responsibility. For example, a person who is not very suable may buy a higher liability limit than she would otherwise need, to make sure that any fellow human being she injures is provided for financially. If you're one of these people, my hat goes off to you in admiration.

The cost of higher liability limits

You may be wondering how much it costs to raise your liability coverage — well, it costs very little. Call your agent and find out for yourself — you'll be amazed! (Don't forget to raise all your liability limits on your other personal policies to the same limit as your car insurance.) Table 5-1 shows an example of fairly typical costs involved in raising liability coverage from $100,000 for two cars, a home, a cabin, and a boat. (The numbers may vary depending on the insurance company and the circumstances of the insured.)

Table 5-1	The Cost of Raising Liability Limits from $100,000
New Liability Limit	**Additional Annual Premium**
$300,000	$100
$500,000	$150
$1.5 million	$300
$2.5 million	$390
Each additional $ million	$90

Coverage beyond $500,000 is sold in $1 million increments under a catastrophic excess policy commonly referred to as an umbrella policy. (See Chapter 15 for more on umbrella policies.)

When you look at what you're spending for the first $100,000 of coverage, you see that you can tremendously increase your catastrophic lawsuit coverage (not to mention your peace of mind) for just a little more money. Additional liability coverage is the best value in the insurance business.

The danger of split liability limits

Most liability coverage for homes, boats, recreational vehicles, and other personal policies is sold by insurance companies as a single limit (such as $300,000) that applies to all injuries and property damage you cause in a single accident, no matter how many people are injured or how much property is damaged. In other words, if you're in an accident, you have one pool of money to pay for *all* your liability.

Liability coverage for car accidents is also available as a single limit, but just as commonly it's sold with *split limits*. With split-limits auto liability coverage, you select three *limits* (the maximum your policy pays):

- ✔ One for injuries you cause to a single person

- ✔ One for all injuries you cause in a single accident involving two or more people

- ✔ One for all damage to property you cause in a single accident

Table 5-2 provides examples of three of the most typical combinations of split limits.

Table 5-2	Typical Split-Limits Policies Sold		
	Example 1	Example 2	Example 3
Injury limit per person	$50,000	$100,000	$250,000
Injury limit per accident	$100,000	$300,000	$500,000
Property damage limit per accident	$25,000	$50,000	$100,000

If you buy a single liability limit of $300,000 on your home, cabin, and boat policies, you should get the same $300,000 limit on your car insurance. If you request that limit from an agent selling only split limits (instead of a single limit of $300,000), here are the split limits the agent may suggest as an alternative:

- ✔ $100,000 per person for injuries you cause

- ✔ $300,000 per accident for injuries

- ✔ $50,000 per accident for all property damage you cause

The danger of buying split-limits coverage is a false sense of security given to you by the injury limit *per accident*. The limit you're actually most likely to exhaust in a car accident is the injury limit *per person*.

Suppose you buy the limits shown in the second column in Table 5-2. Your policy limits you to $100,000 per person and $300,000 per accident for injuries you cause. Here are some hypothetical injury claims, what a jury may award, and what your policy pays with those split limits:

- ✔ You rear-end a car ahead of you with only one occupant, resulting in injuries to the driver's neck and back. Jury award: $250,000. You have a $300,000 limit per accident for injuries, so you're fine, right? Well, your limit per person that you injure is $100,000, so you're out $150,000.

✔ You rear-end the same car, but with two occupants. Both have neck and back injuries, one more serious than the other. Jury awards: $200,000 to one, $50,000 to the other. You guessed it. The policy pays the full $50,000 for the less seriously injured person but only $100,000 for the more seriously injured person, and you're out $100,000 ($200,000 minus the $100,000-per-person limit).

Neither of these scenarios involves catastrophic lawsuits, permanent serious injuries, or death. They are, in short, relatively ordinary. But look at what you would owe with split-limits coverage!

In both accident examples, the total amount of jury awards is within the $300,000 per accident limit. But because the policy also has a per person limit, the judgment costs you astronomical sums of money that you would not have owed if you had a $300,000 single-limit coverage.

Don't forget about legal fees. Legal fees in an accident defense case can run $50,000, $100,000, or more! After you've used up your liability limit per accident, those legal costs come out of your pocket. Every time you're sued for more than your policy limits, you'll get a friendly letter from your insurance company (certified mail, of course) that tells you that after their policy limits have been paid out, you're on your own.

So, how can you avoid the per-person pitfall of split-limits coverage? Because the vast majority of car accidents involve cars occupied by only one person, I recommend one of three strategies:

✔ **Select a per-person limit high enough to meet your lawsuit coverage needs for one person's injuries.** In the two accident examples I just gave, for example, $250,000 to $500,000 of liability coverage per person would have saved you hundreds of thousands of dollars out of pocket for as little as $100 a year in additional insurance costs, if you're insuring two cars.

✔ **Buy *single-limit coverage* — one pool of money large enough to cover all injuries and property damage without a limit on the amount paid to any one person.** Because this includes property damage, and any amount spent to pay for property damage reduces the amount left to pay for injuries, be sure to buy a little extra coverage. The least amount of coverage you should consider is $300,000 to $500,000.

✔ **Buy a second layer of liability insurance, called an umbrella policy, of $1 million or more.** (See Chapter 15 for more on the personal umbrella policy.)

Insuring Your Personal Injuries

Injuries, often quite serious ones, happen in car accidents far more than in any other type of accident — plane, train, industrial, and so on. If you're injured in a car accident, you usually have more than one source from which to collect your medical bills and lost wages. One source may be your own health and disability insurance. Another source may be the personal liability coverage of the other driver, if the accident was his fault and if he has any insurance. But the process of collecting from the other driver can take months or even years. A third source is your car insurance.

You've got two types of coverage in a personal auto policy for your injuries in a car accident:

✔ Coverage for compensatory damages (what your injuries would be worth in a court, including compensation for pain and suffering) for your injuries caused by uninsured or under-insured motorists

✔ Coverage for your medical bills (and lost wages in some states) regardless of fault

I address these separately, because I have different recommendations for each.

Understanding uninsured and under-insured motorist coverage

When you're injured in a car accident caused by another driver, you can legally sue the other driver in most states to collect the fair value of your injury. If that driver has auto liability coverage, his policy pays you on his behalf, up to the liability policy limit he purchased. The economic value of your injury equals your out-of-pocket expenses plus compensation for your pain and suffering.

But what if the other driver has no insurance at all? Or what if the insurance limit he has is less than the costs of your injury? You can get a legal judgment against him and try to collect from him personally. But that can be an expensive, long, drawn-out process. Plus, if he's not worth very much and has a limited income, you may not collect much at all.

Fortunately, your own car insurance policy can solve the problem, if you buy adequate limits of uninsured motorists and under-insured motorists coverage.

- ✔ **Uninsured motorists** are other drivers who are either unidentified (hit and run) or have no liability insurance at all.

- ✔ **Under-insured motorists** are other drivers who have some auto liability coverage but the economic value of your injury exceeds their liability limit.

I see these two coverages as a form of *reverse liability* in that you collect some or all of the economic value of your injuries caused by another driver from your own insurance company, almost as if they were the other driver's insurer. In short, uninsured and under-insured motorists coverage make up the gap between the other driver's liability coverage and the amount of liability coverage he would have needed in order to pay your claim in full — subject, of course, to the amount of uninsured or under-insured motorists coverage you buy.

How do the two coverages work? Say you're injured in a car accident caused by a driver who runs a stop sign. The economic value of your injury is $450,000. Now, assume that you bought $500,000 of both uninsured and under-insured motorists coverage under your own auto policy. For an under-insured motorist, first, you collect for your injury from the other driver's insurance in the amount of the other driver's liability limit (say, $100,000). Then, you collect the balance of $350,000 from your own insurance company under your under-insured motorists coverage. Had the other driver been without *any* insurance, you would have collected all $450,000 under your uninsured motorists coverage.

Buy as much protection for your own injuries (caused by another person) as you buy to cover the injuries you yourself cause to someone else. In other words, buy the same uninsured and under-insured motorists coverage limits as you buy liability insurance limits to the extent those coverages are available in your state. Why? Because you're worth every bit as much as a complete stranger whom you might injure. Cover yourself accordingly.

Saving money on medical coverage

Coverage for your medical bills (and sometimes lost wages and *replacement services* — help around the home you have to hire) is generally offered by car insurance companies. Depending on your state's laws, this medical coverage generally comes in two flavors:

- ✔ Medical payments coverage (plain vanilla)
- ✔ Personal injury protection coverage (banana fudge supreme)

Both coverages are similar in the sense that they pay your medical bills suffered in a car accident, regardless of fault, up to the limit you purchased. Personal injury protection has the added advantage (at a considerably greater cost) of also reimbursing you for some of your lost wages or replacement services. Some states even allow you (for an additional premium) to add together the personal injury coverage limits per car (called *stacking*) to cover a single injury (for example, $20,000 coverage per car × 3 cars on the policy = $60,000 total medical coverage for a single injury).

I don't have space to cover all the different requirements or costs relating to these coverages, but keep in mind three things when buying either coverage:

> ✔ **Check the law in your particular state.** State laws on medical payments coverage or personal injury protection coverage vary dramatically.
>
> ✔ **Buy only as much medical-related coverage as the law requires.** Medical and disability costs should be covered under other policies you have, so having additional car insurance coverage is redundant.
>
> ✔ **Don't buy additional coverage for your medical bills and/or lost wages from car accidents only.** This approach is betting that those particular kinds of expenses will happen just in an auto accident and is a violation of the principle "Don't buy Las Vegas insurance" (see Chapter 2).

Not buying more than minimum coverage limits for either medical payments or personal injury protection is an area where you can save money on your insurance. To fully transfer the risks of medical payments and personal injury, not just those arising from car accidents but from *any* illness or injury, you need major medical insurance and long-term disability insurance — both of which cover financial losses no matter how the losses are caused, rendering special insurance to cover the damages caused only by car accidents superfluous.

If you don't already have major medical and long-term disability coverage in your insurance portfolio, I urge you to consider adding both immediately. (See Chapter 18 on buying health insurance and Chapter 22 on disability insurance.)

Insuring against Damage to Your Vehicle

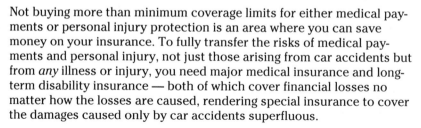

In this section, I tell you how to manage the risks of damage to your vehicle — risks such as fire, theft, collision, vandalism, glass breakage, and so on. The AART non-insurance strategies from Chapter 3, particularly reducing and retaining, apply to managing vehicle damage risks. Here are just a few examples of how to use non-insurance strategies to reduce risks:

✔ Carry an onboard fire extinguisher to reduce the risk of a serious fire.

✔ Always lock your car and install a burglar alarm to reduce the risk of theft.

✔ Park in a locked garage at home and always park in well-lit, nonisolated areas when away from home to reduce both theft and vandalism risks.

✔ Keep a safe distance behind the vehicle ahead of you to reduce the risks of both glass breakage and collisions.

You can use the retaining strategy by either choosing higher deductibles or not buying damage insurance at all and paying all claims out of your own pocket.

Insurance for vehicle damage is usually offered in two parts:

✔ **Collision:** Covers damage from colliding with another object (for example, a vehicle, post, or curb), regardless of fault

✔ **Comprehensive (also known as *other than collision*):** Covers most other kinds of accidental damage to the vehicle, such as fire, theft, vandalism, glass breakage, hitting a deer, wind, or hail.

Both of these coverages are subject to a front-end copayment on your part, called a *deductible*. When buying either or both of these coverages, assume as much risk as you can afford, financially and emotionally (see the nearby sidebar, "Deductible psychology"), through higher deductibles — or don't purchase these coverages at all.

A couple of things to keep in mind here:

✔ **Make sure that the insurance company gives you enough of a price discount for taking the additional risk.** I offer some guidelines for choosing the most cost-effective deductibles, as well as for determining the point where dropping these coverages on an older car makes sense, later in this chapter.

✔ **If you're on a tight budget but still need higher liability insurance limits to protect future assets or income (like if you're a student in medical school), it may make sense to carry higher deductibles even if the money to cover them isn't currently available.** The savings will often pay for most or all of the cost of the additional liability coverage you need. Incredibly, the savings for raising your collision coverage deductible by just $250 (from $250 to $500) is often enough to pay for an extra $200,000 of liability insurance. No matter how tight things are, coming up with another $250 to fix dents is far easier than coming up with $200,000 to cover lawsuits!

Deductible psychology

Make sure that you can emotionally afford a high deductible before changing your policy. I've had a number of clients who chose higher deductibles, but when the loss occurred parting with the money caused them major stress. I have one well-to-do client who could easily replace her new Jaguar out of petty cash but who opts for the lowest deductibles the insurance company offers. She knows herself well enough to be aware that parting with *any* money at claim time would be emotionally traumatic for her.

If your driving record has deteriorated and your premiums are in danger of rising significantly with one more claim, I recommend very high deductibles, such as $1,000. In all likelihood you won't file a small claim — and risk higher rates — so why pay for something you're not going to use anyway?

Choosing cost-effective deductibles

I estimate that the average person has a claim for damage to her vehicle every four or five years, so I advise my clients to choose a higher deductible if the *extra risk* (the difference in deductibles) can be recouped via premium savings within a reasonable time (in other words, four to five years). The number of years it takes to recoup that added risk is called the *payback period.* The formula looks like this:

payback period = the difference in deductibles ÷ the difference in annual premiums

If you're trying to figure out the most economical deductible, look at the hypothetical examples I offer in Tables 5-3 through 5-6 to better understand how to determine the best deductible for you.

Here's an example of how to use a table: Table 5-3 is an example of insurance costs for collision and comprehensive coverage for a 3-year-old Lexus driven by a 47-year-old woman and used for business. Reading across from left to right in Table 5-3:

- ✔ The first row, "Deductible," shows the different deductible choices for both damage coverages.

- ✔ The second row, "Extra risk," shows the dollar amount of the difference between each deductible (the extra dollar amount you'll be at risk for if you choose a higher deductible).

✔ The third row, "Annual premiums," shows the annual insurance cost for each deductible.

✔ The fourth row, "Annual savings," shows the annual insurance cost savings if you choose the next higher deductible.

✔ And the fifth row, "Payback period," represents the number of years it would take without a claim to save, through your reduced premiums, the amount of extra risk you would assume by opting for higher deductibles. The payback period is determined by dividing the extra deductible risk in the second row by the annual insurance premium savings in the fourth row. If the payback period is less than four or five years, choosing the higher deductible makes good sense.

Table 5-3	A 3-Year-Old Lexus Coupe, Driven by a 47-Year-Old Woman for Business	
	Collision	*Comprehensive*
Deductible	$250/$500/$1,000	$100/$250/$500
Extra risk (difference)	$250/$500	$150/$250
Annual premiums	$500/$400/$300	$250/$200/$150
Annual savings	$100/$100	$50/$50
Payback period (extra risk ÷ savings)	2½ years/5 years	3 years/5 years

In Table 5-3, the extra risk, from the second row, to increase the collision coverage deductible from $250 to $500 is $250. The annual premium savings, from the fourth row, to make that change is $100. Dividing the $250 extra risk by the $100 annual savings, you get 2½ years. That means if she goes 2½ years without any claims, she'll save $250 on her insurance costs — the amount of the added risk she took by raising her deductible. Using the rule of choosing a higher deductible if the payback period is less than four or five years, it's clear that raising the deductible makes sense.

The payback period from the example in Table 5-3 — even for the highest deductibles — is only five years for collision and comprehensive coverages, making it logical to take the added risk for both coverages.

Table 5-4 shows a 5-year-old Honda used to commute to work by a 35-year-old man. Although the premiums are less than they are for the more expensive Lexus in Table 5-3, the extra risk of the higher deductibles can still be recaptured in five years and is still worth taking.

Table 5-4	A 5-Year-Old Honda Accord, Driven by a 35-Year-Old Man, 10 Miles Each Way to Work	
	Collision	*Comprehensive*
Deductible	$250/$500/$1,000	$100/$250/$500
Extra risk (difference)	$250/$500	$150/$250
Annual premiums	$300/$200/$100	$150/$100/$50
Annual savings	$100/$100	$50/$50
Payback period (extra risk ÷ savings)	2½ years/5 years	3 years/5 years

Table 5-5 shows an older Chevy driven by a 19-year-old man with three recent speeding tickets whose rates are much higher due to both his age and his driving record.

Table 5-5	A 12-Year-Old Chevy, Driven by a 19-Year-Old Man with Three Speeding Tickets	
	Collision	*Comprehensive*
Deductible	$250/$500/$1,000	$100/$250/$500
Extra risk (difference)	$250/$500	$150/$250
Annual premiums	$1,200/$1,000/$800	$600/$450/$300
Annual savings	$200/$200	$150/$150
Payback period (extra risk ÷ savings)	1⅓ years/2½ years	1 year/1⅔ years

Clearly, with payback periods of two and a half years or less for each deductible, this high-risk driver is better off with the highest deductibles possible. Not to mention that, with three tickets, he won't be turning in small claims anyway, because they may result in his being dropped by the insurance company. Would he be better off not carrying the coverages at all? See the next section for tips on making that call.

In Table 5-6, check out what happens to the insurance costs for this same Chevy if the 19-year-old sells the car to his 74-year-old granny who has never had a ticket in her life. The payback period for the highest deductibles far exceeds the four- to five-year guideline. This driver would clearly be better off with low to midrange deductibles.

Table 5-6	A 12-Year-Old Chevy Cavalier, Driven by a 74-Year-Old Widow with a Clear Record	
	Collision	*Comprehensive*
Deductible	$250/$500/$1,000	$100/$250/$500
Extra risk (difference)	$250/$500	$150/$250
Annual premiums	$150/$100/$50	$75/$50/$30
Annual savings	$50/$50	$25/$20
Payback period (extra risk ÷ savings)	5 years/10 years	6 years/12½ years

Knowing when to drop collision and comprehensive coverage

When deciding whether a vehicle's value has decreased enough to drop one or both of these vehicle damage coverages altogether, you apply the same four- to five-year payback guideline as I explain in the preceding section. The only difference is that the extra risk you're assuming is the full value of the vehicle (less any salvage value collectible from a junkyard).

Assuming an old Chevy has a junk value of $300 and would cost $2,500 to replace with an equivalent automobile, the net risk is $2,200 (the $2,500 value less the $300 salvage value). Dividing the $2,200 risk by the collision and comprehensive premium will give you the payback period. Drop the coverage if the payback period is five years or less.

Evaluating Road Service and Car Rental Coverages

Other coverages offered by most insurers are towing/road-service coverage and loss-of-use/car-rental coverage.

I believe towing/road-service coverage, though inexpensive, is better suited to automobile clubs, like AAA, Amoco, and others. They're good at it, claims are paperless, and they offer a number of other vehicle services — all for a flat fee.

Avoiding the marriage penalty

One of the most common mistakes I've seen agents make when insuring a married couple is to list the policy in the name of only one of the spouses — usually the husband. Besides the obvious sexism, this practice creates a coverage concern: An unnamed spouse has automatic insurance only while she lives in the household. If she moves out, her automatic coverage ends. "But a spouse is covered equally with the partner who's named on the policy. The policy says so!" goes the rebuttal argument. True, but only if the spouse is a resident of the household. Under many policies, if you, the unlisted spouse, are not a resident of the listed spouse's household (for example, if you sepa-

rate for a long period), you may have coverage only if you have your spouse's permission. It's important to know that this exclusionary language is fairly universal, not just in auto policies but in virtually every personal policy (covering homes, boats, and so on).

When you get married, get every insurance policy listed in both names, on page one. If you're either married or separated, check your policies before you read any further — every one of them. If any of the policies are not in both names, call your agent or insurance company as soon as possible and get this omission corrected.

On the other hand, towing/road-service coverage under car insurance is not paperless — you must pay the claim first yourself (usually), then file a formal claim report and wait two to three weeks for reimbursement. Coverage also is often limited to a dollar amount ($25, $50, $75, and so on). And a large number of these claims combined with other tickets and accidents can impair your relationship with your car insurance company. I've seen it happen several times.

Loss-of-use/car-rental coverage is quite important. If a collision or other covered loss deprives you of your car, you probably need a substitute. If your car is badly damaged, or there is a parts delay, that car-rental bill could be several hundred dollars out of pocket. Loss of use covers the daily cost to rent a vehicle while yours is out of commission due to a covered loss. Costs covered typically range from $10 to $50 per day for up to 30 days. I recommend buying at least a $30-per-day benefit.

There is another major benefit to loss-of-use coverage. Any delays by the claims adjuster in getting to your car penalize the insurance company — not you — by increasing the cost of the claim. So it's to the insurance company's advantage to see your car as quickly as possible. And the coverage saves you a lot of aggravation that repair delays would cause you otherwise.

A swing and a myth: Automatic coverage for new cars

I often get phone calls from clients wanting to add coverage for a newly purchased automobile that they've been driving casually for a couple of weeks. When I tell them that they've been driving without car insurance, they reply with a shocked, "But I thought I had 30 days of automatic coverage!" That is often not the case. Yes, you do have automatic coverage for newly acquired vehicles under certain circumstances (for example, if it's the first Tuesday of the month following a full moon). But *assuming* that you have automatic coverage is a huge mistake. I won't bore you to tears describing all the scenarios in which you don't have coverage. Let me give you the bottom line instead.

When adding a newly purchased vehicle to your auto policy, *always* arrange for the insurance on the vehicle to commence prior to the day you transfer the title or the day you start driving the new car regularly, whichever comes first. If you don't, you may be uninsured at claim time.

All personal auto policies provide automatic liability coverage when test-driving a vehicle. That coverage, however, often stops the day you acquire possession. Follow this iron-clad rule and never be caught with your insurance pants down.

Warning: If you're selling a car, don't rely on the buyer to complete the title transfer for you, or you may get a phone call in the middle of the night from the police wondering about your abandoned car that was in an accident involving some serious injuries. Whether you're a buyer or a seller, always accompany the other person to the title-transfer office and request proof of the transfer. Then, if you're the seller, remove the insurance from the car.

Chapter 6

Dealing with Special Auto Insurance Situations

. . . .

In This Chapter

▶ Protecting yourself when renting a car

▶ Avoiding the pitfalls of the company car

▶ Covering antique and classic cars

▶ Buying motorcycle insurance

▶ Insuring your new teen driver

. . . .

Some vehicle risks have their own special set of problems, beyond the usual issues addressed in Chapter 5. In this chapter, I address the special risks associated with renting cars, when the typical personal auto policy covers those risks, and when it doesn't. I address the two uninsured risks you face when you're given a company car. I show you the unfair pitfall found in insurance coverage for antique and classic cars. And I even share a few pointers on motorcycle insurance. Finally, I wrap things up by giving you money-saving tips on insuring a teen driver. If your motor-vehicle situation is a little different from the norm, you'll find the answers you need in this chapter.

We'll Pick You Up: Insuring a Rental Car

Renting a car, whether for business or for pleasure, puts you face-to-face with risks that your personal auto policy may not cover. Here are the four main sources of liability you face when renting a car:

✔ **You have direct liability for injuries or property damage that you cause to others while operating the rental car.** If you run a red light and injure others or damage their vehicle, for example, you're at fault and responsible.

✔ **You're directly liable for damage to the rental car that you cause by your negligent driving.** If you run a red light and damage the rental car, for example, you're responsible for the repair costs.

✔ **You're responsible for damage to the rental car — damage that you did *not* cause but for which you agreed to be responsible when you signed the rental contract.** Every rental contract I have ever looked at makes the renter absolutely liable for all damage *regardless of fault!* This clause has always been nonnegotiable. This means that you're responsible for damages such as hail damage, someone else running a red light and hitting you, someone vandalizing the car by keying it, or someone hot-wiring the car and stealing it. In short, if you return the car with any damage at all, you owe. With the cost of new cars today, that could mean more than $25,000 if the car is totaled or stolen.

✔ **You're liable for the loss of revenues the car rental agency suffers as a result of the car being unavailable to rent while being repaired.** Again, you'll owe this loss of revenue regardless of whether you actually caused the damage. You agree to be responsible when you sign the contract.

In the following sections, I fill you in on your options for addressing these sources of liability so that you're at the least risk possible when you rent a car.

Uncovering how your auto policy covers car rentals

How well do you think your auto policy would cover the four types of liabilities I list earlier? Because personal auto policies vary somewhat, it's always best to check with your agent or insurer prior to renting, but here's the norm:

✔ **Injuries and property damage that you cause as a driver:** Usually you're covered up to your liability policy limit.

✔ **Damage to the rental car that you cause:** You *are* covered only if you have collision and comprehensive coverage on at least one of the vehicles on your policy, subject to your deductible. You are *not* covered otherwise; in this case, you may need to buy the collision-damage waiver coverage from the car rental company (see the next section).

✔ **Damage to the rental car that you didn't cause:** You have contractually agreed to be responsible for all damage, regardless of whether you caused it. Again, you are covered only if you have collision and comprehensive coverage on at least one of the vehicles on your policy, subject to your deductible. You are not covered otherwise.

Be sure to check with your insurance provider prior to renting a car to see exactly how your policy will apply, because policy language varies from company to company. Also, ask your agent to advise you about any state laws that may affect your coverage.

✔ **Rental company's lost income while a damaged car is being repaired:** You may be covered only if you have loss-of-use coverage on at least one vehicle on your policy, and then only up to your loss-of-use policy limit (usually $20 to $50 per day). Your coverage depends on your insurance company. You're covered only up to a limit — for example, $20 a day. If you buy the optional collision-damage waiver coverage from the rental company, loss of use may be covered in full.

Courts have ruled that rental companies can only charge you for their lost income on a car you return with damage if they had no other vehicles available to rent.

Evaluating coverage from the rental agency

If you don't have automatic coverage under your personal auto policy for any damage to a car you're renting, regardless of cause, you should buy the optional *collision-damage waiver* (CDW) from the rental agency.

The CDW coverage supplied by rental car companies usually has two problems:

- ✔ **Cost:** It's usually about $10 per day. If that amount doesn't sound like much to you, consider that the bill comes to $3,650 over the course of a year. Compare that to perhaps $500 a year for collision and comprehensive coverage to insure the same car on your personal auto policy. Ouch!

- ✔ **Restricted coverage:** The average CDW coverage is full of restrictions that you would not tolerate if you were buying personal auto insurance. Often excluded are unlisted drivers, such as a spouse or friend who is sharing the driving with you. Other exclusions include driving outside the permitted geographic area, driving in a careless manner, or driving after drinking anything alcoholic — even a single drink. *Read the fine print before you sign!*

Even if you have insurance coverage for damage to a rental car on your personal auto policy, buying the CDW coverage from the rental agency may be advantageous in two circumstances:

- ✔ **When protecting your auto insurance rates:** One disadvantage of relying on your personal auto insurance policy to pay for damage to a rental car is that if you file a claim for which you are responsible, your rates will usually increase 20 percent to 25 percent for three years (the period of time most insurers surcharge rates for tickets and accidents). You won't see an increase in your personal auto insurance rates if you file a claim under coverage that you purchased from the rental agency. If your driving record is already borderline, filing another claim against your insurance may even lead to your company canceling your policy. If either of those is an issue for you, you may want to consider buying the coverage from the rental agency and saving your personal auto coverage as a backup.

✔ **When renting for business:** Buying the rental agency's coverage is also a good idea when you're renting for business purposes and your employer reimburses your expenses. Because you're using the rental car for your employer's benefit, it seems reasonable that your employer should pay for the insurance and any claim costs.

Covering your rental car with a credit card

Your fancy, new, super-shiny credit card has promised you insurance coverage if you use it to rent a car. How safe should you feel knowing that your card is protecting you and your rental car? Well, some cards offer very broad coverages; others are very restrictive. Some have a dollar limit; others don't.

Most credit card coverages don't pay for damage to a rental car until you prove in writing that your personal auto policy doesn't provide coverage. That can be a major disadvantage, because the entire cost of the rental car damage will be charged to your credit card until you get that proof.

I wouldn't rely on coverage from your credit card unless it does *both* of the following:

✔ Provides *primary coverage,* which means it pays first and ignores your personal auto coverage. Diners Club is an example of a card that does this.

✔ Has no exclusions that could hurt you, such as careless driving, driving after even a single drink, and so on.

One for the road

I once had a client who took a business trip with a friend and coworker to California. My client signed the rental contract and listed his friend as a permitted driver. He bought the CDW coverage from the rental agency. Later, he and his friend went to dinner. Both had a glass of wine with their meal. The friend drove the rental car back to the hotel parking lot where, in the dark, he drove over one of the concrete meridians, causing significant damage to the underside of the car — $3,500 in damage, to be exact.

Although the friend was a permitted driver, the rental agency declined to pay for the damage because of the alcohol-use exclusion and a careless-driving exclusion in their CDW contract. If that wasn't bad enough, guess who the rental agency came after for the $3,500? It was not the friend who caused the accident. It was my client, who signed the car rental agreement in which he agreed to be absolutely responsible for all damage no matter what the cause.

The moral of the story? Know what you're signing. And if you're sharing the rented car with a second person other than a family member, have the rental agreement listed jointly in both names and have the other person cosign the rental agreement, so that you share the damage responsibility.

Best advice? Order a sample policy ahead of time. Read (or ask your agent to read) the policy and all its exclusions, and to make sure it pays first before any other insurance you have. If it does that, with no exclusions of any concern, use the card and decline the watered-down coverage from the rental agency.

As for the four risks associated with renting a car, your personal auto policy covers the first one — injuries and property damage you cause. The credit card coverage should cover the other three.

Getting backup coverage from your personal umbrella

If you don't have automatic coverage under a personal auto policy, you need to accept the CDW coverage from the rental agency or take the coverage your credit card company offers. But you have a $25,000 car you're responsible for and you're concerned about the coverage limitations of either choice. What can you do? Good news! You can find backup coverage with the right personal umbrella policy.

Renting abroad

When you're renting a car abroad, the rental agency offers you two optional insurance coverages:

- Liability coverage, covering your responsibility for injuries and property damage you cause to others.

- Vehicle damage coverage, covering your responsibility for any damage to the rental car. (This coverage is very similar to the domestic CDW coverage.)

Virtually all automobile policies sold in the United States do *not* provide coverage outside the United States, its possessions, and Canada. Therefore, I recommend buying all the coverage you can from the rental agency when you're abroad, including liability coverage for injuries and property damage, as well as vehicle damage coverage for damage to the vehicle you're renting.

However, one exception exists: If you have a personal umbrella policy, you're probably protected worldwide for liability. I've never seen an umbrella policy that did not provide worldwide coverage. To be safe, have your umbrella policy agent confirm this fact before you decline other types of international coverage.

I do, however, recommend that you buy the vehicle damage coverage from the rental agency. Even if your umbrella policy covers the damage, as many do, this additional protection can help you avoid unnecessary hassles and delays in your trip.

Vacationing with friends, family, and expensive vehicles

This type of share-the-expense, share-the-driving arrangement happens fairly frequently among friends and family members taking trips together. Usually, it involves renting something expensive like a deluxe van or a motor home. Anytime you're responsible for a $150,000 motor home, you'd better be sure about the insurance arrangements *before* you get started!

When you rent a vehicle in this type of situation, always do three things:

✔ Have all parties sign the contract so that everyone is jointly liable.

✔ Buy the optional CDW coverage from the car rental agency to avoid possible hassles if the vehicle is damaged.

✔ Most important, check with your insurance agent in advance. Ask if your automobile and umbrella coverage will protect you (as a backup).

Start by checking with the agent or company writing your personal umbrella policy, if you have one. It's a little-known fact that many — but not all — umbrella policies pay 100 percent of the damage to a car you rent, regardless of who caused the damage, as long as the rental contract makes you responsible. The umbrella coverage is usually subject to a deductible, typically $500. (See Chapter 16 for more on choosing the right umbrella policy to cover the liability coverage gaps in your life.)

Relying on this umbrella strategy has one disadvantage: possible claims settlement delays. So don't use your umbrella policy exclusively. Keep it for the nice backup it is.

Put It on My Boss's Tab: Driving a Company Car

If you're fortunate enough to have your employer provide you with a company car, you've got a tremendous perk. These days, it's probably worth at least $400 per month to you. Like the rental car situation, it has a few pitfalls, and employers are seldom aware of them.

What I want you to draw from this section is a healthy fear — just enough so that if you're ever furnished a company car, you'll know that insurance limitations exist. Fully informed, you can avoid those types of uses for which you aren't covered, or you can provide supplemental insurance for the company car through one of the two insurance strategies I lay out for you in this section.

Don't mix business and pleasure

Some owners of small, family-owned businesses or corporations decide to insure a vehicle they use personally under a personal rather than a business auto policy (even though the title to the vehicle is in the corporate name for tax purposes). Personal auto insurance is, on the average, about 30 percent less expensive than business auto insurance, so this does save money on the front end. But it can also lead to large uninsured claims on the back end.

When it comes to large risks, safe is better than cheap. When buying a car that you use for business, the safest approach is to insure the vehicle the same way you title it. Business title? Get a business policy. Personal title? Get a personal policy. You'll avoid all the serious coverage gaps that come with doing it any other way.

When you're furnished a company car, you're insured while driving it for your liability for injuries and property damage you cause to others by your employer's business auto policy. You're covered when driving other company vehicles as well, and even when driving borrowed or rented vehicles on company business.

There are, however, two driving situations that the company business auto policy usually won't provide liability coverage for:

- ✔ When you borrow or rent vehicles for personal use
- ✔ When you injure a coworker riding with you in the company car

If you own and insure another car, the solution to both liability coverage gaps is simple and cheap: For driving borrowed or rented cars, your personal auto policy includes liability coverage automatically. Problem solved!

To protect yourself from the risk of injuring coworkers while driving your company car, ask your insurance agent to add an extended non-owned auto endorsement. The annual cost for this optional coverage is about $25 per year.

If you *don't* own a personal vehicle and the only car in your household is the company car, you've got three possible strategies to choose from:

- ✔ The best (but also the most expensive) and safest is to cover both uninsured liability coverage gaps by buying a named non-owner personal auto policy. Because it is a personal auto policy, you have automatic liability coverage for driving other cars you borrow or rent. And because you're specifically insuring your use of the company car, your liability for coworker injuries is also covered automatically.

- ✔ A second strategy for managing the company car coverage gap has two parts:

    - Have your employer add a broad-form drive-other-cars endorsement to his business auto policy, which covers your liability while driving borrowed or rented vehicles. Make sure you also add all licensed family members to this endorsement; otherwise, they aren't covered.

    - Buy a personal umbrella policy of $1 million or more to cover injuries you cause to coworkers while using the company car. (See Chapter 16 for more on plugging coverage gaps with personal umbrella policies.) Be careful. Not all umbrella policies cover this risk. Be sure you include the company car on the application for the policy.

- ✔ A third strategy is one of the ARRT non-insurance strategies from Chapter 3: avoidance. You can avoid both risks by never driving cars other than the company car and never driving with coworker passengers.

The avoidance strategy works only if you follow it perfectly. If you cheat even once, you risk incurring a catastrophic amount of liability. Because of the difficulty of following the avoidance strategy, I recommend you use one of the first two strategies instead. I mention the avoidance strategy only because I've had clients choose it — although their choice made me extremely nervous.

I Want It My Way: Protecting Your Customized Vehicles

Today, it's fairly common for people to buy vehicles that are highly customized. What do I mean by *customized?* This broad category can include custom paint jobs, captain's chairs, carpeting, high-end stereos, TVs, DVD players, refrigerators, slide-in campers, or pickup toppers. And don't forget the specialized equipment installed in vehicles designed to assist the handicapped, such as wheelchair lifts.

If the equipment is anything beyond that which comes standard from the factory, the majority of auto policies do not insure that extra equipment for damage (for example, loss through theft, fire, vandalism, or collision).

You can, however, insure the custom equipment if you declare it to the insurance company and pay an extra premium. Compare the price against the benefits and decide if it's worth the cost. That way you won't have any surprises if you opt not to cover your customizations and face a loss.

Antiques Roadshow: Insuring Your Antiques and Classic Cars

The biggest concern that owners of classic cars have when insuring them is getting back the full collector's value of the car — not just the book value. For example, the book value on a 1965 Ford Mustang convertible may be $500 for an unrestored car. However, the car may be worth $10,000 in restored condition. So how do you get an insurance company to pay out the $10,000 instead of the $500 for your classic car?

The insurance industry's solution to this problem is an optional coverage they call *stated-amount coverage*. Here's how it works: You collect and send to your insurance company both interior and exterior photos of the car and a market-value appraisal from a competent appraiser. The car is then listed on the policy for $10,000 (or whatever it's worth), and you pay a premium based on that $10,000.

If the car is stolen, how much do you expect to collect? Ten thousand dollars? Not likely. Stated-amount coverage pays the market value of the car at the time of the loss, not to exceed the stated amount (in this case, $10,000). People who buy stated-amount coverage mistakenly expect to receive the appraised value of the car if it is stolen or totaled. In the case of the Mustang, however, if the market has recently soured and the market value of the car is $6,000, you receive $6,000 — not the $10,000 that your premiums have been based on. Now assume that the market for the Mustang has improved, and the car's value is $13,000. How much will you receive? Unfortunately, $10,000 — not $13,000.

Obviously, an inequity exists here. The major pitfall of stated-amount coverage is that it pays the *lesser* of the stated amount and the actual value of the car at the time of the loss. It does not pay any increases in the car's value.

Until the insurance industry comes up with a better solution, I recommend that you adopt the following strategy when insuring antique or classic cars:

- ✔ Do *not* buy the optional stated-amount coverage. Instead, opt for the usual actual cash value coverage that comes standard with the policy.

- ✔ Gather photos of both the interior and exterior, as well as any appraisals, and keep them in a secure place outside the vehicle to prove what you had if the car is ever stolen.

If the car is ever totaled or stolen, the insurance company owes you the *actual cash value* (ACV) — generally interpreted by most claims adjusters to be the market value of your specific vehicle — on the date of loss.. That is where the photos and appraisal come in. You simply bring that documentation to a competent appraiser at claim time, have her give you a new current value appraisal, and submit the photos and the new appraisal to the adjuster for payment. In the case of the examples involving the Mustang, you would receive its actual value at the time of the loss — $6,000 in the first example and $13,000 in the second.

Bottom line: If you adopt this strategy, you get paid properly. Plus, you save the substantial added premium that you would be charged for stated-amount coverage.

Get Your Motor Runnin': Covering Your Motorcycle

Most of Chapter 5 on the subject of automobiles also applies to motorcycles, so this section is brief. Here are my insurance tips for licensed two-wheelers:

✔ **Buy the same liability insurance limits for injuries and property damage to others that you buy for all your other insurance coverage (cars, home, boat, cabin).**

✔ **Buy the same liability limits for guest passengers riding with you, if those limits are available.** If they're not, don't carry passengers!

✔ **Avoid lay-up periods, during which all coverage except comprehensive is suspended for a small premium credit.** It's simply not worth the risk of your forgetting and accidentally driving during the lay-up period, such as on an unseasonably nice day in February, with no insurance.

✔ **Avoid buying more medical coverage than state law requires.** It simply duplicates the health insurance you already should be carrying. Following this tip will save you quite a bit of money on your cycle insurance. (If you don't carry health insurance, you're breaking one of my Chapter 2 rules and gambling with more than you can afford to lose!)

✔ **If it's available in your state, carry uninsured and under-insured motorists coverage in limits equal to your liability limits.**

✔ **If you've customized your cycle, make sure to list the additions on your application.** You may have to pay an extra premium if you want that equipment covered.

✔ **If your cycle is worth enough that you carry collision and comprehensive coverage, follow the guidelines in Chapter 5 regarding how to choose the most cost-effective deductibles.**

To reduce both the chance of — and the seriousness of — injury claims to yourself and others, follow the two best risk management tips I know of:

- ✔ **Prevent serious head injuries.** Everyone on the cycle should wear a helmet. No exceptions.

- ✔ **Minimize the amount of time you carry passengers.** Passenger injuries are the number-one source of lawsuits against motorcycle operators.

Insuring Your New Teenage Driver

That day you've dreaded forever is finally here. Your little darling is now of legal driving age and is doing exactly what all kids his age do to their parents: He's bugging the crap out of you to drive.

In my opinion after insuring hundreds of these new drivers for clients over three decades, there are three steps parents can take to significantly impact their child's success as a driver:

- ✔ Expose your teen to many more hours of driving with a permit under your supervision than the law requires them to have, under every type of condition possible (ideally 30 to 40 hours).

- ✔ Do not okay your teen's licensing until he's responsible in all areas of his life. How responsible he is outside a car is pretty indicative of how he'll drive.

- ✔ After he does get licensed, set limits on his driving in that first year. For example, when he's driving, change his curfew from 11 p.m. to 10 p.m., set the rule that he can't have more than one passenger in the car, tell him he can't drive on the freeway, and so on.

For several other ideas on reducing the risks involving a teen driver, see the latter part of Chapter 3.

Keeping in mind that new teen driver roughly doubles your rates on the car she most often drives if she is an occasional operator and triples the rates if she is a principal operator, here are some tips that will reduce your insurance bill:

- ✔ Keep her as an occasional-use driver for as long as you can. This strategy saves 30 percent off her principal driver rates. (To reap the benefit of this practice, make sure you always have fewer cars than you have licensed drivers in the household.)

- Have her drive the older family vehicle, the value of which is low enough to not need collision or comprehensive. This approach saves 30 percent of her occasional driver cost. (Plus, the older car can handle a few learning-how-to-drive dings and dents.)

- Encourage her to get good grades. If she gets a B average or better, you may be able to save 15 percent on your insurance — check with your agent to see about the incentives your insurer offers.

- Teach her to be a safe driver. If she has no tickets or accidents, you may be able to avoid a 25 percent three-year surcharge, for example.

- If she goes off to college 100 miles or more away from home and doesn't bring a car with her, ask for a distant student credit. This can save you 70 percent to 80 percent on her insurance costs. Plus, she'll be able to drive during vacations and holidays and will be covered at school when she borrows a friend's car.

- When she becomes a driver of her own car, keep it titled in your name until she is officially out of the house. She'll pay 30 percent more on her own policy.

Chapter 7

Insuring Recreational Toys and Trailers

. . . .

In This Chapter

▶ Understanding the automatic coverage of homeowner's policies

▶ Discovering the insurance options for boats and RVs you own

▶ Protecting yourself when renting recreational toys

▶ Understanding how to insure every type of trailer

. . . .

*P*eople love their toys: speedboats, sailboats, pontoons, jet skis, mopeds, all-terrain vehicles, go-karts, golf carts, snowmobiles, campers. . . . The list goes on and on. They're great fun — and they pose some significant risks to the owners, because most of them have little or no coverage under standard auto and homeowner's policies.

When you consider insuring your recreational toys (whether a boat or snowmobile, golf cart or ATV), keep in mind that they all share the same two risks:

✔ **Risk to your personal assets from injuries or property damage you cause others:** This risk has to be insured, and it should be insured at the same limits you buy for your cars and home.

✔ **Risk of theft or damage to the toy itself:** Here the decision as to whether to insure depends on the toy's current value, the cost to insure it, and your tolerance for taking the risk yourself.

In this chapter, I give you the information you need to insure your watercraft, recreational vehicles, and trailers. I also share how you can protect yourself when you're borrowing or renting them from others.

Covering your risk without buying insurance

When managing the risks that come with watercraft, recreational vehicles, and trailers, you can make very good use of the non-insurance techniques I cover in Chapter 3 — avoid, reduce, retain, and transfer (ARRT):

✔ **Avoid:** You can avoid the risk altogether by not buying these toys, although I'm assuming if you're reading this chapter, that isn't an option for you.

✔ **Reduce:** You can reduce the risk by using your toys responsibly, storing them in a safe place, making sure that they're always locked when not in use, and being careful about who you let use the vehicles. Make sure that the guy driving your go-kart is a

safe driver. Just because he's your wife's sister's neighbor, doesn't mean he should be allowed behind the wheel.

✔ **Retain:** If the watercraft, recreational vehicles, or trailers are older, their damage may not be worth insuring against. If you do decide to insure it, you can reduce costs by retaining a portion of the risk — a sizable deductible.

✔ **Transfer:** Transferring works, for example, if you own a boat and are leasing it to others when you're not using it. You can transfer much of the risk of damage to the boat while it's being rented to the renter by use of a contract.

Man Overboard! Insuring Watercraft

A friend once told me the second happiest day of his life occurred when he bought a boat. The happiest day occurred when he sold it! In between those two happy events, here are the kinds of risks he faced — and you face — as a boat owner, along with my advice on how to protect yourself from each.

Covering your liability

The typical homeowner's policy has a liability exclusion for boats, but it isn't all bad news: It includes some exceptions that actually *provide* coverage. The homeowner's boat liability exclusion addresses several different scenarios — owning, renting, or borrowing a boat. I spell it all out in Table 7-1, but keep in mind that the references to boat lengths and horsepower (HP) in the table are for purposes of illustration only — the exact horsepower and boat lengths vary from one policy to the next. Also keep in mind that this section of a homeowner's policy can be confusing, so if you're not sure what you're covered for, talk to your agent.

Your homeowner's policy watercraft coverage may be different from what you see in Table 7-1. Consult your agent or read your homeowner's policy to find out the specifics for your situation. Homeowner's policies vary widely when it comes to boat coverage.

Table 7-1   Automatic Homeowner's Liability Coverage for Boats

	Boats with Inboard or Inboard/Outboard Motors		Boats with Outboard Motors		Sailboats	
	50 HP or Less	More than 50 HP	25 HP or Less	More than 25 HP	Less than 26 Feet	26 Feet or More
Owned	No	No	Yes	No	Yes	No
Borrowed	Yes	Yes	Yes	Sometimes*	Yes	Yes
Rented	Yes	No	Yes	Sometimes*	Yes	No

If you don't own the outboard motor, yes. Otherwise, no.

Many insurers are starting to exclude liability coverage for jet-ski-type one- or two-person watercraft regardless of horsepower due to the disproportionately large number of injuries and deaths involved with these watercraft. They run at very high speeds and are often operated by teens too young to appreciate their danger. If you own or occasionally use one, check with your agent to make sure you're covered, and exercise good judgment regarding its use.

In the following sections, I offer some tips for managing your boat liability risks under your homeowner's policy. The following tips assume coverage identical to that in Table 7-1.

Check with your agent or carefully read your policy to determine exactly what your policy covers.

Here are some non-insurance strategies you can use to decrease the risks involved in operating a boat — whether you own it, borrow it, or rent it:

✔ **Don't mix drinking and boating.** This one doesn't need any explanation.

✔ **If you have a motorized boat, have all users take a boating safety class that's been approved by the U.S. Coast Guard (www.uscg.mil).** In addition to being safer boaters, you usually get a nifty discount (10 percent to 15 percent) on your boat insurance premiums, for the rest of your life.

✔ **If young people drive the boat, make sure that they're well-trained and know exactly what they are and are not allowed to do.** Many boating accidents start with kids goofing off behind the wheel.

See Chapter 3 for more on non-insurance strategies for managing risks.

For boats you own

If you own a boat with an outboard motor of 25 HP or less, or a sailboat less than 26 feet long, you won't need to buy separate boat liability coverage because coverage is included — free — in your homeowner's policy. If you own any other type of boat or motor, you don't have automatic coverage and will need to buy boat liability coverage, either as a homeowner's endorsement or in a separate boat policy.

For boats you borrow

If you operate almost any boat of any size that is borrowed (meaning neither owned nor rented), you have automatic liability coverage. Here are two examples of when this most likely would occur:

✔ Your friend invites your family to go water-skiing with his boat. He does the driving at first, but now he wants to ski, so he asks you to drive. If you carelessly drive the boat in a way that injures him or you hit a swimmer and are sued, where would you get your coverage? Right here — in your wonderful homeowner's policy.

✔ If you go sailing with a friend on her boat and she lets you take the helm, where do you get liability coverage if you cause injuries or collide with another boat? Again, in your homeowner's policy.

For boats you rent

If you rent a boat — say, on vacation — you have automatic coverage for your liability for injuries or property damage in each case except for the following two situations:

✔ If the boat you rent has an inboard motor or an inboard/outboard motor of more than 50 HP

✔ If the boat is a sailboat 26 feet long or more

To get liability coverage for these two excluded types of rented watercraft, you can

✔ **Buy coverage from the boat rental agency, if it offers the coverage.** Many don't.

✔ **Be covered under your existing boat liability policy.** If you own a boat at home for which you have a boat liability policy, it may include coverage for when you rent most other boats. Again, many don't.

✔ **Get the coverage from a supplemental personal-liability policy called an** *umbrella policy* **(see Chapters 15 and 16 for more information).** Be sure to read your policy or check with your agent. Not all umbrellas cover boat rentals. If yours doesn't, shop for a better policy.

When you're renting a boat that is excluded under your homeowner's policy, if you can't get coverage from some other source, then the best non-insurance strategy to practice is to avoid the risk (see Chapter 3). Either don't rent at all, or rent something else for which you *will* be insured.

Covering damage to your boat

Boats — including their motors, trailers, and other equipment — are usually limited in most homeowner's policies to $1,500 of coverage, plus no wind coverage unless they're stored inside a building and no theft coverage away from home. In addition, many of the hazards related to boating — such as collisions, sinking, and hitting submerged rocks — are not covered at all.

If your entire watercraft setup is worth less than $1,500 and you can live with the limitations (regarding wind, theft, and hazards), then you may want to forgo insurance and cover any losses out of your own pocket. If you go this route, make sure that you store the boat in an enclosed building to prevent wind damage, and while you're using the boat prevent theft by securing it well if you leave it unattended.

If you want broader coverage, including coverage for normal boating hazards, buy either a special watercraft policy or a homeowner's endorsement with *open perils coverage* (which covers every kind of loss or damage to your boat with just a few exclusions, like wear and tear, intentional damage, and so on). Annual premiums are about 1 percent to 2 percent of the value of the boat and equipment. The deductible is at least $100, however. Choose a higher deductible if you save enough on the premium to justify taking the extra risk.

Many boat buyers buy the boat, motor, and trailer at a discounted package price. Yet most freestanding boat policies ask you to declare a separate value for each item — the hull, the motor, and the trailer. Because any one of the three can be stolen, make sure that the amount you insure each for is the retail cost to buy the item by itself. Be sure to include something, typically $300 to $500, for miscellaneous boat equipment (anchors, oars, life jackets, fuel tanks, seat cushions, depth finders, and so on). And don't forget to include sales tax in your values.

Insuring Recreational Vehicles

When I refer to *recreational vehicles,* I mean motorized vehicles not licensed for road use, such as ATVs, go-karts, golf carts, mopeds, snowmobiles, and so on. (Even those little motorized cars for kids, like Power Wheels, fall in this category.) All motorized vehicles — except those used for service to the home itself (such as riding lawn mowers) — are excluded from homeowner's property coverage. Why? Because these vehicles present a greater-than-average risk.

Unlike watercraft — where there is some coverage for small watercraft under a homeowner's policy — there is no automatic liability coverage for owned recreational vehicles. The one exception is when you use the vehicles on your residential property or on vacant land you own — in both of those cases, your homeowner's insurance will cover you.

Most homeowner's policies provide liability coverage for any borrowed or rented recreational vehicles, regardless of size or horsepower, if they aren't licensed for road use. So you're covered when you rent a golf cart at your local course, for example, or when you rent snowmobiles on your Rocky Mountain winter vacation.

If you drive to and from the golf course or if you live in a community that allows golf-cart use on local streets, your homeowner's policy may not cover your liability for your road use automatically. Newer versions of homeowner's policies recognize the growing use of golf carts in retirement communities for local transportation to and from the grocery store, for example, so they've made an exception for such use if it complies with local traffic ordinances and community association rules. If your homeowner's policy doesn't cover you, you can arrange coverage through your auto policy. When in doubt, check with your agent.

The only time you need to buy liability coverage for your use of recreational vehicles is if you own them yourself (as opposed to borrowing or renting them), and you're using them off your own land. So, for example, if you plan to go snowmobiling out on your neighbor's fields, and someone gets hurt, you're not covered under your homeowner's policy.

Most insurers offer liability and optional theft or collision coverage for recreational vehicles. Some offer the coverage under a homeowner's policy endorsement; others offer a stand-alone recreational vehicle policy; and still others cover them as a special endorsement to your car insurance policy. The coverage is usually equally good under any of the three choices, so price them all with your agent.

Even if you buy full insurance coverage for a go-kart, almost all policies exclude racing, both organized or informal, and coverage is difficult to come by.

Avoiding the Hidden Danger of Recreational Rentals

Even when you've arranged liability coverage for injuries and property damage you cause to the public while renting boats or recreational vehicles, you don't have liability coverage for damage to the rented item itself. (See the exclusion in your homeowner's policy for property that is in your custody.)

Here's an example of the problem for a boat rental that also applies when renting recreational vehicles of all types: You're on vacation and you see a boat that you want to rent. If you're like most people, you scribble your signature on a contract without reading it. (Who has time to read? You're on vacation!) You pay a damage deposit, usually about $500, and you assume that if you damage the boat, you'll just lose your deposit. Then you're off, operating a boat that you may be unfamiliar with, on a body of water that you may also be unfamiliar with.

Your uninsured liability for damage to the boat itself occurs in two ways:

✔ Your legal liability for damage you actually cause to the boat when operating it yourself

✔ Your contractual liability in which you agreed to be responsible for anything that happens to the boat, even when the damage is not your fault

"Okay, but the worst that can happen is that I'm out the damage deposit," you say. Not true, unless the damage is less than the damage deposit. The damage deposit is just a deposit. If the boat is destroyed in a tornado, or if you hit some submerged rocks causing an engine fire that burns the boat, you're liable for the cost of the repairs or the cost to replace the boat.

Now, assume you're sharing the rental with a friend. You're both driving the boat, and you're splitting the cost. But you signed the contract; he didn't. Your friend drives recklessly and seriously damages the boat. Who does the rental agency go after? You — because you agreed to be responsible for anything that happens! Ouch!

How can you protect yourself? Read the contract before you sign it or have it faxed to your insurance agent. If the contract makes you responsible (most rental contracts do), there are two ways to protect yourself:

✔ **Buy the optional insurance from the rental agency, but only if it covers all the damage you're responsible for.** Often, it does not.

✔ **Rely on coverage in your umbrella policy.** If it doesn't cover damage to any boat you rent, find an umbrella policy that does. The good ones do. (See Chapter 16 for tips on buying the right umbrella policy.)

Up the creek without a policy

I rented a 28-foot sailboat, worth $30,000, on Lake Pepin in Southern Minnesota. I paid the $500 damage deposit and was told that amount would be all I owed if I damaged the boat. When I read the contract, I pointed out to the gruff character behind the desk that his contract made me responsible for the entire $30,000 — not just for the $500 — if any serious damage should occur. He scoffed, "Don't worry about that! The owner has the boat insured. All you'd owe is the $500 deductible. She'd collect the rest from her insurance company." He's correct. But what he *doesn't* know is how quickly the insurance company would send me a registered letter and a copy of the rental contract I signed, demanding that I reimburse them for all repair costs, or even for the cost of buying a new boat. And I would owe them every penny!

That is exactly what would happen (not a pretty picture).

Always read rental contracts. See if you're responsible for just your deposit or for the entire boat. If you're responsible for the entire boat, you need to arrange for insurance. *Do not rely on verbal statements from rental agents.* And don't assume that the optional insurance the rental agent offers is comprehensive — that it covers all damage you're responsible for. Make sure there's no dollar limit on the coverage (such as a $2,000 limit on a $30,000 boat). Read the policy exclusions. Make sure the policy doesn't exclude something important. If the policy has either a dollar limit less than the boat's value or if it excludes anything you're doing, don't buy it.

On the Road Again: Managing Trailer Risks

Trailers come in just about every size, shape, and color you can imagine. There are pop-up tent trailers, horse trailers, utility trailers, boat trailers, and trailers to haul recreational vehicles. There are rental trailers for household moves. And of course there are camping trailers with self-contained living quarters. Some of these are towed from place to place; others are parked at an owned or leased property and used as vacation homes.

Finding liability coverage

The good news is that, when you're hauling any trailer — whether you own it or not — liability coverage from your auto policy fully extends to the trailer automatically for the same liability limits as you carry on your vehicles at no additional charge. The bad news is that the free coverage from the auto insurance policy ends as soon as the trailer is disconnected from the vehicle. A homeowner's policy does extend liability coverage to your trailer when it's at your residence or temporarily elsewhere, like a camping trailer at a campground.

Premises liability coverage ends, however, for a camping trailer away from home if you own or lease the land on which it sits (such as an owned lake lot or a trailer park lot leased for the summer). For a modest charge (less than $20 per year), you can get an extension on your homeowner's policy, providing liability coverage to the trailer and the lot on which it sits.

Never park a camping trailer on a vacant lot you own or lease long-term without endorsing your homeowner's policy to extend liability coverage to that lot.

Covering damage to your trailer

Trailers are typically covered only up to a $1,500 limit on a homeowner's policy. Like watercraft, there is usually no windstorm coverage if they are outside a building and no theft coverage away from home. If your trailer is worth under $1,500, if you can protect it against wind damage in the open and theft damage away from home, and if you can live with paying your homeowner's deductible if the trailer is damaged or stolen, don't buy additional insurance.

You can get full collision and comprehensive coverage on your trailer by adding the trailer and its value to your auto policy. However, it's usually less expensive to insure a boat or RV trailer on the same form you use to ensure the boat or RV.

Personal property being hauled in a camping trailer is covered under the homeowner's off-premises coverage for the same perils that the homeowner's policy covers — you get little or no breakage coverage. If you add special perils coverage to your homeowner's policy, breakage coverage would apply to all but glassware and other highly breakable items.

However, if the trailer is parked on a lot owned or rented long term (such as a lakeshore lot), there may not be any theft coverage when you aren't there. In that case, reducing the risk may be your best choice. When you leave the trailer for any length of time, take high-theft items with you (such as your portable TV, computer, and so on), and spend the extra money on a quality lock.

Chapter 8

Getting What You Deserve for Automobile Claims

In This Chapter
▶ Documenting your claim to collect top dollar
▶ Working with the insurance adjuster effectively
▶ Maximizing your settlement
▶ Getting more than book value when your car is totaled

*T*he majority of claim disputes or unhappiness, based on my years of observation, arise from claims for damage to automobiles, homes, and personal property. This chapter focuses on your automobile damage claims. (Turn to Chapter 14 for home and personal property claims.)

Your automobile claim is underpaid or denied by an insurance company for three main reasons:

✔ **The type of claim being submitted isn't covered at all or not fully covered by your particular policy — although it would have been fully covered by a more comprehensive policy.** This situation is the most common.

✔ **The type of claim being submitted is never covered by any policy.** This situation rarely occurs.

✔ **The claim is mishandled by the insurance company.** This situation occurs enough that you need to be aware of the problem.

The majority of the other chapters in this book focus on the first bullet — protecting yourself by having coverages that are right for the unique risks in your life. This chapter's focus is on the last bullet. In this chapter, I show you what to do to make sure that your automobile claim will be paid in full.

When You're at Fault: Collecting from Your Collision Coverage

You've just been involved in a collision, and you have collision coverage on your auto policy. Collision coverage pays to fully repair your car or replace it if it's a total loss (minus your deductible, of course), regardless of who's at fault. If you're the primary cause of an accident and your car is damaged, there are only two places to get the money for repairs — collision coverage or your kid's piggy bank.

You report the claim either to your agent or directly to the insurer. A claims adjuster contacts you. If your car is drivable, you may be asked to get one or two estimates, or the adjuster may inspect the car herself and write her own estimate.

Here are a few of the common problems you may encounter during this process and what you can do to solve them:

- ✔ **You don't like the shop that the insurer recommends.** Most insurance companies have relationships with body shops that they've found to be easy to work with, as well as reasonable in their estimates and in negotiating repair costs. In most states, though, you have the right to pick the shop of your choice, and you can insist that your insurance company work with that shop.

  Some shops are known to be price gougers. It benefits everyone if you avoid those shops — keeping repair costs reasonable keeps premiums down.

- ✔ **The adjuster demands that you get two or three estimates.** Requesting one estimate is reasonable — get it from your preferred body shop. If it's not inconvenient, getting a second estimate helps keep shops honest. If you prefer not to get a second estimate, you may have the right to refuse and request that the insurance company send an appraiser to work out a repair price with your shop, especially if your car is not drivable. As for a third estimate, refuse — it's totally unreasonable of the adjuster to ask that of you.

- ✔ **Your preferred shop won't honor the adjuster's estimate.** Unfortunately, this situation occurs often. When an adjuster is busy, he'll write an estimate and hand or mail you a check for that amount. At first, you may be happy to have such prompt service. Then you bring your car in, and the body shop refuses to repair it for the amount the adjuster gave you. The body shop often points out damage that the adjuster missed. Don't worry — just call the adjuster and ask him to work out a new repair price with your shop and issue you a second check.

Never accept an estimate and payment before your preferred body shop agrees to do the repairs for that amount.

✔ **The body shop wants additional money from you before it will release the car.** The shop may do this for one of two reasons:

- The adjuster may have approved additional damage, but the second claim check has not arrived. If so, the solution is to sign a form (available in every body shop) authorizing your insurer to bypass you and pay the shop directly for the additional cost. Then most shops will release your car without further problems. If the shop still won't release your car, the best bet is to charge the additional amount to your credit card.

- A second possibility is that the shop may be trying to pull a fast one. All reputable shops know that any supplemental repairs must be approved by the adjuster. If the shop surprises you with demands for more money when you arrive, it did the repairs without an authorization. The shop is hoping that you'll be so desperate to get your car released that you'll either pay the difference yourself or protest so loudly to your insurance company that it will pay just to appease you.

  If the shop did not get an approval, the shop is the bad guy. *Don't pay them.* Sign an authorization for your insurance company to pay additional amounts, if any, to the body shop. The shop then has to do what it should have done and try to work things out with your adjuster. But then it's the shop's problem, not yours.

✔ **The insurer won't pay for new parts.** You have a nice, clean, low-mileage, 8-year old car. It's banged up. The adjuster's estimate is for used parts, but you want new parts. The insurance company is within its rights to replace your used parts with used parts. You have the right to make sure that the parts are in good condition, and you can refuse to allow them to be used if they aren't. You also have the right to demand new parts, although you'll have to pay the difference between the cost of new parts and the cost of used parts. Think of it this way: The insurance company is within its rights when it only pays for used parts because it only has to replace what you had — and your parts certainly had some wear and tear on them by the time you were in the accident.

✔ **Getting cash when you won't be making the repairs.** The insurance company, not you, gets to choose whether to repair, replace, or pay cash. That said, most insurers still let you choose cash if you prefer. Companies differ on the amount of cash they pay — some pay you the full repair cost; others pay what they call an *appearance allowance* to compensate you for the loss in value of your damaged car. If you're not happy with the amount of an appearance allowance, go to a dealer. Show the used-car manager your car. Ask him to write on his letterhead both the preaccident and postaccident values of your car. You're entitled to receive the difference between these two values if you decide not to repair the car (assuming that value is less than the repair costs).

Deciding whether to file a small claim: How insurance company pricing works

You back into a post and cause $973 in damage to your car. You have a $500 collision coverage deductible. You file the claim and collect the $473. Four months later, your auto insurance premium comes with an at-fault accident surcharge of $300 a year for three years. In short, you end up paying $900 to collect $473.

You aren't happy. Why didn't someone warn you so that you could have paid the claim yourself? And how unfair that the dollar amount of the rate increase for your minor accident could exceed what you collected in your claim! Here's why that happens and how you can protect yourself in the future.

When you buy car insurance, you get grouped, and share losses with, people similar to you in age, location, use of car, and driving record (tickets and at-fault accidents). When any of these factors change, you move to, and share losses with, a different group of drivers. (Remember when you turned 25 and your rates dropped 30 percent? On that day, you weren't a better driver than the day before, but you transferred to a group of more experienced drivers who have fewer accidents and lower premiums.)

Similar changes in your insurance rate happen when you move from one city to another, or change the use of your cars, or when you get tickets or are in an at-fault accident. You simply change groups. When you hit a post and file a claim, you change groups — just like when you get a couple of speeding tickets.

Before you file a small claim with your insurance company, find out first how much more you'll pay over the next few years in insurance premiums. If it's greater than the claim value,

you're probably better off paying the claim yourself. Note that some insurance companies forgive the charge for the first at-fault accident if you've been insured with them a while. Other companies won't charge for at-fault accidents unless the amount they spend exceeds a certain threshold — typically $500 or $1,000.

Your agent, if you have one, should always warn you of the impact it will have on your future rates when you report a small claim. He can estimate for you the extra costs of reporting the claim and help you decide if it's in your best interest to do so.

Remember: Never file a small claim for an accident you cause without first knowing the total impact on your rates — unless there's even the smallest injury. If there's any kind of injury, *always* file the claim, no matter how small, or you could void your liability coverage for that injury.

A good agent will look at the entire family driving record when deciding to report a small claim. Maybe this minor accident, combined with a speeding ticket from two months ago, will jump your rates $1,500 over three years. Maybe the family driving record is so bad that one more accident will cancel your policy and force you into high risk insurance where the rates are double what you're paying now. Under these circumstances, you may not even report a $2,500 accident. It may be cheaper, in the long run, to pay for it yourself.

If you do have a poor driving history, it may make sense not to carry collision coverage or to have high deductibles. Why pay for coverage that you aren't going to use?

When It's the Other Guy's Fault: Considering Other Factors

When you're in a collision caused by the other driver, you often have the choice between using your own collision coverage (if you have collision coverage) or collecting from the other driver's liability insurance (if he has liability insurance). If you have no collision coverage on your car, you only have one choice: to collect from his insurance (or from him, personally, if he has no insurance).

Collision insurance pays to repair your car if it's damaged in an accident, regardless of who's at fault.

As a general rule, if your damage is caused by the other driver and you have collision coverage, you should collect from your own coverage, especially if your car is not drivable. Your insurance company will almost always be faster and easier to deal with, because you're its customer. And, unlike with the other driver's insurance company, your claim won't be delayed because of an investigation (see "Proving your version of the accident," later). Also, you'll spend less in the long run, in spite of your collision deductible, in states where *subrogation* (see the "Sub-ro-what?" sidebar) and *comparative negligence* (see the "Comparative negligence: Assigning blame" sidebar) are allowed.

Sub-ro-what?

You're in a wreck. Another driver caused the accident, but you choose to have your insurance, under collision coverage, pay for the damage to your vehicle. Your legal rights to seek reimbursement from the other driver are transferred to your insurance company. This transfer of rights is known as *subrogation.* Your company gets compensated by the other driver's company.

When your insurance company subrogates against the other driver, it usually tries to get your deductible reimbursed too, saving you a lot of hassle. For various reasons, it often collects less than 100 percent of the amount that it spent fixing your car. Whatever percentage it collects, you get the same percentage of your deductible back. The bad news is that the collection process often takes six months or more. So when you spend your deductible, don't look for the cash to come back to you anytime soon.

Comparative negligence: Assigning blame

Most states use *comparative negligence* to apportion fault in an auto accident. Comparative negligence takes into account the fact that not all accidents are 100 percent the fault of one driver. If you rear end someone who is sitting at a red light, you probably would be assessed 100 percent of the fault. But if you pull from a stop sign into the side of a passing car, you may be assigned 85 percent of the fault, and the other driver may be assigned 15 percent.

The percentage of fault assessed the lesser at-fault driver depends on how much opportunity that driver had or should have had to avoid the accident. There's no hard and fast rule about fault.

If you have collision coverage and you live in a comparative negligence state, you're almost always better off using your collision coverage, paying your deductible, and letting your insurance company subrogate against the other driver or insurance company — unless the other driver is 100 percent at fault. After subrogation, your net cost will always be less than collecting directly from the other driver's insurance.

One of the biggest drawbacks to collecting from the other driver's insurance is the delay in getting paid. Before the other driver's insurance company can pay you, it has to interview the other driver and investigate the accident. That can take two weeks.

To expedite the process, you can

- ✔ **Call and report the claim directly to the other driver's insurance company or agent.** When you aren't the other company's customer, the company may very likely take a few days just to get the claim reported and set up, so you'll save time by getting the process started right away.

- ✔ **When reporting the accident, get the other driver's insurance company's okay to pay for a rental car.** If it balks and you need a rental, get one anyway and let the insurer know about it. Why? Because when the company is paying for a rental car, it speeds up your claim processing. Without a rental car, its slow processing hurts you; with a rental, delays hurt the insurance company. If the accident is the other guy's fault, his insurance owes you both for the cost to repair you car and the cost of a replacement vehicle. Some insurance companies claim they don't cover your rental. That's baloney — if the company balks, send the bill directly to the other driver.

Navigating the Total-Loss Maze

When the costs to repair your car exceed your car's value, you have what's known as a *total-loss claim.* (If you want the full-blown details on how an insurance company figures this out, check out the nearby sidebar, "How you know if your car is really totaled.")

If your car is a total loss, the *actual cash* value (that is, the preaccident market value) of your specific car at the time of loss needs to be established. Remember, this is different from book value. *Book value* is the average selling price of a car like yours, with similar features and mileage, in a cleaned up, dent-free condition. Various used car guides list these prices.

You should know three things about book value:

- ✔ It's the *average* selling price for a car like yours, in your area, which means there were plenty of cars that sold for more — some even much more. Your mint car could be one of those. Of course, the reverse could also be true.

- ✔ It's a guide — it says so right on the cover — not a bible.

- ✔ It doesn't always take into account the supply and demand factors in your particular area. A sports car in Alaska may not be worth as much as a sports car in Los Angeles.

How you know if your car is really totaled

Your insurance company must determine three values before concluding that your car is a total loss:

- ✔ The value of your car at the time of the accident

- ✔ The total cost to repair your vehicle

- ✔ The amount a salvage yard would pay for your car

Your car is a total loss if the repair cost exceeds the car's preaccident value minus any salvage value. For example, let's say your car's preaccident value was $5,300 and the repair estimate is $4,800. At this point, it seems like the insurance company is $500 better off repairing your car. But now factor in salvage value. The salvage company bid is $850. The insurance company will *total out* your car because its net cost to do so is $5,300 (paid to you) less $850 (which it will get from the salvage company). Your insurance company ends up losing $4,450, which is $350 less than the $4,800 it would have had to pay to fix the car.

Now suppose the repair estimate was only $4,000. The insurance company would probably still total it, because of *hidden damage.* Most estimates to repair seriously damaged cars underestimate the final costs because all the damage can't be seen until repairs are started and the outer parts are removed. What starts out looking like a $4,000 repair often ends up costing closer to $5,000 or $6,000.

Keeping your car after it's been totaled

Suppose you have a nice car. It's your baby. You've cared for it, maintained it, changed the oil every 3,000 miles. It's been a great car. Suddenly, it's in an accident. The front end is banged up and needs new parts. It can be repaired and be as good as new, but your insurance company won't pay for repairs. The insurer is calling it a total loss and offering you $5,300 for your baby. You protest, but the repair estimate is $5,800 — plus possible hidden damage. You're heartbroken. Is there anything you can do?

Yes, even though the insurance company won't generally volunteer this fact: You can accept the $5,300 (less your deductible) and keep the car by paying the insurance company what it would have received from the salvage yard (say, $500). You now still own your banged-up car and have $4,800 you can use toward repairs. You then can either not repair all the damage, or do what most people do — find a quality, small shop that, with the aid of used parts, can probably repair the entire car for $4,800 or less. Remember this strategy. It really works!

For all these reasons, the book value will be different from your specific car's preaccident market value. (You can check out the book value of your car at www.kellybluebook.com.)

The pre-accident value of your car is what you would have to pay to replace it with a car almost exactly like yours. Therefore, your insurance company needs to check with used-car dealers to see what price your car, preaccident, would sell for. Push the insurance company to get at least three estimates from local dealers. (But be warned: The dealers may give the company a price that's *lower* than the book value.)

To get the best settlement offer possible, check with at least three dealers yourself. Clip out any newspaper used-car ads for cars similar to yours. When you call dealers, talk only to the used-car manager, whose opinion will carry more weight than a salesman's. Then write down the manager's name, the dealership's name, the manager's phone number, and his estimate of what he would sell your car for. If your car is really mint and you have good photos, pay a personal visit to the dealership. The photos will help you get a higher estimated value.

Next, average those three estimates and any newspaper prices to come up with your own estimate of your car's preaccident value. Then sit on it. When the adjuster makes you an offer, if it's equal to or greater than your average estimate, smile at your good fortune. If the offer is less than yours, pull out your information and insist that he either accept your number or, at the very least, average your number with his. If he balks at that, enlist the aid of your insurance agent.

When your car is stolen

A stolen car is deemed a total loss if it's not recovered. But the majority of stolen cars are recovered, usually with damage. If that happens to you, remember that, even though your car was in a collision, the initial cause of loss was theft. Therefore, you will owe your theft deductible rather than your collision deductible. And the theft deductible is usually lower.

Also, because the insurance company doesn't want to pay you for your car and then have it

be recovered, the company typically will wait to settle as long as three to four weeks. Even if you don't have loss-of-use coverage (car rental), because of this added wait, most policies will pay something (usually $15 a day) toward your cost of renting a car, starting 48 to 72 hours after you report the claim. Remember that in case the company forgets to offer it to you.

When you buy a car, you also have to pay sales tax, title fees, and so on. Be sure that the insurance company pays you for all those added costs. And don't forget the prorated share of your license plate fee, based on the number of months until your plates would have expired.

In a total loss situation where the accident was caused by the other driver and where your car won't be repaired, simultaneously file a claim with the other driver's insurance and your own collision coverage. By filing both claims, you'll get two offers for the value of your car, and you can take the highest one.

Dealing with Insurance Adjusters

An *insurance adjuster* is the person empowered by an insurance company to investigate your claim, when you file one, and to determine how much you are entitled to receive. Not only do adjusters have to determine whether you have coverage for your claim, but they also have to work to make sure that the repair or replacement costs are reasonable. Finally, they have to communicate to you — clearly — the settlement offer and how the offer was calculated.

I find that most adjusters do a good job of knowing their coverages and knowing how to control costs. When they fall short, it's most often in one or more of the following areas:

✔ **Communicating:** Some adjusters don't explain how they arrive at the settlement, which is especially important if it's less than what you had expected. Sometimes adjusters don't tell policy holders what to do if repair shops or contractors won't honor the adjuster's estimate, or if there's additional damage that the adjuster missed.

✔ **Getting an agreed price on an auto repair:** Some adjusters just mail a repair estimate and a check, putting you in the awkward position of having to find a body shop to do the work for that price.

✔ **Being reachable:** Sometimes getting in contact with the adjuster is almost impossible, and you aren't given an alternative way to reach someone familiar with the claim, such as the adjuster's supervisor.

The number-one complaint I get from customers is the amount of phone tag they have to play to reach adjusters. You can eliminate most of that frustration by getting the following information the first time you contact the adjuster:

- Claim number

- Date of the accident

- Adjuster's name and phone number(s)

- Name and phone number(s) of the adjuster's supervisor

Don't hesitate to call the adjuster's supervisor if you need to reach someone right away or if you're having a problem with the adjuster.

Here are some things you can do to make your claim go more smoothly:

✔ **Request the direct-dial phone numbers for the adjuster and the adjustor's supervisor when the adjuster first contacts you.**

✔ **Never accept payment for any auto repairs without the adjuster and your body shop agreeing to a price.**

✔ **If you can't reach the adjuster, or you aren't unhappy with her for any reason, call her supervisor.**

✔ **If you don't think the adjuster is doing a good job, call the supervisor or even the claims manager and request that she reassign your file to another adjuster.** You don't have to accept poor performance.

✔ **If you have an agent, don't hesitate to ask for help with any kind of problem that you're having, especially if you feel the settlement offer is too low.** A good agent has the skills to negotiate, on your behalf, to improve an unfair settlement offer.

Resolving Claim Disputes

If your auto damage claim is unjustly denied, go to your agent for help. Many agents have the expertise and skills to be an effective advocate for your rights, and they often succeed in getting claims paid. If that fails, you can mediate, arbitrate, file a complaint with your state insurance department, or even sue your insurance company. (See Chapter 14 for more on those options.)

But what if the adjuster agrees that you're covered but disputes the amount of your claim? Fortunately, your policy has a simple, inexpensive solution built into the policy provisions — the *appraisal clause.*

Virtually every personal policy — auto, home, boat, and so on — contains an appraisal clause. Few people know about it, and even fewer people use it. In this section, I explain how to use the appraisal clause if you and your insurance company don't agree on how much your claim is worth.

Use the appraisal clause *only* after the best attempts of you and your agent to settle the claim for a fair amount have failed.

Either you or your insurance company may request an appraisal if you fail to agree on the dollar value of a covered claim. If you're requesting one, you simply send the insurance company a letter with your request.

Each party picks an appraiser to represent his position. The two appraisers independently choose a disinterested umpire to resolve things if the two appraisers can't reach an agreement. Each party pays for his own appraiser and splits other appraisal expenses (including the umpire's cost, if needed).

The good news is that you aren't forced to accept the insurance company's offer. Also, the process is considerably cheaper and faster than lawsuits or arbitration.

For *most* property valuation disputes, you don't need an elaborate group of three solemn judges. You just need a fair, unbiased, and disinterested person with excellent knowledge regarding the subject of the dispute — someone both parties are comfortable with — to act as the umpire. Both parties agree to abide by the umpire's decision.

Part III

Home Sweet Home: Understanding Homeowner's Insurance

The 5th Wave   By Rich Tennant

"Wait a minute. He sold you a homeowner's policy that covers us in the event Hell freezes over?"

In this part . . .

Most people live a significant portion of their lives in and around their homes, whether those homes are single-family residences, condominiums, town houses, or apartments. They fill these places with the necessary and unnecessary stuff of their lives. Losing a home and/or the stuff in the home would be catastrophic.

In this part, I show you ways to insure against a loss, how to expose gaps in your current coverage, and how to minimize the risk of a loss ever occurring. I also give you information on insuring your home business and collecting what you deserve if you have a claim.

Chapter 9

Understanding the Basics of Homeowner's and Renter's Insurance

*H*omeowner's insurance policies are outstanding values — they offer tremendous amounts of coverage for very little money. But they're also, in my opinion, the most dangerous personal policies you can buy, because they have the largest number of exclusions and limitations.

When you're buying homeowner's insurance, you have to figure out which risks you're exposed to that fall outside the basic box of coverage. Then you can develop a strategy for dealing with those risks.

Most people make the mistake of shopping for their insurance based on price alone. What they usually end up with is the wrong coverage for a cheaper price! (See Chapter 4 for more on the right way to buy insurance.)

To buy the homeowner's insurance you need, first you have to understand something about the basic homeowner's policy. In this chapter, I explain the fundamentals of homeowner's insurance. In Chapters 10 and 11, I show you the different types of coverage gaps and how to protect yourself from them.

Introducing the Six Parts of a Homeowner's Policy

All homeowner's policies have six major coverage parts:

- ✔ **Coverage A:** Covers damage to or destruction of your residence. (***Note:*** This coverage does not apply to renter's insurance policies.)

- ✔ **Coverage B:** Covers damage to or destruction of detached structures. (***Note:*** This coverage does not apply to renter's insurance policies.)

- ✔ **Coverage C:** Covers damage to, destruction of, or theft of personal property anywhere in the world.

- ✔ **Coverage D:** Covers the added living costs you incur as a result of a loss covered by Coverage A, Coverage B, or Coverage C (such as lodging and meals).

- ✔ **Coverage E:** Covers non-vehicle personal liability for injuries and property damage at home and anywhere else in the world.

- ✔ **Coverage F:** Covers medical payments to guests injured on your premises, regardless of fault.

In the following sections, I fill you in on each of these six coverages.

Note: When I refer to *homeowner's insurance,* I also mean renter's insurance (except for Coverage A and Coverage B, which don't apply to renters).

Coverage A: Insuring your home

If you arrange the coverage on your residence properly, the insurance company fully repairs or replaces your home if it's damaged or destroyed by a covered cause of loss — such as a fire, tornado, or whatever your policy happens to cover.

If you insure your home for *less* than its full replacement cost, you need to be aware of two possible claims penalties:

✔ **The first penalty occurs if you are under-insured for a** *total loss* **(the complete destruction of your home).** Say your home — which you bought five years ago and insured for $275,000 — burns to the ground. The cost to rebuild that house in today's market is $350,000. Because you insured the house for $275,000, you suffer an out-of-pocket loss of $75,000.

✔ **The second penalty for under-insurance occurs when your home is partially damaged.** Say you purchased a beautiful, hundred-year-old, two-story home for $300,000 a decade ago. You insure it for $250,000 — the purchase price of $300,000 less the $50,000 lot value. Were you to build this home new today, it would cost you $500,000. Let's assume that you have a kitchen fire with extensive smoke and water damage, and that the total cost to repair your home is $150,000. Your insurance company pays you $100,000. You're out $50,000! Why?

The vast majority of homeowner's policies will only pay the full cost to replace partial damage to your home if you insure your home for at least 80 percent or more of the cost to rebuild new. If you insure your home for less than 80 percent of the home's full replacement cost, your claim settlement will be depreciated. On older homes, that may reduce your claim settlement by 35 percent or more. In this example, the cost to completely rebuild your 100-year-old home isn't the $250,000 you insured your home for, but $500,000. Because $250,000 is far less than 80 percent of $500,000, your settlement will be depreciated.

Translated into English, the policy essentially says that if you insure your home for its depreciated market value (in this case, $250,000), the insurance company settles with you on a depreciated basis at claim time. The $50,000 penalty in this example represents the amount of depreciation deducted from the repair costs.

If, on the other hand, you insure your home for its cost to build new (or at least 80 percent of that value, according to the formula in the policy), the insurance company settles your claim for the full replacement cost of the damage — up to your policy limit.

Always insure for 100 percent of the estimated new replacement cost. Paying the extra premium is far easier than facing thousands of dollars in losses out-of-pocket at claim time from either not having enough insurance to rebuild if your home is destroyed or having your repair costs substantially depreciated on partial losses.

Also, add a home replacement guarantee, if it's available. (See "Guaranteeing you'll have enough insurance to rebuild," later in this chapter, for more information.)

Coverage B: Insuring detached structures (garages, barns, swimming pools, and more)

Virtually all homeowner's policies extend 10 percent of Coverage A — the residence coverage — to detached structures. In other words, if your home is insured for $200,000, you've got up to $20,000 worth of coverage for any detached structure — for no additional charge. Examples of detached structures include garages, pole barns, in-ground swimming pools, decks, and fences. (Always check your policy to see what's counted as a detached structure — policies vary.)

The Coverage B coverage for detached structure has two pitfalls:

✔ **The possibility of under-insurance:** If the structure can't be replaced for the 10 percent automatic coverage you get under Coverage A, and that's all the coverage you have, you could be left holding the bag.

Make sure your detached structure limit equals the total replacement value of *all* detached structures on your premises.

✔ **The business exclusion:** Many insurance companies exclude any detached structure used even partially for business.

Here's an example from my own files that illustrates both pitfalls: Bob and Bobbie have a home insured for $150,000. They have a four-car, detached garage with an upstairs loft. If they were to build this garage new today, it would cost them $35,000. They have automatic coverage from their homeowner's policy that covers their house in the amount of $15,000 (10 percent of $150,000). To be properly insured, they have to buy an additional $20,000 of detached-structure coverage (Coverage B) to bring their total coverage to $35,000.

In addition, Bob is self-employed — he owns and manages several rental properties. The detached garage, besides storing vehicles, also houses business equipment like lawn mowers, snowblowers, and so on. Plus, his business office is located upstairs in the loft portion of the detached garage.

Now, what if a tornado comes through destroying their $35,000 garage? Because they bought the extra $20,000 coverage, they do have $35,000 of insurance. The adjuster shows up with a $35,000 check the next day, right? Wrong. Because Bob stored business equipment in their garage, the insurance company could deny their *entire* claim.

Excusing the exclusions

I'm often asked why there are so many property exclusions and limitations in homeowner's policies. One reason is fairness. ***Remember:*** Insurance is just a mechanism where people facing similar risks pool resources (pay premiums) into a large pot (the insurance company). It's from that pot that compensation for damages from fires, thefts, lawsuits, and so on is paid. Insurance companies don't pay claims, really — *we* do, with our premiums. The insurer is simply a middleman. The company collects money from those of us who don't have losses and redistributes it to those who do.

It's important that people who share losses be similar in the risks they face. That way, people with greater risks than the norm aren't being subsidized by those with normal residential risks. For example, people with vast amounts of jewelry have considerably more jewelry claims than the usual homeowner. If jewelry coverage were unrestricted in the policy, the rates for non-jewelry owners would go up every time the jewelry owner lost or had another piece stolen.

Contrary to public perception, then, these exclusions and limitations are not in the policy to be nasty. They're there primarily to make sure that the premiums will be fair to all payers. Most of what is limited or excluded in the basic policy can be insured for an extra charge.

Remember: Read your policy to find out what is limited or excluded, before a serious loss happens, so that you can properly modify the policy to cover those things that otherwise would not be covered.

This situation certainly doesn't seem fair, but it's how the coverage often works. The equipment had nothing to do with causing the destruction of the garage. Yet, all the insurance company has to prove to deny the claim is that the garage was even *partially* used for business purposes.

If you have a detached structure on your home premises that is even remotely used for business other than for storing business vehicles, you must find out if your policy has this business use exclusion. If so, be sure to request an endorsement to your homeowner's policy that permits that business use.

Coverage C: Insuring your belongings

Two ways exist to value personal belongings for insurance purposes: *actual cash value* (used) and *replacement cost* (new).

Buy the replacement cost option! It's generally only about 10 percent more expensive but you'll receive 30 percent to 40 percent more at claim time. If the total cost of replacing your belongings after a major loss is $100,000, with replacement cost coverage, you'll get $100,000 (minus your deductible). With actual cash value coverage, you'll probably get anywhere from $60,000 to $70,000, after deducting depreciation. Believe me, at claim time you'll be glad you bought the better coverage.

One requirement of the replacement cost coverage is that you actually do replace the damaged or stolen property. Until you do replace it, the insurance company only pays you the depreciated or used value.

For residence owners, the basic homeowner's policy comes standard with personal property coverage of 50 percent to 75 percent of your Coverage A building limit. (The exact percentage varies, depending on the insurance company.) If you have a lot of high-end personal property, the automatic coverage provided under the homeowner's policy may not be enough.

Be sure you evaluate the contents-coverage limit on your policy and customize it to your needs. Don't just take what comes automatically with your policy — it may not be enough. (Later in this chapter, I give you some tools to help estimate what your belongings are worth.)

Coverage D: Insuring additional living expenses

Your house is blown away by a tornado. Even your kitchen sink is in the next county. You check into a motel and call your insurance agent. You'll need a place to live until you rebuild. You'll need to eat your meals out. You'll need a daily massage to soothe your shattered nerves. But you won't have much in the way of utility bills. And you won't be buying any groceries. Some of your living expenses will go way up. Others will shrink. The difference between the two expenses — the *additional living expense* — is covered by Coverage D.

This helpful coverage pays the *additional* — not the total — expenses you have to incur for lodging, meals, utilities, and so on as a result of a covered loss (such as a fire, smoke, or windstorm) that causes you to vacate your home. It usually will pay these costs for up to the policy limit, if any, or 12 months, whichever is exhausted first. With some insurers, the benefit is unlimited (always a plus); with others, the benefit is a percentage of the Coverage A building limit.

Though higher limits are available, the odds of exhausting the base benefit are really slim, so almost no one buys more.

Coverage E: Insuring your personal liability

Though the cost of coverage for your personal liability for injuries and property damage that you cause represents a small part of your total homeowner's bill, in my opinion this is just about the most important coverage in the policy. Why? Because it covers lawsuits and the cost of defending against lawsuits, and because it's so comprehensive, covering most of your non-vehicle personal liability worldwide.

Here are some examples of claims that Coverage E would cover, including some from my own files:

- ✔ Your 6-year-old spills red punch on the neighbor's white carpet, which requires a $3,000 carpet replacement.
- ✔ You get sued by a neighbor who, in spite of your repeated warnings, has allowed his child to climb your fence and harass your German shepherd. The child gets bitten, and you get sued.
- ✔ Your riding lawnmower kicks up a rock, hits a neighbor, and injures her.
- ✔ A child is hurt while you're babysitting her.
- ✔ In a baseball game, your teenage son throws errantly to home plate and hits another player in the face, causing a loss of vision. That player grows older, still suffers from a loss of vision, and sues five years later for $100,000.
- ✔ You hit someone in the face playing racquetball.
- ✔ You're snowboarding and collide accidentally with a skier who sues for injuries.
- ✔ Playing golf, your errant tee shot hits a bystander in the head. (Happens to me all the time.)

The bottom line? Coverage E is great coverage! Most homeowner's policies include the first $100,000 of coverage at no extra charge.

The two biggest mistakes I see people make with Coverage E is not buying more than the $100,000 of free coverage, and not setting their personal liability limits to match their other liability policy limits (on cars, cabins, boats, and so on).

You don't know where the lawsuit may come from, so you want the same amount of coverage protecting you no matter where it comes from. You wouldn't want different liability limits for different policies any more than you'd want different liability limits for different days of the week!

How much liability coverage should you buy? Here are some considerations:

- ✔ **Your suability factor:** How suable you are is affected by the size of your bank account, your income, your future income, and your asset prospects (in other words, inheritances). In short, your suability factor represents how likely it is that an attorney for the person you injure will come after you personally if you don't have enough insurance. (See Chapter 5 for more on suability.)

- ✔ **Your comfort zone:** How high do you need the limits to go for your own peace of mind?

- ✔ **Your sense of moral responsibility:** Many people with a modest income and few assets buy high liability limits to be sure that anyone they may hurt gets provided for. If you're one of these thoughtful people, I tip my hat in admiration and respect.

The insurance cost of higher limits is minimal. Additional liability insurance is truly one of the best values in the insurance business. An extra $200,000 costs only about $15 a year; an extra $400,000, only about $25 a year!

So, how much liability coverage should you buy? Here's my bottom line advice regarding liability limits: Choose a liability limit that considers your current and future assets and income, feels emotionally comfortable, satisfies your sense of moral responsibility to others, and matches what you would expect if you were the one suing. Bottom line: In my opinion, anyone with less than $500,000 liability coverage is under-insured. Most people should have limits of $1 million or more.

Whatever limit you decide on, be sure to adjust your auto, boat, and personal liability limits to match.

Coverage F: Insuring your guests' medical bills

This is the sixth and final (and least important) homeowner's coverage part. Let me start with what this is not: It is *not* health insurance for you or your family. Instead, it's what I call *good neighbor coverage*. If a guest gets hurt on your premises, even if the injury is caused by her own carelessness, this coverage pays her medical bills up to the coverage limit (usually $1,000).

You can increase the limit for an extra premium, but I would save your money. Odds are, most of the people you invite into your home have health insurance already. If they're seriously hurt and may sue, your personal liability coverage responds. Just be aware that you have this coverage if you have an injured guest. As I said, good neighbor coverage.

Choosing the Right Homeowner's Property Coverages

Coverages A, B, C, and D of homeowner's policies cover property damage to your dwelling, detached structures and their contents, and any increase in living expenses related to property damage. That's how homeowner's policies are similar.

How they differ is in the *kinds* of losses they cover. All homeowner's policies cover damage from fire or a windstorm, for example. But only some policies cover water damage from cracked plumbing or toilet overflows. And none automatically covers damage from a flood or an earthquake, though both coverages can be purchased.

To choose the homeowner's policy best suited to your needs, you need to know which causes of loss are covered and which are not.

Understanding the causes-of-loss options: Basic, broad, and special

When you have a homeowner's claim for damage to your property, the first question is, "Was the cause of the damage covered by the policy?" If "yes," your claim is paid. If "no," your claim is denied. Most insurance companies offer three choices for the types of losses covered:

- ✔ **Basic form causes of loss:** Very limited coverage. Limited to a handful of covered causes of loss, including fire, wind, vandalism, and very limited theft. This option is rarely sold or purchased anymore.

- ✔ **Broad form causes of loss:** Covers about 15 causes of loss. From my experience, the vast majority of the kinds of loss that damage a home or contents are covered. If you have a loss that's on the list, you're probably covered. If the cause of the loss isn't on the list, you're probably not covered.

✔ **Special form causes of loss:** The best. Covers any accidental cause of loss unless that cause of loss is specifically excluded. (Damage from floods, groundwater, sewer backup, earthquakes, and a few other causes of loss aren't covered.)

Here are some examples, many from my own experience, of losses *not* included in the broad form list that *are* covered by the special form:

✔ **Massive interior water damage from roof leaks to a town house:** Claim of $30,000 paid.

✔ **Interior damage to ceilings and walls caused by melting ice and snow that backed up under the shingles:** Claims have averaged $4,000 to $10,000.

✔ **Scorched counters or floors from hot pans dropped onto them:** Claims to replace counters and floors run $5,000 or more.

✔ **Paint spills on furniture:** The average claim runs $2,000.

✔ **Spills of any liquids on oriental rugs:** Claims to replace rugs range from $600 to $20,000.

Probably the most unusual example I've heard of involved someone who took a month-long winter vacation in Florida. To keep his pipes from freezing back home in the cold North, he set his thermostat at 50°F (10°C). Shortly after he left home, the thermostat malfunctioned and never shut off. The combination of 90°F (32°C) heat and winter dryness warped all the floorboards in the house, requiring all the flooring to be torn up and replaced. Most of the floor coverings — tile, carpet, and so on — which had to be removed to get at the floor, also had to be replaced. If that loss happened today, the claim could easily be in excess of $75,000.

Neither "thermostat malfunction" nor "excessive heat" is on the list of covered losses on the broad form. But the special form covered the loss in full because "thermostat malfunction" is not on the list of exclusions. The annual extra insurance cost for the special form over the broad form? Probably $75 a year. (I'd say the homeowner with the faulty thermostat got his money's worth!)

I flat out suggest that you *not* buy the basic form coverage — it's way too restrictive. I like broad form coverage because the majority of your losses will be covered. But my favorite is the special form, because it puts you in the driver's seat — no matter how bizarre the cause, from Martian invasions to some kind of damage from new cybertechnology, your loss is covered (unless it's specifically excluded).

Introducing the six most common homeowner's policies

If you looked at a typical menu of homeowner's policies available from most insurance companies, you would see six entrees, ranging from light fare to a full-course meal. Each of these six options is referred to as a *form*. One form is designed specifically for renters, one is specifically for town house or condominium owners, and the other four are for owners of private residences.

Table 9-1 shows the six homeowner's forms most commonly used in the industry, the type of buyer they're designed for, and the causes of loss covered under each (basic, broad, or special).

Table 9-1	The Six Homeowner's Policy Forms		
Type of Buyer	*Form Number*	*Building Coverage*	*Contents Coverage*
Homeowner	1	Basic	Basic
Homeowner	2	Broad	Broad
Homeowner	3	Special	Broad*
Renter	4	N/A	Broad*
Homeowner	5	Special	Special
Town house or condo owner	6	Broad*	Broad*

*The special form is available as an option at an additional cost.

To choose the homeowner's form best for you, first determine what type of buyer you are — homeowner, renter, or town house/condominium owner. Then determine the causes of loss you want covered — basic, broad, or special — for the building and again for the contents.

For example, if you rent, you would choose homeowner's form 4. It comes automatically with broad form coverage. You can buy the special form for an extra charge. If you're a homeowner and you want special form coverage on your structures but you're comfortable with broad form coverage on belongings, you would choose homeowner's Form 3.

Which form do most insurers sell and 90 percent of homeowner's buy? Form 3, covering buildings with the special form and contents with the broad form. The logic behind this decision is that the structure is the biggest property risk, and totally exposed to the elements, whereas most contents are more protected by being inside. It's a reasonable argument. I think Form 3 is a reasonable choice for most people.

If you have expensive personal belongings, fine arts, expensive rugs, paintings, or antiques, or if you simply like having the best, special form contents coverage is the best choice for you. It's only about 10 percent more expensive than broad form coverage.

Here's how to get special form coverage for both your home and contents:

- ✔ **If you own a home,** you have two choices: Buy a homeowner's Form 5, if available, or buy a Form 3 and add a special perils contents endorsement.

- ✔ **If you own a town house or condo,** buy homeowner's Form 6, add a special perils endorsement to Coverage A (building coverage), and add a special perils contents endorsement. (I devote an entire chapter — Chapter 12 — to the special needs of town house and condominium owners.)

- ✔ **If you rent,** buy homeowner's Form 4 and add a special perils contents endorsement. (For more on insurance for renters, see the next section.)

Buying Renter's Insurance

People who buy renter's insurance (technically homeowner's Form 4) do so when they don't own the structure they occupy, but they do own the personal property in the structure and they're concerned about that property being stolen. Specifically, they're concerned about their most prized possessions — their 52-inch high-definition flat-screen TV, top-of-the-line stereo system, or $3,000 customized bicycle. That fear of being ripped off is what draws many people to look into buying renter's insurance. And yes, if they are burglarized and have these valuables stolen, there will be coverage.

But renter's insurance is much more than just theft coverage. The policy has all the coverages of a full-fledged homeowner's policy, except for structural coverage. If you have a kitchen fire, and while your place is being restored, you have to live elsewhere, you'll have coverage for additional living expenses. If you cause that fire and damage the structure that you're renting, you're liable for that damage and your liability coverage under the renter's insurance will pay for repairing that damage. The liability coverage also will defend you and pay any judgments against you for injuries to guests who fall on your newly waxed floor. And often overlooked is that that same renter's liability coverage applies anywhere else, too. For example, it will defend and pay any judgment against you caused by injuries you cause in sporting activities (racquetball, touch football, baseball, tennis, skiing, and so on).

Valuing your belongings

One of the mistakes most people make when they insure their belongings in a renter's policy is to totally under-insure them. They buy $10,000 or $15,000 of coverage but can never replace everything they own for close to that amount.

I recommend that you use the 200 percent method for valuing personal property. Total up the replacement value of all your major items — furniture, appliances, television, stereo, and so on — and then double that number. You'll end up with an amount high enough to replace all your major possessions and still have an equal amount of money available to replace all your other possessions, such as clothing, dishes, silverware, towels, and other miscellaneous household items — items that are easy to overlook, but that you'll still need to replace if something happens to them. That amount will also be high enough to replace bicycles, ski equipment, and other sporting gear, as well as tools.

Always buy the optional replacement cost coverage so that, in the event of a major loss, the insurance company will pay you enough to replace everything brand-new. Otherwise, you'll be paid the depreciated value for all your possessions — typically 40 percent less.

Evaluating your causes-of-loss options

Homeowner's Form 4, for renters, automatically includes a broad form causes of loss coverage (refer to Table 9-1), but, for a reasonable additional fee (typically less than $100 per year), you can change that form to a special form so that all losses are covered other than the exclusions. You should definitely consider this option if you have a lot of high-end furnishings or property you use away from home, such as customized bicycles.

In Chapter 10, I introduce you to the homeowner's policy coverage limitations and restrictions on certain types of personal property. Be sure to read that chapter to see if any of those limitations and restrictions apply to you, and follow my recommendations.

Choosing a liability limit

The standard renter's policy comes with $100,000 of personal liability coverage — not nearly enough to cover someone's serious injuries or loss of life that you cause.

Giving your college kid a place to live without losing the roof over your own head

My client Ken called me one day. His college-age son, with a couple of friends, was moving into an apartment off-campus. The landlord was requesting a parent's signature on the lease to guarantee the rent payments. Ken wisely faxed me the lease.

If he had cosigned the lease with his son, Ken would have not only guaranteed the rent payments but would also have taken on all the other obligations of the lease. For example, if his son and his friends had a party in the apartment and someone was badly injured, Ken's assets would have been exposed to lawsuits. Similarly, if someone had too much to drink at a party and had a car accident seriously injuring others on the way home, Ken again could have been dragged into a lawsuit.

Ken was not too happy about those possibilities, and I advised him not to sign the lease but instead give the landlord a separate document that guaranteed that, if the rent payments were not made by his son, Ken would take responsibility for them, which is all the landlord was really looking for anyway. Avoiding the risk is often better than insuring it!

Had Ken already signed the lease, the only way to fully protect Ken would have been to extend his homeowner's and umbrella liability policies to a second location — namely the college apartment. The insurance cost per year to do this would have been about $25.

I have two recommendations with regard to personal liability limits:

- ✔ **Buy at least $300,000 and ideally $500,000 of coverage.** The cost is unbelievably cheap — typically $20 to $25 a year!

- ✔ **Make sure that you buy the same liability coverage on your renter's policy as you buy for your car insurance liability.** Both liability limits are protecting the same assets and same income.

If you have a high income or the potential for a high income in the next few years, I recommend that you consider an umbrella policy (see Chapters 15 and 16).

Establishing Property Coverage Limits

Insuring your home and contents properly to get the very best payout at claim time means insuring both for their full replacement cost. You probably have a pretty good idea of the market value of your home, but where do you find the replacement value? And how in the world do you compute the cost of all your furniture, clothing, appliances, and other belongings without taking six months off from work and consuming a drawer full of pain-reliever for all the headaches you'll have?

In this section, I give you tools that can help you establish the approximate replacement cost of your home and its contents.

Determining the replacement cost of your home

The *replacement cost* of your home is the cost to rebuild it. Most insurance companies and/or their agents will estimate the replacement cost of your home using a computer program designed for that purpose. But how can you be sure their estimate is accurate?

Insuring your home for its replacement cost is important, to avoid serious penalties at claim time. But you also don't want to spend more than you need to by over-insuring your home. The most accurate way to estimate your home's replacement cost is to spend $200 to $500 (or more) and have a professional appraisal done. But that strategy is tough on the budget. And it doesn't exactly follow the "Keep it simple" principle from Chapter 2.

I recommend two strategies to cross-check your agent's estimate:

- ✔ **Double-check the agent's worksheet.** Have the agent send you her worksheet. Make sure all the features and square footage are correct. Many times the information is not correct. It's your job to make sure that it's accurate.

- ✔ **Use your home mortgage appraisal.** If you've financed or refinanced your home recently, you paid for an appraisal and you're entitled to a copy of it. If you don't have a copy yet, call your mortgage company and request it. True, the appraisal is for market value, not cost new, but in almost all appraisals, the appraiser also includes the appraiser's esti-mated replacement cost.

  Their numbers are typically conservative, so be sure your building insurance equals or exceeds the mortgage appraisal's replacement cost estimate. For example, if the insurance agent calculates the cost, new, of your home at $278,000 and your bank appraisal estimated it at $262,000, I'd be comfortable with the agent's number. But if your bank appraisal estimated the cost, new, at $175,000, I'd make an issue out of that big difference. If you send the agent your bank appraisal, I'll bet you can get her to adjust her number downward.

I've found that the larger and/or more customized your home is, especially if it's an older home, the more likely it is that the insurance company's estimate is wrong. Determining the replacement cost of your home is a difficult process, but definitely worth your time.

The replacement cost is what you're after — not the market value. It might cost you a lot more to rebuild your home than you could sell the home for.

Guaranteeing you'll have enough insurance to rebuild

You've done your homework. You've double-checked your agent's replacement cost estimate and made appropriate coverage corrections. Suddenly, your home burns to the ground. You've insured your home for $258,000, but after the fire, the true cost to haul all the debris and rebuild is $292,000. You tried your best to buy the right coverage but your out-of-pocket loss is $34,000! Good news! This problem has a great solution — an optional home replacement guarantee, usually called *extended replacement cost coverage*.

Extended replacement cost coverage has three requirements you must comply with in order for the guarantee to be honored at claim time:

- ✔ You initially insure your home for 100 percent of its estimated replacement cost as determined by your agent or insurance company (with your input, of course — see the preceding section).

- ✔ You agree to an inflation rider that annually adjusts your coverage limit by the construction cost index for new homes in your area and you pay the premium increase each year.

- ✔ You notify your insurer anytime you spend $5,000 or more in structural improvements and agree to the change in coverage and higher premium that results.

Be careful. Many people forget about the third requirement, which voids their guarantee. However, spending $5,000 or more is reportable only if it makes your home more expensive to rebuild new. Examples of expenditures that do not void your guarantee are replacing worn-out items like roofs or heating and cooling equipment, or cosmetic changes to your home that increase your enjoyment and probably increase the market value, but don't affect the replacement cost at all (such as replacing kitchen cabinets or stripping off wallpaper and repainting walls with contemporary colors).

As a result of the lessons of Hurricane Andrew, many insurers have capped their home replacement guarantee (usually 125 percent of your building coverage). Unlimited coverage, though, is still very available. I like the unlimited coverage, especially if you have an older home where the exact replacement cost is difficult to determine.

When insuring your home, always double-check the insurance agent's replacement cost estimate so you don't over-insure your home and, thus, pay too much for your insurance. And always buy the optional extended replacement cost coverage, without a cap if possible.

Estimating the cost to replace belongings

The most accurate way to determine the cost of replacing all your belongings is to take a full inventory of *everything* that you own. No one does that — but there are two methods that can get you close enough, whether you own or rent.

The 200 percent method

I like this method and use it a lot because you can do it in 30 minutes or less:

1. **Add up the estimated new cost for all the major items in your home — furniture, stereo, TVs, appliances, computers, and so on.**

2. **Double the total.**

   This will insure that you not only have enough coverage to replace all the major items you own, but that you have an equal amount available for all the smaller items — clothing, dishes, linens, athletic equipment, seasonal and stored items, and so on.

3. **Add to that the values of any exceptional property or collections, artwork, tools, home workshops, and so on.**

Keep it fast and simple. Use your best guess on values, or it won't get done.

The percent of building-value method (for homeowners only)

Oddly, the vast majority of homeowner's insurance buyers accept the amount of contents coverage that comes with their homeowner's policy (usually 70 percent of the building-coverage value). Why? Partly because it's easy, and partly because most people have no idea of the significant value of property they've accumulated over the years.

If you accept the percent of building-value method as a means of determining the amount of content coverage you have, make one modification. Inflate your contents limit by the value of any exceptional property: fine arts, collectibles, antiques, tools, and so on.

Don't accept as gospel the estimates of others when they value your property, and don't automatically accept the stock coverage that comes with your policy.

Choosing your deductible

The usual deductible that comes with a homeowner's policy is $250 per claim. Most insurers allow you to increase the deductible to $500, $1,000, or more, in exchange for a lower premium. When deciding how big a deductible to carry, use three criteria:

✔ How much can you comfortably afford, financially, out of cash reserves?

✔ How much can you emotionally afford? (If parting with that much of a deductible would bring on tears, it's too high!)

✔ How much premium credit are you receiving for taking the extra risk?

It's been my experience that the average home property claim typically occurs once every seven to ten years. My advice is to pick the deductible that has a seven- or eight-year *payback period.* Here's how to determine the payback period:

1. **Subtract the lower deductible from the higher deductible.**

2. **Subtract the lower premium from the higher premium.**

3. **Divide the number in Step 1 by the number in Step 2.**

   If the result is 8 or less (meaning that you'll recoup your added risk in eight years less), pick the higher deductible.

Documenting Your Claim

Suppose your house burns to the ground, along with every shred of your belongings. Or suppose you come home to an empty house after that cheap moving company steals most of your furniture. What do you do?

Reducing your risk

Here is a list of things you can do to reduce risk, to reduce the chances of having a claim at all, and to reduce the severity of any claim you do have. You can save on your insurance premiums by putting some of these tips into effect.

✔ Install a UL-approved smoke detector on each floor. Replace the batteries yearly. (Doing it on your birthday is an easy way to remember.)

✔ Install a UL-approved dry-chemical fire extinguisher in the kitchen for grease fires. Check it periodically to make sure it's fully charged.

✔ Install dead-bolt locks on all access doors.

✔ Install a motion-detector alarm.

✔ Install a central burglar-and-fire alarm (the premium savings are huge for this one — 10 percent to 20 percent).

✔ Have your fireplace, flues, and chimney cleaned regularly to prevent chimney fires (and all the horrible interior smoke damage that results).

✔ If you want a wood stove, buy a UL-approved one and have it professionally installed.

Don't leave it unattended. Have it professionally cleaned annually.

✔ Change your locks immediately if your purse or keys are ever stolen.

✔ Install a sump-pump system to prevent damage from groundwater, which is excluded by virtually every homeowner's policy. (Be sure to buy optional sump-pump failure coverage.)

✔ Keep trees trimmed so they're safely away from the house.

✔ Keep walkways clear and safe.

✔ If you have a swimming pool, make sure it's surrounded by an approved fence. Take out the diving board (where most injuries occur). Add a locking pool cover to prevent unauthorized use.

✔ Buy your kids membership to a health club offering a supervised trampoline instead of buying a trampoline yourself, to avoid all the potential liability for injuries to the neighbor kids.

✔ Install a carbon monoxide detector.

"No problem," you say. "I read *Insurance For Dummies,* and I bought all the right coverages. The replacement cost on building and contents. The home replacement guarantee. The special causes-of-loss form. I'm set." Here's the catch: Without documentation, even great coverage won't get you an easy — or full — claim settlement.

Here are some easy ways of documenting your home and its contents:

✔ Take photos of the exterior of the house and any detached structures.

✔ Take photos of any special structural features in the interior, like stone fireplaces, built-in buffets, custom woodwork, and so on.

✔ Take a photographic inventory of all your personal property. Take pictures of every cupboard and closet with the drawers open. Don't forget storage areas, the basement, and property in garages and other structures.

✔ Keep your home blueprints, if you have any. They're wonderful for making sure you get exactly the house you had. (It wouldn't hurt to put a copy of your home appraisal and photos with the blueprints.)

Having photos, blueprints, and other documentation won't help at all if they burn up in the fire. So be sure to keep them off premises.

Chapter 10

Avoiding Homeowner's Personal Property Pitfalls

In This Chapter

▶ Identifying the three types of homeowner's coverage gaps

▶ Arming yourself with gap management strategies

▶ Examining the coverage restrictions on a case-by-case basis

▶ Applying the gap management strategies to each restriction

*A*ll homeowner's insurance policies provide coverage for personal property. Pricing for the coverage has two components:

✔ **Base premium:** The base premium is designed to provide coverage for the types of low-hazard property common to everyone — furniture, clothing, appliances, electronics, and so on.

✔ **Supplemental premiums:** Supplemental premiums are designed to cover higher-hazard property not covered much or at all by the base policy — such as jewelry, silver, boats, and business equipment.

The good news is that this dual pricing is fair; people with only low-hazard property don't pay extra to subsidize those with high-hazard property. The bad news is that consumers with high-hazard property often naively just buy the basic homeowner's policy, off-the-shelf, without customizing the coverage — so their high-hazard property is either poorly insured or completely uninsured.

In this chapter, I fill you in on the types of personal property *not* covered well by the basic homeowner's insurance policy. I also show you creative ways of getting the best coverage for your money.

Most of my advice is based on the coverages and limitations found in the vast majority of policies, but there *are* differences from one company to another. Be sure to read *your* homeowner's insurance policy and, ideally, discuss it with a professional.

Exposing the Three Major Coverage Gaps

You have homeowner's insurance, so all your stuff is covered, right? Unfortunately, no. There are three reasons that some of your personal property may have little or no homeowner's coverage:

- ✔ The basic policy sets a dollar limit on that type of property.
- ✔ Certain causes of loss are excluded.
- ✔ The property is unique and difficult to put a value on.

Here's a personal example that illustrates all three problems: My bride of 30 years, Judith Marie, owns a top-quality, half-carat, solitaire diamond engagement ring, worth — today — about $4,000. Our basic homeowner's policy (without any customization), has a $1,000 limit on jewelry theft (the *dollar limit*). In addition, the policy has an exclusion for any loss of the stone from its setting (the *excluded cause of loss*). Finally, even if $4,000 of coverage were available, the burden of proof rests with my wife and me to prove the quality and value of the ring in order to be paid that value (making it *unique and difficult to value*). Can you imagine how difficult that would be? Depending on quality, a half-carat diamond is worth from $1,000 to $10,000. How would you prove to an adjuster your diamond's quality if the ring or the diamond is gone? A photo can't. A bill of sale can't.

Dollar limits

In the Coverage C section of your homeowner's policy — the section covering personal property — you can find a list of property subject to limitations. It should look something like this partial list:

- ✔ Theft of jewelry: $1,000
- ✔ Theft of silver: $2,500
- ✔ Theft of guns: $2,000
- ✔ Damage to or theft of coins: $250
- ✔ Damage to or theft of stamps: $500
- ✔ Damage to or theft of boats, motors, and trailers: $1,000

If you don't want to be a victim of the personal property coverage limitations of your homeowner's policy, reading the list in your policy is imperative. Almost all the limitations can be eliminated for an extra premium charge.

Excluded causes of loss

Damage to or loss of your personal property may not be covered for two reasons:

- ✔ **The cause is specifically excluded from coverage in the policy language.** For example, your policy may have a loss-of-stone exclusion for jewelry, excluding coverage for a stone that slips from its setting.

- ✔ **The cause is not in the list of covered causes of loss, if your policy contains a basic or broad cause-of-loss form.** Under the basic or broad form (see Chapter 9 for more information), any loss not appearing on the list won't be covered. So, for example, if you have a paint spill that ruins your valuable Persian rug, and "paint spill" isn't one of the listed, covered causes of loss, it wouldn't be covered.

Read your policy to find out which items of your personal property are not covered for certain causes of loss so you can use insurance or non-insurance strategies to close the gap.

Valuation problems

Even if no dollar limit exists on an item of personal property, and even if the cause of your loss is fully covered, a third obstacle to collecting the full value of your property is the difficulty in proving the value of it. Antiques, original art, and collectibles are examples of items that have this problem. How do you prove to the adjuster that your stolen painting was an original Picasso and not a copy? How do you prove its value after it's gone?

Arming Yourself: Successful Strategies for Protecting Your Personal Property

So how do you protect yourself from being burned by one of the personal-property coverage problems common with homeowner's insurance? In this section, I offer up three insurance strategies and one non-insurance strategy to help you.

Raising your dollar limit

For some personal property with dollar limits, insurers offer you the option (for an additional premium) of increasing that dollar limit to a maximum value that better suits your needs. It's quite common, for example, to be able to increase your typical jewelry theft limit from $1,000 to $2,500 or $5,000, or to increase sterling silver theft limits from $2,500 to $10,000 or $15,000.

Raising dollar limits is not usually an expensive proposition. A $5,000 jewelry theft limit, for example, typically costs $25 a year. A $10,000 sterling silver theft limit may cost you $50 a year.

If the limit you buy adequately covers what you own, this strategy solves the dollar-limit problem. It won't help with the cause-of-loss or valuation problems, however.

Scheduling your valuables

A strategy that addresses all three problems of dollar limit, cause of loss, and valuation is to specifically list (or *schedule*) certain valuables as an amendment to the basic policy. A value for each item is declared and a premium is paid. Here's how this addresses all three problems:

- ✔ The dollar-limit problem is solved by insuring the scheduled valuable for its full value.

- ✔ The causes-of-loss problem is solved because almost any cause of accidental loss, no matter how bizarre, is covered (other than a handful of exclusions).

- ✔ The valuation problem at claim time for hard-to-value items (such as jewelry and fine art) is solved by providing the insurance company with credible appraisals at the time the insurance is arranged.

Because scheduling addresses all three problems so well, it's usually the best strategy for many types of valuables — but not always.

The three advantages of scheduling valuables are

- ✔ Having the broadest possible special (everything-is-covered-but-a-few-exclusions) causes-of-loss coverage

- ✔ Having no deductible

- ✔ A smoother easier claim settlement.

The disadvantage of scheduling is that you lose inflation coverage if the item increases in value. For example, if the particular style of your scheduled antique table becomes quite fashionable, and the table's value skyrockets, you only collect the scheduled amount. To solve the inflation problem, you can get your items reappraised every year, if you're willing to go through the hassle and the expense. No one — absolutely no one — does so, and neither will you. If you're dealing with personal property that doesn't have a dollar limit under the policy (such as artwork or antiques), you can get around this inflation problem without having to get annual appraisals (see the next section).

Buying special perils coverage

A strategy for partially dealing with the problem of excluded causes of loss is to expand the covered causes of loss to approximately the same as the covered causes of loss under a schedule by buying an optional coverage called *special perils contents coverage* (see Chapter 9). Special perils coverage broadens the coverage on all your personal property so that anything that accidentally happens to your belongings, no matter how bizarre, is covered unless the cause of the loss is one of those specifically excluded (for example, a flood, an earthquake, breakage of fragile items, and a few others).

If you have a lot of treasures, I recommend adding special perils for its broader coverage and also because it usually adds only about 10 percent to your homeowner's insurance bill. See Table 10-1 for some examples of how you could benefit at claim time with this better coverage (ignoring the deductible).

Table 10-1	The Benefits of Special Perils Coverage			
Loss Description	Amount of Claim	Amount Paid under Typical Homeowner's Policy	Amount Paid under the Special Perils Endorsement	Comments
Red wine spilled onto Oriental rug	$1,500	$0	$1,500	No exclusion for red wine stains.
Free-standing shelving unit topples, destroying TV and stereo system	$7,500	$0	$7,500	Breakage exclusion applies only to glassware and fragile items.

(continued)

Table 10-1 *(continued)*

Loss Description	Amount of Claim	Amount Paid under Typical Homeowner's Policy	Amount Paid under the Special Perils Endorsement	Comments
Loss of the diamond from an engagement ring	$4,000	$0	$1,000 (or whatever the jewelry dollar limit is)	The special form covers the loss but still has a dollar-limit problem.
Roof leak ruins stamp collection	$2,800	$0	$500 dollar limit	There is a dollar limit on stamps. They must be scheduled to cover the full dollar loss.
Rain soaks almost all personal property while the roof is being replaced	$35,000	$0	$35,000	No exclusion for rain damage.
Dry cleaner ruins wardrobe by shrinking it during cleaning	$20,000	$0	$20,000	"Shrinking from dry cleaning" is not an exclusion.

As you can see, the special perils endorsement won't solve all your claims problems, such as the dollar limit problem. But it surely puts a dent in them.

In the following sections, I tell you about the many types of personal property that either have restricted coverage under a basic homeowner's policy or face unique risks that require special handling. I show you how to use these insurance and non-insurance strategies to protect yourself.

Covering Portable Items

Homeowner's policies do a pretty good job of protecting stationary personal property when it's contained safely within the walls of your home. The most common causes of loss — fire, wind, vandalism, and theft — are covered even under the most basic of policies. But the homeowner's coverage falls short when it comes to certain types of belongings that you carry with you, such as cameras, jewelry, musical instruments, guns, and furs.

Cameras

Cameras and their accessories are a good example of a type of property that's more vulnerable away from home. Because people take them wherever they go, cameras are subject to breakage or loss, water damage, and other unusual risks not covered by your basic homeowner's policy. In addition, there is almost no coverage for business use — a problem for those who occasionally make money from their gear, by filming weddings, for example. Some good news: Homeowner's policies usually have no dollar limit for camera gear.

Here's my advice for managing the risk of photographic equipment:

✔ **If your investment is modest, retain (self-insure) the losses.** In other words, just figure that if something happens to your camera, you'll pay to repair it or get a new one.

✔ **If you *own* expensive gear but either no longer use it or wouldn't replace it if it were lost, retain any losses yourself.**

✔ **If you own expensive gear and you do want insurance to replace it if it's lost or damaged, buy better coverage than the primary homeowner's policy offers.** You can do one of the following:

   • Specifically insure the camera gear — this is called *scheduling* it.

   • Buy the special perils endorsement, which covers all your personal property — not just cameras — for more causes-of-loss than the basic homeowner's coverage.

Both of these strategies cover camera gear for any accidental damage, unless the cause of loss is one of just a handful of excluded causes. Scheduling offers the advantage of having no deductible on claims (see the "Scheduling your valuables" section, earlier in this chapter, for more information).

If you do schedule, be sure that the values you declare are replacement costs *new* — not used values. Also be sure to add sales tax to the value you declare, if applicable where you live.

If you use your equipment, even occasionally, to make money, the only way to cover it is to schedule it. Make sure that you add an endorsement for business use.

Jewelry

Besides being portable, personal jewelry has two other unique problems: Items are usually small and easily lost, and jewelry often can only be valued under a microscope. Jewelry is also subject to two policy limitations;

- ✔ A dollar limit for theft — usually $1,000 per claim — not a limit per item
- ✔ No coverage for the loss of a stone from its setting (a very common claim)

For managing the dollar limit on theft problem, the strategy of raising the dollar limit on jewelry coverage is available from most insurers, usually to a limit of $5,000 to $10,000. Insurers vary, but common pitfalls of this strategy include

- ✔ **No broader causes of loss being covered.**
- ✔ **A per-piece limit of $1,000 to $1,500.**
- ✔ **The burden of having to prove the value of what you lost — very difficult to do with unique jewelry.** If you can't prove what you lost, you're vulnerable to the insurance company replacing what you lost with a lesser-quality item or gem.

The insurance company normally replaces your gem with another gem, instead of cash. This claims practice significantly reduces the number of fraudulent claims for "stolen" jewelry.

The strategy of scheduling jewelry items works better because

- ✔ Almost every accidental claim — including the loss of the stone or even the loss of the entire piece — is covered.
- ✔ There's no deductible.
- ✔ An appraisal is required to schedule an item, so there's no dispute over what you lost. You simply take the most recent appraisal to the jeweler who is doing the replacing. She uses the appraisal to closely match what you lost.

The only negative of scheduling, besides the cost and hassle of getting an appraisal, is the danger of being under-insured if the value of your jewelry increases. You can protect yourself by updating your appraisals and increasing your coverage limit every three to five years. Out of scores of jewelry claims, I've only had two clients get paid less than the appraised value; in both cases, their appraisals were over ten years old.

If you've had a piece of jewelry insured by the same insurance company since the original appraisal was done, you can call the jeweler who did the appraisal and request an updated value. You don't have to prove you still have the piece because it has been continuously insured.

The strategy of buying the special-perils causes-of-loss coverage option is only partially effective for jewelry. Though it broadens the kinds of loss covered, it doesn't help with the dollar-limit problem.

I find non-insurance strategies — avoid, reduce, or retain — very helpful when it comes to personal jewelry risks:

- ✔ **Avoid** the risk for seldom-worn jewelry that you eventually want to pass on to your kids. Pass it on now, while you're still here to enjoy them enjoying it — and the risk now belongs to someone else.

- ✔ **Retain** (self-insure) smaller jewelry items — especially those you won't bother replacing if anything happens to them.

- ✔ **Reduce** the risk to your jewelry by putting expensive, seldom-worn pieces in a safe-deposit box. Reduce the risk of the loss of stones from their settings by regularly having the prongs checked.

There usually is no way to transfer the risk to someone other than through insurance.

The burglary risk is reduced significantly when you install a central burglar alarm. Hide expensive pieces to further reduce the risk — the first place the burglar looks is in your jewelry box. (My longtime client Mary — God bless her — showed me her favorite hiding place: her freezer! Did she microwave her jewelry when she wanted to wear it?) If you hide it, don't forget where you hide it. (I'm guilty of that one!)

My recommendations for managing your jewelry risks are:

- ✔ **Retain the small stuff — especially items you wouldn't replace.**

- ✔ **Schedule items worth $1,000 or more — especially those you would replace.** Don't forget to add sales tax to the value of the item.

- ✔ **Add up the values of the items under $1,000 that you would replace, if you want them insured, and then raise the jewelry dollar-limit high enough to cover those items, or to the maximum available from the insurance company.** When you talk to your agent, impress her with the technical name for this: *blanket unscheduled coverage.*

Still get appraisals for the unscheduled jewelry items you're covering under the blanket coverage and store the appraisals off-premises. The insurance company won't require an appraisal from you at the time you buy the coverage as they will for scheduled items, but being able to prove what you lost will greatly enhance your claim settlement.

✔ **Store pieces you seldom wear — especially heirlooms — in a safe-deposit box.** Insurance can only pay cash. It won't begin to replace the sentimental value of your treasures.

✔ **If you have a lot of jewelry, reduce the burglary risk by hiding it and/or adding a central burglar alarm.** Consider installing a safe, but be sure it's part of the building (built into the wall or in the floor, covered by a rug).

TECHNICAL STUFF

How jewelry claims work

You've done all the right things. You obtained a quality appraisal from a certified gemologist on your diamond wedding ring for $4,200, which feels good because you only paid $3,200 for it. You scheduled it for $4,200. You even added the sales tax to the value. Six months later, the ring is stolen. You're very happy you bought *Insurance For Dummies* and followed my advice — until, that is, you discover that the cost to the insurance company, through its wholesale connections, to replace this ring is only $2,100. You're outraged! You insured your ring for $4,200 and paid an additional premium. You want a $4,200 ring. The insurance company refuses. Then you demand $4,200 cash. They offer $2,100 cash. More outrage!

What can you do? Nothing. Jewelry is appraised at retail and settled at wholesale. That's how the system works. Pricing for scheduled jewelry is discounted because of this fact.

A few insurance companies sell *agreed-amount* jewelry coverage and would pay you the $4,200. But those jewelry policies are much more expensive.

I actually like the current system. You benefit in three ways:

✔ Reduced insurance premiums.

✔ Reduced fraud, preventing people from profiting from a claim (collecting $4,200 cash for a ring that cost $3,200 six months earlier).

✔ Some inflation protection. Your $4,200 ring will increase in value each year. But if you're like most people, you won't get updated appraisals each year. Your appraisal won't need updating more than every five years until the $2,100 wholesale price has increased in value to match the $4,200 insured amount. (If, five years from now, the retail value of the ring is $8,400 and wholesale value is $4,200, you still have enough insurance at $4,200.)

You need to know and understand how the system works so you won't be disappointed at claim time. *Remember:* What's really important is that insurance replaces what you lost — and it will, up to the scheduled amount.

Musical instruments

The good news with musical instruments is that homeowner's policies neither contain any dollar limits nor have any added causes of loss excluded. But if you own an expensive instrument, it is subject to two coverage pitfalls:

 ✔ No damage or breakage coverage in the basic homeowner's policy

 ✔ Limited coverage at home and virtually no coverage away from home if the instrument is used even partially for business

You can get damage or breakage coverage by either scheduling the item or buying the special perils option for all your belongings. Coverage is similar under either choice. Scheduling has the advantage of no deductible, a particularly popular feature with parents of 8-year-olds.

If you use your instrument even occasionally for business, the only way to avoid the homeowner's policy dollar limits on business property is to schedule it *and* add the business-use endorsement.

It's quite common for parents to rent instruments rather than buy them, especially for a child's first instrument. The rental agency requires you to insure the rental and offers you insurance on the $800 violin you're renting — typically $4 to $8 a month added to your rental fee. That's $48 to $96 a year. You can schedule the $800 violin under your homeowner's policy for $4 to $8 a year! That's the way to go — always. Be sure to include the rental agency as loss payee on the schedule so its interest is properly covered.

Guns

If all you own is a handgun, a standard shotgun, or a hunting rifle, you can probably skip this section. The basic homeowner's policy usually has a dollar limit on theft of guns — typically $2,000 to $3,000 — and no added exclusions. Business-use restrictions exist that won't be addressed here (for detectives, bounty hunters, and mafia hit men), but you can find out about them in *Hired-Gun Insurance For Dummies*.

You've got two reasons to buy better gun coverage:

 ✔ You may need to raise the basic dollar limit for theft.

 ✔ You may need broader coverage, especially for guns used recreationally (for example, if you hunt and lose a gun overboard while sitting in a duck boat).

If you have both needs, scheduling the gun is the best choice. If you don't need broader coverage, just raise the theft limit. If the insurance company's optional limit isn't high enough, you need to schedule.

I have 400 clients, with almost no gun schedules, and very few increased gun limits. Why? Because gun claims rarely occur. And because preventing the loss, with a high-quality gun safe, is so effective. By the way, locking guns in a safe not only reduces the risk of theft but, more important, keeps your children, grandchildren, or anyone else from accessing the guns and hurting themselves or others.

Many people have elaborate gun collections, often including vintage guns. If you fall into this category, here are my recommendations to help improve future claim settlements, whether you schedule the guns or just increase the limit in your policy:

✔ Take good photos of each piece with the name and serial number listed. Store a set off-premises to document what you had at the time of your claim.

✔ Get appraisals on the collectible guns and also store these appraisals off-premises.

Furs

If you have valuable furs, you should know that your policy probably has a dollar limit for theft of furs included in the jewelry dollar limit of, usually, $1,000. That's a problem if a burglar takes your jewelry and furs in the same burglary.

Because most fur thefts occur away from home, preventing the theft risk by keeping the fur with you at all times is probably the best strategy. If you do still want insurance, I recommend you schedule the item for its full value. Besides the increased dollar limit, you'll also broaden coverage for nearly every accidental loss (including tears, stains, dry cleaner damage, and so on).

To schedule a fur, you'll need a furrier appraisal. If you want your claim settled for the cost, new, and have purchased replacement cost coverage on contents with your basic policy, make sure that the appraisal is for the new (not used) value.

Covering Artwork and Antiques

Because the value of fine art and antiques is based both on authenticity and condition, good documentation is essential. Can you imagine owning an original Picasso worth $2 million, having no documentation, and trying to get that amount from the insurance adjuster after it's stolen?

Another problem common to fine art and antiques is valuation. Replacing this type of property usually isn't even possible. What is the replacement cost of a Picasso? What's the replacement cost of your antique, hand-carved table? Even if it *can* be replaced with a new, identical table, doesn't its historical value often exceed — sometimes far exceed — the value of a new table?

Because replacement cost coverage just doesn't apply to these types of items, most insurance policies now settle these losses for the market value at the time of the loss. That's good news for you. The bad news is that the burden of documenting what you have falls entirely on your shoulders. Yet another difficulty with insuring this kind of property is that the value can increase while your coverage remains static, especially if you schedule the items. With each passing year, your coverage becomes more and more inadequate.

So, how can you solve the problems of documenting and valuing your fine arts and antiques, and still be protected against under-insurance due to inflation? You can choose between two methods of insurance: scheduling or not scheduling.

Scheduling is the strategy used and recommended exclusively by the insurance industry for insuring this type of property. It requires you to document what you have at the time you insure it by providing a credible appraisal and, often, a photograph. The item is then scheduled for the appraised amount and an extra premium is charged.

Here are the advantages of scheduling your fine art and antiques:

- **The documentation problem is solved in advance of any claim.** Items in the schedule are valued at their market value.

- **Most insurers — for fine art only — include *agreed amount* coverage (meaning, they pay you the scheduled amount for a theft or total loss with no value argument).**

- **You have the option to add breakage of glass and other fragile items to the schedule.** If breakage is a big concern, scheduling the item with breakage coverage is the best course of action.

Annual appraisals done easy

I had a client once who, instead of investing in real estate or the stock market, invested hundreds of thousands of dollars in original art. When I asked him why, he said that art values more than keep up with inflation, virtually never decline, and, unlike stock certificates, can be a source of visual warmth and pleasure every day. What a great idea! He scheduled all his paintings and also solved the annual appraisal problem: He simply bought every single painting from one art dealer who, as part of the deal, annually provided me, with no prompting, an entire list of all the paintings including up-to-date values. If you collect art and can do the same thing, scheduling is the perfect strategy!

Scheduling leaves you vulnerable to the inflation problem, unless you're willing to incur the time, expense, and hassle of new appraisals almost every year. Virtually no one is willing to appraise items yearly — and it completely violates one of the rules of the road in Chapter 2, to keep it simple.

The second insurance strategy is one I devised for my clients in order to solve the inflation problem without the hassle and expense of new appraisals. It has three parts and works only if your homeowner's policy has no dollar limits on paintings, collectibles, and antiques. Very few homeowner's policies have a dollar limit on these items, but be sure to check yours just in case.

Here are the three parts:

- **Buy the optional special perils coverage endorsement for your personal property.** It raises your total homeowner's cost about 10 percent to 15 percent and gives you coverage for any accidental loss, except for a few exclusions. It covers losses not covered by a basic homeowner's policy, like paint spills on the antique rug or piano, water damage to your paintings or antiques from a roof leak, and so on. It has very broad coverages — not only on fine arts and antiques, but for all your other belongings as well.

- **Increase your total homeowner's limit for Coverage C — personal property — high enough to cover all these valuables as well as all your other personal property.** Most homeowner's policies, in a total loss, don't have enough contents coverage to pay for all these treasures and all your other belongings.

- **Get photos of everything and appraisals on all items where authenticity is vital to a claim settlement.** Store the photos away from home, at work or in a safe-deposit box. If you don't follow through on storing this critical documentation off-premises, this strategy will fail you and you'll be extremely disappointed at claim time.

Creatively managing an inherited art collection

Suppose you inherit such a high-value art collection that you don't want to deal with the hassle and expense of protecting it, yet you want to maintain ownership for posterity. Transferring (see Chapter 3) is an excellent risk-management technique for this type of situation. Here's how it works: Contact places such as art museums, historical societies, and the like. Tell them they can display your artwork in exchange for assuming the risk for any loss or damage. If someplace agrees, get the deal in writing.

If you're successful, you avoid the insurance problem — hundreds of dollars in premiums — and the expense of the high-end security you would need to properly protect your collection. You gain peace of mind by not having all those expensive items in your home. You maintain the ownership of the items to pass on to future generations. And, finally, you can still enjoy your art by visiting the museum anytime during normal business hours. In fact, they may even give you a key to the place!

With this method, you don't need to get regular appraisals. When you do have a claim and need a current appraisal to document the claim value, you bring your original appraisals with the photos to a dealer or appraiser. A hidden benefit of this method: The cost of the valuation is completely paid for by the insurance company as a claims-adjusting expense!

Here are my bottom-line insurance recommendations for insuring artwork, collectibles, and antiques:

- ✔ **For high-end pieces (for example, expensive paintings), especially if you can get your appraiser to agree to send you annual value updates, I recommend scheduling.** Scheduling fine arts makes for a far easier claim settlement, with no arguments about value, as opposed to not scheduling, where you must prove the authenticity and value of what you lost.

- ✔ **For glassware or other highly-fragile items, including antique glass, I recommend scheduling if you want breakage coverage.** Remember to add optional breakage coverage to the policy when you schedule.

- ✔ **For most other treasures, I recommend the three-part plan — *but only if you faithfully keep the necessary documentation away from home.***

If you have any kind of property that's quite valuable and could be stolen, like jewelry or fine paintings, install a central burglar-and-fire alarm. Installation costs are often $200 or less. The monthly cost to monitor the alarm is about $30. You reduce the risk of losing an irreplaceable treasure, and you receive 10 percent to 20 percent off your homeowner's bill.

Covering Collectibles

Collecting — anything from baseball cards to bottle caps, from coins to comic books, from stamps to sterling silver — is all the rage and has been for years. But this type of property has insurance pitfalls. In this section, I show you how to protect yourself from the pitfalls, case-by-case.

Coins, money, and more

We all want to collect money — the more of it, the merrier! What you need to know is that your homeowner's policy wants nothing to do with your money — or almost nothing. The policy has a dollar limit on money, typically $200. That's $200 for *everything* — not just what's in your wallet. If it even looks, tastes, or smells like money, it's included in the $200 limit — for example, banknotes, bullion, gold, silver, platinum, coins (including coin collections), and medals.

Yes, you can increase the $200 policy limit, or, in some cases, schedule collections — for a fortune in premiums, but I never recommend either strategy because proving your loss is nearly impossible. (Imagine losing that wonderful coin collection. Now imagine proving to the adjuster the exact coins you had, what their condition was, and the current value of each.)

If you insist on keeping any money collectibles at home, my suggestion is to hide your collection very well. Strongly consider installing a central burglar alarm or a home safe. If neither approach is an option for you, put the money items in a safe-deposit box, where they aren't insured but where the theft risk is extremely remote.

Stamps and valuable papers

Another item insurers don't want to cover is anything valuable contained on a piece of paper. They'll cover the blank paper — they just don't want to cover what's *on* the paper. So the homeowner's policy has another dollar limit, usually about $1,000 for this type of property. Stamp collections are a good example. Some other examples include manuscripts, passports, tickets, letters of credit, and deeds.

Yes, you can raise the dollar limit on this type of property. You can even schedule stamps, but I don't recommend it. Prevention is better. Getting a safe-deposit box is a good option. Some of my clients have installed in-home fireproof safes to protect their stamps or valuable papers.

Make sure your safe can't be removed from your home. It should be built into the wall or floor.

Cards, comics, and other collections

People used to collect just stamps, or coins, or art. These days, anything goes: CDs, books, antique toy trains, soldiers, Barbie dolls, baseball cards, comic books, miniature Christmas villages, porcelain dolls, teddy bears, and Beanie Babies. Some people even collect old insurance policies!

The biggest problems with collections are documentation and valuation: proving what you had and putting a value on it. If you have a claim, every policy has a requirement that you make a detailed inventory of what you lost. It's a nightmarish task.

Say a fire destroyed your 2,000-card baseball card collection and you're asked for an inventory from the claims adjuster. You spend days putting together your list. Now, how do you value it? The value of each card will fluctuate wildly, depending on condition. Because your collection is destroyed, how do you prove to the adjuster that your 1952 Mickey Mantle rookie card was the mint one worth $12,500 and not the bent, folded, crinkled one worth $75? The burden of proof is on you. If you can't prove condition, you'll probably end up getting paid for average cards when many of yours were mint.

To get what you deserve for your collections at claim time, you need to:

- ✔ Document every item to prove its existence for the claims inventory and to prove its condition for the valuation.

- ✔ Authenticate the originality of items whose value depends on their originality.

- ✔ Make sure your policy limit on belongings is high enough to cover all your collectibles and all other normal personal property.

- ✔ Make sure that the kinds of losses that can damage your collections (breakage for porcelain dolls, water damage for baseball cards, and so on) are covered.

Here are suggestions that will allow you to do all of this and still keep it simple:

- ✔ Check your homeowner's policy under Coverage C, personal property. Are your collections subject to any dollar limitations that could hurt you? If so, either raise the limit or, better yet, switch your insurance to an insurer whose policy does not have these dollar limits. Most do not.

- ✔ Don't schedule collections and spend a lot of money on appraisals if the values can change quickly, making your schedule obsolete overnight. Here are two exceptions to this rule:

  - • If you need breakage coverage

  - • If the values are high-end and dependent on proof of authenticity.

  If you do schedule, insist on the fine arts form so at claim time the insurer has to pay out the scheduled amount regardless of current value.

- ✔ Take a close-up photographic inventory. A digital or video camera works best for extensive collections like books, comic books, or sports cards. You can probably film your whole collection in one sitting. (It's also easy — and cheap — to add to as your collection grows.) Then at claim time, you can make up your inventory of what you lost from the photos. The photos will also document the condition. Be sure to store photos away from home!

- ✔ If any or all of your collection's value depends on proving authenticity or mint condition, get an appraisal just once that does so. Store the appraisal off-premises with the photos. A signed statement from a credible dealer works fine. To enhance the appraisal, consider attaching an individual photo.

- ✔ Buy the optional special perils contents coverage for the broadest possible coverage on your collection (if you don't schedule).

- ✔ Determine the approximate value of your collection, add it to the estimated value of your belongings, and raise your Coverage C personal property limit as needed. (See Chapter 9 for how to estimate the value of your contents.)

- ✔ Do whatever you can to reduce the risk of loss to your collections. For example:

  - • Don't store moisture-sensitive collections, like old record collections, in a damp basement where they can warp (as I'm currently doing) or be subject to water damage. Instead, seal them in airtight, plastic zipper bags. (This works well for comic books, too.)

  - • Put breakables out of the flow of traffic and, ideally, in protective storage — cabinets or trunks.

If you follow these suggestions, especially the one about having a photographic inventory, your satisfaction on any claim involving a collection will improve substantially. If you do nothing at all, you'll have a major hassle and get paid less than you deserve. Enough said.

The Wares: Silver, Gold, or Pewter

All homeowner's policies have a dollar limit on theft — usually $2,500 to $5,000 — of silverware, gold ware, and pewter ware, including plated ware. This dollar limit applies not just to flatware, but also to accessory pieces like tea sets. It even applies to trophies.

The policy limit is usually adequate if your pieces are plated. But the limit is inadequate if you have solid sterling, solid gold, or solid pewter.

So how do you protect your wares? The most common insurance-industry solution for insuring silver, gold, and pewter is to get it appraised and then schedule it on the policy as you do with jewelry. The problem I have with this solution is that these wares are a commodity, and they go up and down in value. If you schedule each of your silver pieces, for example, when silver prices go up, you're immediately under-insured on every piece. And when silver prices drop, you're over-insured.

Even if you decide to schedule your silver, gold, or pewter, don't spend money for an appraisal. Just contact a dealer for a current price list, or bring a couple of pieces down to the store for a ballpark estimate. Because the values fluctuate daily, an exact price isn't necessary. These wares have a low chance of loss. What can happen to them? Fire and theft. Fire is fully covered, without limit, which means theft is your only insurance concern.

Silver, gold, and pewter aren't like jewelry — they don't need to be examined under a microscope. They more closely resemble camera gear. They usually have a manufacturer and pattern name, and you can generally look up prices in a book.

I don't recommend scheduling your silver, gold, or pewter. You have better options:

- ✔ **If you don't use your wares every day,** hide them. Hiding works, but if you want more security, add a central burglar alarm.

- ✔ **If you do use your silver, gold, or pewter regularly,** or you just prefer to keep it displayed, you probably need to insure it. Check with a dealer first to see what it's worth. Then, because theft is the only cause of loss with a dollar limit, raise your theft limit from the basic limit (typically $2,500) to the true, current value of your silver. Round up a bit so that you're covered if prices rise.

If your silver, gold, or pewter was a gift and you either wouldn't replace it or are comfortable replacing it with silver plate, you can skip the extra insurance and live with the $2,500 policy limit.

If you increase the silver limit and don't schedule your silver, the burden of proof, as usual, is on your shoulders at claim time to prove what you had. Here's how to protect yourself:

- ✔ Take photos and write the name of the manufacturer and the pattern on the back of the photos.

- ✔ Get appraisals just once for any pieces that don't have that information, not to prove value but to prove that the piece is solid silver, gold, or pewter.

- ✔ Store the photos and appraisals off-premises along with a single piece of flatware to prove what you had.

Failure to maintain documentation will cause you, at the least, claims hassles — and probably lead to your claim payment being inadequate.

Don't feel like you have to follow just one strategy. Maybe some silver you're comfortable hiding, some you want to display and would replace if it were stolen, and some you display but wouldn't bother replacing. If so, combine these strategies.

Covering Business Property at Home

Homeowner's policies are designed for residential — not business — risks, so it's no surprise that coverage for business personal property is minimal — typically $2,500 at home and $250 away. Also, there is usually a complete exclusion for business data — both on paper and electronic media.

The definition of *business* in most homeowner's policies clearly includes your regular job. But does it include part-time jobs, home babysitting, or summer lawn jobs? Unfortunately, that's subject to interpretation. Because the policies are vague, the courts have gotten involved: They've defined *business,* as used in homeowner's policies, to mean an activity that both earns revenue and is continuous.

So, a once-a-year garage sale would not be a business. But my friend Bobbie's garage sales, which she's conducted out of her garage for the whole neighborhood, once a month for 20 years, may be a business, and the $2,500 limit would apply. Similarly, your 12-year-old son's use of your $600 lawnmower to do a few summer lawn jobs probably isn't a business because it's not continuous. But your 18-year-old son's $10,000 investment in landscaping equipment, pulled on a utility trailer and used year round, may be a business.

If you have an incidental home office (with a desk, filing cabinet, computer, fax, and so on) and you telecommute from your regular job, you're also subject to the business-property limitations of the policy.

If the business property coverage that comes with your homeowner's policy (typically $2,500) is enough to replace all you own or use at home and you never take for-business items off-premises, you're set. Just remember to read your policy and make sure you know what the dollar limit is.

If some of the business property at your home is owned by your employer and furnished for your use, see if your employer is covering it already or can cover it. You won't need supplemental insurance if the items are already covered.

If you own substantially more than $2,500 worth of business property, or take more than $250 worth of business property away from home, or if you have a lot of business data at risk, here are some things you can do:

- ✔ **If you have more than $2,500 at risk at home, increase your business property on-premises coverage high enough to cover your exposure.**

- ✔ **If you take more than $250 worth of business property out of your home, try to reduce the risk by taking less.** Home insurers seldom offer an option to buy a higher limit. If they do, it's pretty pricey. The one exception is laptop computers. If you own a laptop, you can avoid the $250 limit by scheduling the laptop — a strategy I recommend for every laptop owner. Be sure to include a business-use endorsement and get special perils coverage, because computers can be damaged easily through a variety of causes. The cost is only about $5 per $1,000 of coverage, with no deductible.

- ✔ **If you have business data at risk, the best strategy is to back up your data.** Sure, you can buy optional data coverage when you schedule a computer, but re-creating lost data is such a hassle! You're better off backing up and storing a copy of the backup away from home.

For a more in-depth look at managing risks associated with a full-fledged, home-based business you operate from your home, see Chapter 13.

Chapter 11

Protecting Yourself from Major Homeowner's Exclusions

. . . .

In This Chapter

▶ Managing excluded property losses

▶ Protecting yourself from homeowner's liability exclusions

▶ Making sense of the new mold coverage restrictions

▶ Understanding the National Flood Insurance Program

. . . .

*H*omeowner's insurance policies are extremely comprehensive in coverage. They cover the majority of property and liability claims related to residences (see Chapter 9), but they do have limits. Even the broadest homeowner's property coverage — special perils coverage — has a handful of excluded causes of loss, including:

✔ Any kind of earth movement, such as earthquake, tremors, landslides, mudflows, and sinking or shifting

✔ Water that enters the house at or below ground level, such as a flood, runoff from heavy rains, sewer backup, and foundation seepage

✔ Ordinance or law requirements that either increase the cost of repairs or require demolition

✔ War or nuclear risks of any kind

✔ Other causes of loss for which no coverage is available, including wear and tear, neglect, insects, intentional damage, failure to protect the property after a loss (see the nearby sidebar, "Protect your property, protect your claims"), and off-premises power failures

 I address in this chapter only the exclusions that you can actually do something about or for which optional coverage is available. I don't address here exclusions covered elsewhere in this book like boats, recreational vehicles, and trailers (which I cover in Chapter 7).

Protect your property, protect your claims

An insurance policy is a binding legal contract. In order to be a valid contract, both parties agree to do certain things for the other. The obvious obligations are for you to pay all premiums by the due date and for your insurer to pay your covered claims when they occur.

But your obligations don't end with the premium payment. You can find your obligations (called *conditions*) in the back of every insurance policy, and you're required to comply with each of them. If you don't, you jeopardize your claim settlement if your noncompliance affects the claim.

One condition that most people are unaware of is the obligation to protect the property from further loss once a claim has occurred. If you don't, any resulting damage may not be covered. Here are some examples:

✔ Not acting to put a tarp over the hole in your roof caused by a storm, which leads to an additional $20,000 interior water damage

✔ Not moving high-value items to a safe place after a fire on one side of the house has made easy access to the interior possible, leading to a theft of six original paintings valued at $52,000

✔ Not changing the locks on your house after someone stole your purse with your keys inside, leading to a major burglary of $35,000 of stereos, TVs, and other property after the burglar entered using the stolen keys

Following any kind of property claim, you *must* take immediate, reasonable action to prevent further damage to your property, or you likely won't be covered for the additional damage. If you incur expenses in the process, the insurance company should always reimburse you, as long as you promptly notify them, the costs are reasonable, and you get their approval.

Earth Movement Exclusions: Shake, Rattle, and Roll!

You have three strategies to choose from to protect yourself from earth movement, a normally uninsured cause-of-loss:

✔ **Avoid the risk completely.** Don't live near a fault line, don't live on or near an active volcano, and don't buy or build a home on a steep hill vulnerable to mudslides. If you do, you have to be willing to live with the consequences. This strategy is my favorite because avoiding a major risk is always easier, cheaper, and more failsafe than the other choices.

✔ **Reduce the risk through preventive construction design.** Like California residents who build homes that can handle some earth shifting without causing major damage, spend what you need to spend so that when nature brings its wrath, your house is built to take it. (This is my second-favorite strategy, but it only works when you're building a new home.)

✔ **Buy earthquake insurance.** If you live in a high-risk area, you need to buy earthquake insurance. Yes, it's expensive. But not carrying the insurance violates one of the major guiding principles in Chapter 2 — don't risk more than you can afford to lose. Consider taking a large deductible on your homeowner's policy and applying the annual discount toward purchasing earthquake coverage.

Water, Water Everywhere: Ground Water Exclusions

Water can enter your home at or below ground level by a true flood — where a nearby body of water, usually a river, overflows its banks — heavy surface runoff, foundation seepage, or sewer backup.

You can avoid the true-flood risk by living nowhere near a body of water or by living on top of a mountain. You can significantly reduce the basement water risk from runoff or seepage with landscaping, gutters, and so on. You can also use my personal favorite approach: adding a sump-pump system. You can reduce the sewer backup risk by installing a one-way valve that allows sewage to flow out, but not in.

There are only two types of insurance available today to cover ground water risks, and neither covers the entire risk. The first is a sump pump failure/sewer backup endorsement you can add to your homeowner's policy. The other is participating in the National Flood Insurance Program. In the following sections, I cover both insurance options, but if you just want the bottom line, here are my recommendations:

✔ **If your home is at risk for serious groundwater damage from flood or heavy rains:** Buy federal flood insurance, with a policy limit at least high enough to cover your maximum probable loss. Then reduce that amount by the value of all furnishings, carpet, wall coverings, and so on, below ground (if you have no walkout), because those items won't be covered.

Be sure to buy coverage well in advance of any potential flood, because the National Flood Insurance Program policy has a 30-day waiting period.

✔ **For almost everyone else with any potential risk from rain runoff or seepage:** Install a sump-pump system with a guarantee from a reputable firm with good references. An excellent resource is the National Association of Waterproofing Structural Repair Contractors (phone: 800-245-6292; Web: www.nawsrc.org). Certified contractors are best because they've undergone extensive additional training. Having a sump-pump installed is far less expensive than you'd guess. And it costs considerably less than uninsured water damage claims.

Also, buy optional sump pump failure homeowner's coverage for the lesser of the maximum probable loss or the maximum coverage available.

Preventing the nightmarish mess of a sump-pump failure is far better than the alternative, so look into the cost of a backup battery or even a full backup system. I had a backup system installed to my town house and I sleep a lot better at night — especially when it's pouring outside.

If you don't have or want a sump pump, buy at least some sewer backup coverage unless you can prevent a backup with a one-way valve in your sewer pipe, or unless the lowest level of your structure is unfinished. Buy enough to cover the maximum probable loss or the maximum available, whichever is less.

Read on for more on sump pump failure and sewer backup endorsements, as well as the National Flood Insurance Program.

Protecting yourself with sump pump failure and sewer backup endorsements

Sump pump failure/sewer backup coverage varies significantly from one insurer to the next, but I can tell you how the coverage typically works. These endorsements cover water damage, including cleanup. The sump pump coverage applies only if you have a sump pump, and only if the sump pump fails to handle the intruding water. It usually even covers failure caused by power outages. The sewer backup coverage covers damage and cleanup anytime the sewer backs up. The basic limit for these two coverages, usually sold together, is $5,000 with limits available to $50,000 or more with some insurance companies.

These endorsements address the seepage and surface runoff problem. *This insurance coverage is not intended to apply to true floods.* Avoid insurers who offer watered-down versions of this coverage. Some of these endorsements exclude any failures caused by you (for example, if you accidentally overload a circuit, cutting power to the pump) or situations where the unit fails to work properly without your knowledge (for example, if the motor burns out and you have no way of knowing the pump is fried).

Signing up for the National Flood Insurance Program

Homeowner's policies don't cover flooding or ground water damage from heavy rains. With the private insurance industry unwilling, for a number of reasons, to offer flood insurance, Uncle Sam stepped in to offer coverage to homeowners, either directly or indirectly through a select list of participating insurance companies who act as the government's agent. Premiums start as low as $119 per year. The only requirement to be eligible is that you must live in a community that participates in the National Flood Insurance Program (NFIP). Some communities don't (but, in my opinion, all should).

NFIP coverage doesn't cover just any ground water entering your home. To be considered a *flood* and, thus, be eligible for coverage, the water damage must be substantial enough to damage either two properties, including yours, or just your property if your property covers two or more acres. So, unless you have two or more acres, if you get flooded from heavy rains but none of your neighbors do, the flood policy you purchase won't cover the damage. (In that case, you probably would not have had damage if you had a sump pump.)

The two federal flood programs

The federal government offers two flood insurance programs:

- ✔ **Emergency program:** The emergency program is for homes in communities that are applying for participation in the NFIP but have not yet been accepted. The emergency program's sole purpose is to allow homeowners in those waiting communities to at least get some flood coverage until the community is officially NFIP-approved.

  In the emergency program, prices are higher than they are in the regular program, and less coverage is available. The maximum available coverage through the emergency program is $35,000 for dwellings and $10,000 for contents — maximums that may be inadequate. Change your maximums as soon as your community gets NFIP approval.

- ✔ **Regular program:** The regular program is for homes in communities that are active NFIP participants. The maximum coverage limits in the regular program are more reasonable than they are in the emergency program: $250,000 for dwellings and $100,000 for contents.

The quirks of flood insurance

Flood insurance differs from homeowner's insurance in several key ways:

- ✔ **There is a 30-day waiting period between the date you apply for flood insurance and the effective date of coverage.** Be sure to apply early — don't wait to apply until you're laying sandbags around your house to keep out the river that's about to overflow.

- ✔ **A $500 deductible applies separately to building and contents losses ($1,000 deductible total if you're covering both).**

- ✔ **Claims are paid on a depreciated basis, not replacement cost.** Structural losses can be paid at full replacement cost only if your building coverage limit is the lesser of the NFIP policy maximum coverage of $250,000 or 80 percent or more of your home replacement cost.

✔ **You can buy insurance coverage for the building only (if you're a landlord, for example), contents only (if you're a tenant), or both the building and the contents (if you're a homeowner).**

✔ **Building and contents limits are bundled together (from a minimum of $20,000 on the building and $8,000 on contents to a maximum of $250,000 on the building and $100,000 on contents).**

✔ **Coverage for basements is very limited.** A *basement* is defined as having all four sides below grade. The NFIP policy covers only basement structures, including equipment (such as furnaces, water heaters, and air-conditioners). It does not provide coverage for finished walls, floors, and ceilings. Belongings in the basement are completely excluded, except for large appliances (such as washers, dryers, and freezers).

If your basement is a *walkout* (the floor of one side is at grade level), you may be fully covered if your home is not in a "high risk" flood zone as defined by the national flood program (if in doubt, check with your agent). On the other hand, if you own a *split-level* where a lower level is half in the ground and half above ground, the flood policy considers that a basement because the floors of all four sides are below grade.

How to buy flood insurance

To buy flood insurance, start by going to www.floodsmart.gov. You can input your address and find out immediately if your home is in a low, moderate, or high-risk flood zone. If you're in the low- to moderate-risk zones, you can even get a quote and/or find an agent who sells flood insurance in your area.

Don't overlook flood insurance just because you're in a low- to moderate-risk zone. According to the Federal Emergency Management Agency (FEMA), about 25 percent of flood losses occur in low- to moderate-risk zones!

You can and should buy flood insurance from your homeowner's agent if he's certified by FEMA to sell flood insurance. (Not all agents are certified, and not all insurance companies participate in the NFIP.) If your agent doesn't handle flood insurance and you need the coverage, change agents. Because flood is a major risk for those people facing it, if your agent is a serious professional, he'll be certified to sell flood insurance.

If you are on the fence about your need for flood insurance, here's a way you can get some coverage and keep your costs down: Start by choosing your building and contents coverage limits lower than your homeowner's limits, at depreciated values rather than replacement cost. And don't include in your valuations any finished areas below grade on all four sides because there is little or no coverage for those areas. Estimate the maximum probable loss for structural and contents damage and choose a bundled building and contents limit high enough to cover the maximum probable loss for both.

Flood insurance vs. disaster assistance: Why flood insurance is best

Many people wonder why they should purchase flood insurance when the government provides disaster assistance through low-interest loans. Having flood insurance is a much better idea than relying on federal disaster assistance. Here's why:

✔ **Flood insurance provides immediate help.** Disaster assistance involves hours of waiting in line, tremendous paperwork, and a wait of many months before you see any money.

✔ **Flood insurance provides coverage even for local rains or runoffs.** Disaster assistance requires a presidential decree before it goes into effect.

✔ **You don't have to pay back flood insurance after you get your settlement.** Most disaster assistance is in the form of a loan that must be paid back.

✔ **Flood insurance coverage limits are much higher.**

✔ **Flood insurance is less expensive.** The usual cost of a flood insurance policy that pays you a maximum of $50,000 is $166 per year. The cost to repay a $50,000 disaster loan is $3,840 per year for over 20 years!

It's the Law: Managing Ordinance Risks

All municipalities have building codes, and those codes often change after a house is built. So, if your structure is damaged, you may very likely be required to upgrade the damaged area to satisfy current codes.

The good news is that the code improvements usually mean a safer, better-quality home. The bad news is that much of the extra costs are often out of your own pocket, because most homeowner's policies cover the added costs of municipally required upgrades only up to 10 percent of your homeowner's coverage limit for your residence. And some insurers completely exclude coverage altogether.

The picture gets even worse if there is a demolition requirement. A demolition ordinance requires that, if more than a specified percentage of the home is damaged, the house can't be repaired — it has to be completely demolished and rebuilt. Say you own a home in a city that requires the home to be demolished and rebuilt if 25 percent or more of it is damaged. The replacement value of the house is $240,000. You're unaware of the law in your city, but you diligently insure your beautiful home for its full replacement cost. You have a kitchen fire that damages one-third of the house. Your insurance company happily sends you a check for the $80,000, the cost to repair the damage. It adds 10 percent of the building limit for ordinance coverage (or $24,000). So you get a total of $104,000 from the insurance company. But the replacement cost, including all the mandatory building code improvements, is actually $300,000. Add to that the cost to demolish the home and haul it away ($35,000). So your total expenses are $335,000. That means your out-of-pocket loss is $231,000!

The good news is that you can get supplemental coverage from most insurance companies under an ordinance and law endorsement to your homeowner's policy. This endorsement usually allows you to raise the automatic coverage that comes with your homeowner's policy from 10 percent of the building coverage to 25 percent, 50 percent, 75 percent, or even 100 percent.

So, for example, if you're insuring your home for $200,000, your automatic ordinance and law coverage will be $20,000 (10 percent). If you estimate that it will take an extra $50,000 to rebuild your home according to new building codes, you'll need an ordinance and law endorsement of 25 percent (25 percent of $200,000 building coverage equals $50,000.)

Estimating the effects of building ordinances on your insurance coverage is tricky at best. This is one area where it pays to have an expert insurance agent to work with you on your whole program (see Chapter 4).

The home vacancy exclusion

If your home is vacant (devoid of furniture) for 60 consecutive days, your vandalism and glass breakage coverage is suspended, which means if someone then breaks into your home, smashes all the windows, and trashes the house, you have zero coverage under your homeowner's policy. Some of the newer homeowner's forms won't even cover damage from an ensuing fire that's started by the vandals!

Vacancy is most common in homes that have been for sale for a long time. The sellers have moved on, taking their furniture with them. It's not uncommon for these homes to be vacant for a year or more before they're sold. Of course, the homeowner has had significant coverage gaps since the 61st day of vacancy if that's true.

The best solution to this problem is to do everything possible to keep furniture in the home. (The courts have held that the amount of furniture has to be adequate for someone to actually live there.) I also recommend that you install a central burglar and fire alarm so that, if anyone does break in, the police will be there in less than five minutes.

If the house is in a cold part of the country, add a temperature sensor to the central alarm service so that, if the temperature dips below a certain level, your alarm company will be notified. This strategy will greatly reduce the chance of pipes freezing and cracking and flooding the house, which may not be noticed for weeks or months.

Liability Exclusions: Making Sure You're Covered

Homeowner's policies have a variety of liability exclusions, and in this section I fill you in on the major exclusions, show you how they can hurt you, and give you strategies for minimizing your possibility of being uninsured in a personal lawsuit.

My advice in this section is based on a *typical* homeowner's policy. Every insurer differs slightly from this norm. So you need to be sure to read and understand *your* specific homeowner's policy.

Every homeowner's policy has a few exclusions that I don't cover here, because there's not much you can do about them — exclusions like war and nuclear-related liability, communicable diseases, abuse (sexual, physical, mental), and anything related to the buying or selling of illegal drugs. All you can do is avoid these activities. Optional liability insurance just isn't available for something like a nuclear blast you set off!

The business exclusion

Homeowner's policies exclude coverage for injuries or property damage you cause in any way related to business — your own business or someone else's. (See Chapter 13 for a more detailed analysis if you actually operate your own business from your home.)

The courts have defined *business,* as used in the homeowner's policy, as any activity for which there is both revenue and continuity. Naturally, anything arising from your job or occupation fills that definition. But so can income you earn on the side. If you have a single garage sale, it's not a business. If you have one once a month for ten years, it probably *is* a business. If you baby-sit occasionally, it's not a business. If you're a nanny for another family's children, it is a business. If you're part of a babysitting co-op where you take turns watching each other's children and no money is exchanged, it's not a business. But if you decide to quit your job and have a home day care, you have a business.

The problem with having your activity defined as a business is that, if you're sued for injuries or property damage arising from those activities, your homeowner's policy won't cover you. It won't even pay for your defense.

That means you would have coverage for none of the following situations:

✔ You're working as a nanny or daycare provider, and the children in your care are injured.

✔ You have a weekly garage sale and someone is electrocuted when using an iron she bought from you.

✔ You're sick and working from home, and your boss sends a courier to deliver work to you; the courier slips on your icy driveway and is injured.

✔ You spill hot coffee on a coworker at work and injure her.

As the last two examples show, this exclusion applies not only to self-employed people but also to people who cause injuries or damage as someone else's employee, whether at home or at work!

Here are some strategies you can take to help prevent the business exclusion from hurting you:

✔ **If you're an employee and you want coverage for injuries you cause to someone while on the job, buy the business pursuits homeowner's endorsement.** It costs about $5 a year, and I think every employee should buy this.

✔ **If you telecommute or have an incidental office at home, buy an incidental office liability endorsement.** It costs only $10 to $25 a year. Many of these endorsements include extra coverage on your business furniture and equipment.

✔ **If you host weekly neighborhood garage sales, consider avoiding the risk of uninsured injuries by stopping the sales.** The money you make isn't worth the potential uninsured lawsuit. You can either give the items to a worthy cause and play golf on Saturdays instead, or sell your stuff only occasionally, maybe at someone else's neighborhood garage sale. By no longer doing it regularly, it won't be a business.

If you aren't willing to give it up, either buy a small business policy (which costs at least $300 a year) or have your agent or insurance company state, in writing, that they won't exclude coverage for your garage sales.

✔ **If you're caring for other people's children regularly, either at your own home or in their home, you *must* buy childcare liability insurance.** It's available from one or more of these four sources:

✔ An endorsement to your homeowner's policy. Check here first — if available, it's normally the least expensive option.

✔ Small business policies from insurance agents.

✔ A state office that licenses childcare.

✔ An association of childcare providers.

> ✔ **If your children earn money from home doing something that has a regular pattern (babysitting, lawn care, and so on), get a written statement from your insurer that your kids' activities won't be excluded as a business.** If your insurer won't do this, change insurance companies. Some insurers have customized and broadened their homeowners policies so that children's business activities are not excluded as long as their earnings are modest (for example, under $2,000 a year, with no employees).

Whatever you're doing that produces income — whether you're an owner or an employee — deal with the business exclusion now, even if it means stopping your activity if you can't get affordable insurance. The cost of an uninsured lawsuit can be ruinous. This is the number one insurance coverage gap I see when I review insurance programs.

The exclusion for renting part of your home

The homeowner's policy excludes coverage for injuries to any roomers or boarders when more than _two_ of them live in your single family home. A good example is a homeowner who rents the three upstairs bedrooms to college kids. If one of the kids gets injured at your home and sues you, you have no coverage. If you're the homeowner, you only have two choices to protect yourself:

> ✔ Cancel your homeowner's policy and get a more expensive, commercial policy for rooming houses.

> ✔ Don't rent to more than two individuals at a time.

Note that the exclusion doesn't apply if you rent occasionally — for example, if you rent out your home for a week during a Super Bowl when hotel rooms are scarce. And it doesn't apply if you rent part of your home as an office, school, studio, or garage.

The exclusion for any other premises you own or rent

The Homeowners policy covers your primary home but not other locations you rent long-term or own, such as vacation homes or rental properties. The easy solution is to include liability coverage with the policy you buy on the other location. Or you can extend your primary homeowner's liability coverage to the other location with an endorsement costing about $15 a year if you occupy the house, or about $25 per year if you're renting it to others.

The loss assessment exclusion

The loss assessment exclusion denies coverage for assessments for injuries or property damage made against you by a community of home, town house, or condominium owners of which you are a member. If you own a home, town house, or condominium that is part of an association, you can buy optional loss assessment coverage as an endorsement to your homeowner's policy that covers some but not all of these assessments. (See Chapter 12 for more details on how loss assessment coverage actually works.)

Because these loss assessments can be quite substantial and because the cost of the coverage is minimal (less than $25 per year), I always recommend that anyone who is part of a homeowner's association buy the maximum — usually $50,000 worth of coverage

The contracts exclusion

The homeowner's policy excludes liability coverage for all contracts, oral or written, but it also has two nice *coverage givebacks*. A coverage giveback means that the exclusion in your policy is nullified — or the insurance company's excuse for not paying you in a given circumstance is taken away. These givebacks apply to the following written — not oral — contracts:

- ✓ Contracts that involved the ownership, maintenance, or use of a location you have insured, such as your home

- ✓ Contracts in which you assume the liability of others *prior to* any claim (for example, you rent a chainsaw and in the rental agreement you agree to protect the hardware store if it's sued for any injury that occurs while you're using the saw)

I have a wheelchair-bound client, Betty, who owns a beautiful two-story home on the Mississippi River. The house has an elevator to help her navigate between floors. In her contract with the elevator maintenance company, she unknowingly agreed to defend them and pay any judgment against them for any lawsuit arising from an elevator injury.

The first coverage giveback for written contracts will do what she contracted to do because the contract has to do with the maintenance of her home. So, if someone is injured in the elevator when a cable snaps, the homeowner's liability coverage will defend and pay any judgment against Betty and, because of the elevator contract, it will do the same for the elevator maintenance company.

Good neighbor property damage coverage

Every homeowner's policy includes a very useful supplemental coverage called *damage to property of others*. It covers up to $1,000 (depending on the insurance company) for damage you or your kids cause to other people's property, including property in your custody, and there's no deductible. It even covers intentional damage (pranks) by your children if they're under a certain age (the age varies from one company to the next). This coverage applies if your 10-year-old throws a rock through the neighbor's window, or if you cut down a tree limb and it crashes through your neighbor's sunroom, or if your dog chews apart the neighbor's new couch. If your neighbor does any of this damage to your property, remember that he has this coverage, too, if he has a homeowner's policy. Just ask him to report the claim — that's all there is to it.

These two coverage givebacks won't cover all your written contracts. But a good personal umbrella policy will cover most of the liability you assume when you sign a contract. (See Chapters 16 and 17 to learn more about the contractual coverage of umbrella policies for all types of personal contracts.)

The property in your custody exclusion

Homeowner's policies exclude coverage for damage to the property of others in your possession, whether you rent it (for example, when you rent a boat), occupy it (when you borrow a friend's cabin for the weekend), or use it (when you borrow your employer's laptop computer). There is one coverage giveback — coverage for fire, smoke, or explosions you cause, such as for a kitchen fire you cause in your rented apartment. (See the preceding section for more on coverage givebacks.)

When you know that this pitfall exists, you can protect yourself, at least partially. Here's how:

- ✔ **Buy a personal umbrella policy that plugs this gap by covering damage to property you don't own that is in your care.** (See Chapter 16 for more information.)

- ✔ **When renting equipment, boats, and so on, if the value of what you're renting exceeds what you're willing to pay for out of pocket, buy coverage from the rental company, if you don't have an umbrella policy that covers it.**

> ✔ **When using other people's property on a long-term basis, like a laptop computer, you can specifically insure it on your homeowner's policy (called *scheduling*).** Be sure to list the owner as a *loss payee* on the policy to protect the owner's interest.

The workers' compensation exclusion

Workers' compensation is an insurance program of state-mandated benefits that employers provide employees, usually covering the employee's medical bills and lost wages from a job-related injury or illness. Workers' compensation is no-fault coverage.

To collect benefits, an injured person must only meet two requirements: He is your employee, and he has been hurt on the job. If an employer fails to buy a workers' compensation policy, he has to pay, out of his own pocket, the same benefits to the injured worker that the policy would have paid.

If you have no employees but you hire contractors or laborers who do not have their own workers' compensation policies, I recommend buying *contingent workers' compensation* (CWC) coverage — especially if you're affluent and very suable. A very small number of homeowner's insurers offer CWC coverage as a policy endorsement for a nominal charge. If your homeowner's insurer doesn't offer CWC coverage, find one that does — or buy a CWC policy from your state workers' compensation insurance pool, if it's available. Some companies included CWC for small exposures — another good reason to have your agent find the best company for you.

CWC works like this: If any injured contractor ever sues for workers' compensation benefits, this optional coverage completely defends you and, if you lose, pays the state-required benefits.

Your state may have a law exempting homeowners from this risk. Check with your state insurance department or the Department of Labor if in doubt.

The mold exclusion

Historically, damage *caused by* mold has never been covered under homeowner's insurance but mold cleanup resulting from covered water damage has been covered. However, as a result of a couple of high-profile successful lawsuits, homes worth hundreds of thousands of dollars were declared total losses by the courts because of "hazardous" mold infestation. Insurers were forced to demolish the homes and rebuild at their expense. The courts' decision has led to a very strong reaction from the insurance industry, which immediately began to also exclude or severely limit claims for mold cleanup that are part of a covered water damage claim.

There's very little consistency in the insurance industry in the way they limit or exclude mold claims. Some companies completely exclude property claims involving mold; others also exclude liability claims (such as defending you if you're sued because a guest staying in your home suffered severe lung damage as a result of an asthma attack from breathing in some mold you didn't know existed in your basement).

Other companies include a modest amount of mold coverage on the policy, most commonly $10,000 on property losses and $50,000 for liability claims. I'm especially concerned about the limitation on liability claims because a lawsuit involving a serious injury from mold inhalation could easily exceed $50,000.

For mold to grow, it needs water. So the key at claim time to avoid getting burned by this exclusion/limitation is to make sure that all the water has been removed — not just the obvious water on the floor but also hidden water, such as replacing the sheet rock that has wicked up water and replacing moldings. If a water damage claim is covered by your homeowner's policy, even though the policy may not cover the cost to remove mold, the insurer is obligated to pay to repair and replace any parts of the home that have been damaged by water. If you're diligent about getting rid of the water at the time of the claim, you shouldn't have to worry about future mold problems.

A good strategy for protecting yourself against large mold liability claims is to buy a personal umbrella policy that will defend and pay any judgment against you for any losses that exceed the small coverage limit that you have on your homeowner's policy. I represent companies that have agreed to do just that, so I know that step-down umbrella coverage is available in the personal umbrella marketplace. (See Chapters 15 and 16 for more on how umbrella coverage works.)

Chapter 12

Insuring Your Condominium or Town House

*T*he single biggest change in the housing market in the past 30 years has been the movement away from single-family homes toward town houses and condominiums. A new type of homeowner's policy, often referred to as the *homeowner's form 6*, has been created to meet the special needs of town house or condominium owners.

The good news is that there is a special policy for those who own town houses or condos. The bad news is that, unless you have a great agent who knows what he's doing, your policy may have serious coverage gaps. (See Chapter 4 for tips on finding a great agent.)

In this chapter, I fill you in on what these coverage gaps are and why they exist, and then I tell you how to work around them. I end the chapter with a section on vacation properties — condos and timeshares — and the special challenges they present. With the information in this chapter at your fingertips, you're sure to get the coverage you need for your condo or town house.

Defining the Problem

First things first: Let me give you a definition of what I mean by town houses and condominiums. Town houses and condos are individually owned, residential units, similar to apartments, that are part of a complex of similar units attached together in one or more buildings.

The usual distinction between the two is that town houses have their entry doors open to the outside, have other adjacent units only on either side but not above or below, and are often multilevel. Condominiums, on the other hand, are more like apartments: They open to a common hallway, are usually one level, and normally have adjacent units on either side, as well as above and/or below. From the outside, town houses look like single homes attached at the sides; condominiums look like apartments in an apartment building.

The similarities between condos and town houses are that:

✔ In addition to the ownership of their individual units, *unit owners* (people who own town houses or condos) also own a proportionate interest in common areas like lawns, driveways, weight rooms, clubhouses, swimming pools, and so on.

✔ All the unit owners band together to form a homeowner association. A board of directors made up of elected unit owners acts on behalf of the association.

✔ Several documents define the rights, obligations, and operating policies of the association (primarily the bylaws and declaration documents).

Identifying the master policy shortcomings

One of the functions of the association is to arrange insurance coverage — both property and liability — for the entire complex of buildings; the insurance policy is called the *master policy.* The master policy insures all structures, including the majority of the structure owned by each unit owner. Each unit owner is responsible for insuring her own belongings, *plus any part of her unit structure not covered by the association master policy.* And that's where the problem arises.

In the vast majority of associations, a significant structural coverage gap exists between the association's master building insurance policy and the unit owner's personal homeowner's policy. And the truth is, this gap is usually the result of a misperception on the part of the unit owner.

The unit owner believes — usually mistakenly — that he's responsible for insuring his personal belongings only, and that the association's master policy pays for everything structural in the unit (after a policy deductible of typically $5,000 or $10,000).

Discovering the unit owner policy gap

But the reality, most of the time, is that the association master policy covers, at a minimum, the bare interior walls of your unit and the bare floors. That makes you responsible for some or all of the interior of your unit. If you have a basic homeowner's policy that only covers the contents of the unit and, say, $5,000 of building coverage, this could be a *big* coverage gap — I've seen the gap be as large as $300,000! Can you imagine discovering such a gap only after a fire destroys most of your unit? Sadly, that's when most people find out.

The gap is not, as you may expect, spelled out in the master policy. Instead, you'll find it in one of your association documents, usually the *declaration* (which defines which part of your unit the association will insure). This makes sense given that the board of directors of the association determines exactly which part of each unit is insured by the master policy and which part is the unit owner's responsibility. The master policy pays only what the association documents require it to pay.

Here are some typical examples of items that you, as the unit owner, may be responsible for replacing — things often *excluded* by the association master policy:

- ✔ **Everything but bare walls and floor.** You're responsible for drapes, carpet, hardwood flooring, bathroom ceramic tile, wall coverings, built-in appliances, cabinets, countertops, plumbing fixtures (like tubs and toilets), lighting fixtures, and more!

- ✔ **Any structural improvements you make.** Examples include finishing the basement, adding a deck or porch, upgrading a kitchen, and so on.

- ✔ **Any improvements made by any unit owner since the unit was built.** This is extremely difficult to determine if the unit is older and especially if it's had several owners before you. Someone on the board of directors may be able to tell you what an original unit looked like.

Solving Problems with Proper Unit Owner's Insurance

The homeowner's policy created specifically to meet the unique property and liability risks of town house and condominium owners has six types of coverage — I review four of them here because these four coverages are most affected by town house or condominium ownership:

✔ Coverage for damage to the unit structure (Coverage A)

✔ Coverage for any detached buildings, like sheds or garages (Coverage B)

✔ Coverage for belongings (Coverage C)

✔ Coverage for injuries and property damage you cause (Coverage E)

See Chapter 9 for a review of the six coverage parts of homeowner's insurance and the two causes-of-loss forms I recommend — broad form and special form.

Home sweet home: Building coverage

There are two components you must consider when buying building coverage (Coverage A) on your unit-owner policy:

✔ The amount of building coverage you need to cover the interior of your unit that is *not* covered by the association master policy

✔ The kinds of claims, or causes-of-loss, you want covered

Enough is not enough: Picking your Coverage A limit

Start by reading your association declaration with the help of your trusted insurance agent to see what your obligations are. The next step is estimating the dollar amount of your potential obligations. Whether you do it on a computer or using plain old paper and pencil, make two columns: On the left, list every structural item you're responsible for; on the right, list your estimated cost to replace each item.

Be sure to include the labor to install.

Add up the amounts in the right column, round that number up by about 20 percent (to cover any errors you made in estimating the cost), and that's the amount of structural coverage you need. See Table 12-1 for an example, but keep in mind that this is just an example — you may need more than $4,000 to replace your carpet, for example.

Table 12-1	Estimating Building Coverage
Structural Item	*Replacement Cost Including Labor*
Carpet	$4,000
Wallpaper	$3,500
Lighting fixtures	$6,000
Plumbing fixtures	$7,500

Structural Item	Replacement Cost Including Labor
Hardwood floors	$12,000
Cabinets	$10,000
Subtotal	*$43,000*
Addition 20%	$8,600
Total	**$51,600**

In this case, you would buy about $50,000 of Coverage A.

Special coverage is very special

The coverage that comes automatically with the majority of unit-owner policies is the *broad causes-of-loss form,* covering your claims only if they appear on a list of about 15 covered causes of loss. Anything not on the list isn't covered. I don't recommend this as an option for insuring a structure.

For insuring a condominium or town house unit structure, request the optional *special form* (also known as *special perils*) that covers any accidental cause of loss if the cause is not on a small list of exclusions (flood, earthquake, and so on). The special form is very inexpensive — only about $1 per $1,000 of coverage. (See Chapter 9 for more on special perils.)

Special perils building coverage also improves your coverage for both deductible assessments and loss assessments.

If you're exposed to flood or earthquake risks, you can find out how to manage those risks in Chapter 11.

Detached structures: From Fido's house to the toolshed

Some garages that you buy with town houses are attached to the first level of your unit; many are in a separate or detached structure. To determine your insurance responsibility for garages, read the association's declaration. If you're required to insure the garage, increase your Coverage A (building coverage) if the garage is attached; if the garage is not attached, buy the appropriate amount of Coverage B.

Be sure to include in the Coverage B limit all other detached structures you're responsible for, like sheds, permanent docks, fancy dog houses, fences, and so forth.

Getting personal: Insuring your stuff

One thing common to every association's declaration is the unit owner's sole responsibility for her personal belongings. Here are my bottom-line recommendations for insuring your belongings:

- ✔ Buy a limit high enough to replace what you own.

- ✔ Buy the optional replacement-cost coverage so your claims will be paid on a new cost basis rather than a depreciated value.

- ✔ Upgrade the covered causes-of-loss from broad form to special form so that any cause of loss (other than a few that are specifically excluded) is covered (such as interior water damage from leaky roofs).

Do these three things and you'll have enough to replace everything you own following a major loss. Plus, you'll have more causes of loss covered.

Turn to Chapter 9 for suggestions on measuring the replacement value of your personal property. And see Chapter 10 on how to insure items of special value that are limited in coverage in all homeowners policies (jewelry cameras, sterling silver, and more).

Liability: You're liable to need it

When it comes to your personal liability for injuries or property damage, be consistent. Buy the same limit that you buy for other policies you own. After all, you're protecting the same assets and the same income — yours! You wouldn't want different liability limits on different policies any more than you would want different car insurance liability on weekends than what you have for the rest of the week.

If $500,000 is the liability insurance limit you buy for your car insurance, buy the same $500,000 for homeowner's liability, too. (See Chapter 9 for tips on choosing a liability limit that's appropriate for you.) And consider an extra layer of liability coverage of $1 million or more under a personal umbrella policy. (See Chapters 15 and 16 for more on umbrella policies.)

Assessing Your Assessments

Two things that all homeowner's associations have in common are loss assessments and deductible assessments. They're as inevitable when you own a condo or town house as death and taxes. *Loss assessments* occur when there is not enough money in the association bank account to pay the bills — usually when the bills exceed expectations. And one of the reasons associations have unexpected bills is inadequate insurance coverage. *Deductible assessments* occur when the association assesses the payment of the master policy deductible against one or more unit owners.

Loss assessments

When the association suffers a loss beyond the limits of its property or liability insurance coverage, it assesses you, the unit owner, with a bill to help pay for that loss. Therefore, the term *loss assessment.*

Suppose you own a unit and there are 100 units in your association. Table 12-2 shows examples of how you could be assessed when an insurance claim is not fully covered.

Table 12-2	Possible Association Assessments			
Claim	*Claim Amount*	*Insurance Pays*	*Assessment*	*Your Share*
Guest drowns in pool	$2 million	$1 million	$1 million	$10,000
Injured worker sues for workers' compensation	$700,000	None — not covered	$700,000	$7,000
Complex destroyed by tornado	$20 million	$14 million	$6 million	$60,000

The bad news is that this all sounds pretty scary — and it is. The good news is that unit owner's policies offer some coverage inexpensively, and you can use one of the ARRT risk management strategies, loss reduction (see Chapter 3), to lower the chances of an assessment ever occurring for an insurance claim.

Two problems can arrive in your mailbox — in the form of a bill — if you ignore the risk of loss assessments in your insurance coverage:

 ✔ The typical unit-owner policy has only $5,000 of loss-assessment coverage. This means that if the association sends you a big, ugly assessment (say, for $50,000), your unit-owner policy will pay only $5,000 of that — not much help. In the three examples in Table 12-2, you could have needed up to $60,000 of coverage.

> ✔ The insurance company only pays that $5,000 if the cause of the loss is covered by your unit-owner policy. In the three examples in Table 12-2, your policy covers lawsuits and tornadoes but not workers' compensation claims. Even if you bought extra loss-assessment coverage, it wouldn't cover your assessment for the injured worker.

In the following sections, I cover three strategies you can take to address these problems: changing the association's insurance program, buying enough loss-assessment coverage, and getting better building coverage.

Changing your association's insurance program

The better your association's coverage is, the better your chances of avoiding an uninsured assessment.

What kind of insurance should your association have? Here's a list of coverages and/or policies that I think every homeowner's association should have, as a minimum:

> ✔ Building insurance for the full replacement cost of all buildings required to be insured by the association, including replacement-cost coverage (so claims settlements are not depreciated), an agreed-amount coverage (which waives any penalties for under-insurance on partial losses), and, if available, a building replacement guarantee if rebuilding costs exceed the insurance amount.
>
> ✔ Flood and/or earthquake coverage if there is the danger of either one happening where you live.
>
> ✔ Public liability insurance of $1 million, or whatever limits are required for an umbrella policy.
>
> ✔ An umbrella liability policy with at least $2 million limits.
>
> ✔ Worker's compensation insurance, even if there are no association employees (to cover claims brought by injured independent contractors, covering all defense costs and judgments).
>
> ✔ Non-owned automobile liability coverage (which protects the association from lawsuits arising out of car accidents caused by people running errands on behalf of the association in their own personal cars).
>
> ✔ Directors and officers liability coverage, for two reasons:
>
>> • People nice enough to volunteer their time to serve on the board should be given this coverage so they have insurance in case they make an honest mistake and are sued for it.
>>
>> • If the director makes an error that could lead to a possible loss assessment, this coverage may cover the error and keep the loss assessment from being passed to you.

> ✔ A fidelity bond, to protect the association from the dishonesty of anyone handling money, including an outside management company, if you use one.

Each association is different, so remember that your association may have insurance needs in addition to these.

As the unit owner, you have every right to ask for proof from the board that it has every one of these policies. If the association does not have one or more of these, write to the board and express your concerns — you may be able to reduce your chances of a possible loss assessment.

Buying loss assessment coverage: Not too much, not too little, but just right

Loss assessment coverage is cheap. About $20 a year for the maximum most insurers offer — $50,000 of coverage — so buy the maximum.

Buying better building coverage

You need to buy the broadest possible unit-owner building coverage — special-perils coverage — in order to have the most possible types of claims covered by loss-assessment coverage. Your loss-assessment coverage only pays for those assessments where the cause of the loss is a cause covered by your building coverage (Coverage A).

Always add the optional sump pump failure/sewer backup coverage. Not only will that cover those types of losses in your own unit, but it will also cover assessments for those losses.

Even if you add earthquake coverage to your policy (which you should do if you live in an earthquake-prone area), you need to add loss-assessments-for-earthquake coverage to your policy because earthquake assessments are not covered by regular loss-assessment coverage. For example, suppose an earthquake crumbles the complex and causes $4 million in damages. The association failed to buy earthquake coverage. There are 100 unit owners in the association: $4 million divided by 100 units equals an assessment of $40,000 to you and all other owners. If you've purchased the optional earthquake damage coverage on your unit-owner policy and at least $40,000 of loss assessment from earthquake coverage, your policy pays the full assessment.

Deductible assessments

In the past few years, two trends have emerged when it comes to association master-policy deductibles:

> ✔ **The deductibles have been increasing to save on insurance costs.** Deductibles of $10,000 are becoming the norm.
>
> ✔ **Individual unit owners are being assessed the entire deductible if the claim is confined to their unit (your dishwasher overflows, damaging your hardwood floors) or if the unit owner caused the loss (you cause a kitchen grease fire).**

Say you're an owner of a beautiful town house. You cause a kitchen fire with $50,000 total fire and water damage. Between the association master policy and your unit-owner policy, your claim was paid in full, and you're happy as a clam. Then two months later, you're hit with a bill from your association for $10,000 — the entire master policy deductible! You submit the bill to your homeowner's insurer, which declines your claim, leaving you responsible for the entire $10,000 assessment.

Here's why: A basic unit-owner homeowner's policy limits coverage for loss assessments to $1,000 but it only covers assessments made association-wide — it doesn't cover assessments against individual unit owners. Even if you buy extra loss-assessment coverage, the policy still requires association-wide assessments in order to compensate you. It also limits deductible assessments to $1,000.

There is no uniform solution that all insurance companies have agreed to. The *norm,* however, is to offer an optional endorsement called *deductible assessment coverage* (or something similar). There's no requirement that the assessment be association-wide so it does cover individual assessments such as the one in this example (as long as you had purchased at least $10,000 of coverage).

Make sure that you add this coverage to your unit owner's policy in the amount of your association's master policy deductible. Be sure to check with your insurer as to how they handle this risk — it may do things a bit differently.

Building Damage Claims: What's Mine Is Mine and What's Yours Is Yours

Suppose that your association's declarations require the association to insure the majority of your unit and for you to be responsible for insuring carpets, drapes, wallcoverings, and improvements you made to the unit. Now, suppose that a fire damages both the property that the association is responsible for *and* the property that you're responsible for. If that sounds complicated, it's because it is.

If you want your claim to go smoothly, you have to be assertive. Because you have the strongest personal relationship with your unit-owner insurance company, ask them to act as the front man on your claim — have them handle their own claim as well as act as an agent for you in dealing with the company insuring the association. This way, you'll only have to deal with one insurance company — yours. Plus, your insurance company will be responsible for dickering with the association insurance company over any disputed areas — they'll agree to resolve any differences between them, without your having to get involved.

You may get some resistance to this request at first, but keep at it. This request is perfectly reasonable. You and your association have paid for the services of insurance professionals — they're the experts, and they should be willing to do their job.

The best way to improve your odds of getting a hassle-free, full settlement is to buy the best possible coverage. No matter how nice your insurance company is, no matter how caring your adjuster is, they will not pay you for coverage you don't have.

I see and hear a lot of people criticizing their insurance companies when their claim is either denied or underpaid. Trust me: In nearly every instance, the coverage is what was lacking — not the insurance company.

Risk Doesn't Take a Vacation: Covering Condominiums and Timeshares

The last thing you want to think about when you've just bought a great new condo or timeshare in Boca is insurance. Somehow insurance and coconut oil go together about as well as oil and water. But risk doesn't take a vacation, and neither can you when it comes to insuring your vacation property.

There are two main types of vacation property: condos and timeshares. I cover both of them in the following sections.

Vacation condos

This section applies to homeowner's of all different types. Maybe you've bought a seasonal vacation condo on the beach in Maui or at a ski resort in Aspen. Someone else manages the property and all the regular maintenance is taken care of, so you can have fun when you're at the condo instead of having to do chores!

All the risk-management strategies I recommend earlier in this chapter apply to vacation condos and timeshares. But there are two exceptions that require special handling:

- ✔ You own your condo with friends.
- ✔ You rent your condo to other people when you're not there.

When you own a condo with your friends

Vacation property costs money, especially because it's usually located in a prime location. To save money, you may have decided to go in on the condo with some of your very best friends. Sharing the costs of a vacation condo offers lots of advantages, true, but it comes with one major disadvantage: The insurance is often set up incorrectly.

Here's an example from my own files. My clients Desi and Lucy bought a Colorado condo with their ski-buff friends, Fred and Ethyl. (Okay, so I changed their names to protect their identities.) Desi and Lucy didn't call me at the time, because Fred and Ethyl said that they would take care of all the insurance. In my annual review of Desi and Lucy's insurance program, the subject came up. At my urging, they got me a copy of the insurance policy from their friends. Here are the pertinent coverages, as arranged by Fred and Ethyl:

- ✔ Fred and Ethyl were the only ones named on the policy. As a result, Desi and Lucy's 50 percent ownership in the building and contents were completely uninsured.
- ✔ The unit-owner building policy coverage limit was only $1,000, with no special-perils endorsement.
- ✔ The liability limit was only $100,000 and again, Desi and Lucy were uninsured.
- ✔ There was only $1,000 of loss-assessment coverage — far too little. And there was no optional deductible assessment coverage.
- ✔ The personal property limit was $45,000. The replacement cost was $80,000.

So how much did it cost to plug all five gaps? Would you believe only $100 per couple per year! As is often the case, a little extra premium to do the job well can save potential out-of-pocket losses of hundreds of thousands of dollars. The added premium is peanuts in relation to the risks being protected.

When you're renting out your condo

Vacation condos are often rented by the association management when the owners aren't using them. If you allow your unit to be rented, your insurance coverage may be suspended due to rental exclusions in the policy.

Bottom line: If you're renting your vacation property even occasionally, check with your agent or insurance company and buy the optional rental coverage.

Vacation timeshares

If you have a timeshare, you've purchased a period of time (say, a week or two) in a vacation condo that you co-own with others. You can use the unit during your allotted time, swap your time for another period of time in the same complex, swap your time for time in another unit somewhere else in the world, or even rent your unit out during your time period.

The condo association manages and insures the whole complex, including liability coverage. Most association policies cover your liability for community injuries (such as a drowning at the swimming pool), but they usually don't cover your liability for injuries or property damage you cause arising out of your personal use of your unit (for example, if your guest is burned in a kitchen fire).

Your homeowner's policy won't cover your personal liability if you own, rent, or occupy another location on a regular basis. If you have deeded ownership, as most timeshares are, you aren't insured during your personal occupancy — one week or two weeks — by your homeowner's liability coverage. So how do you cover your liability for your time in your timeshare?

- ✔ **To cover yourself when you're using your unit during your allotted time, the safest thing to do is to endorse your homeowner's policy to extend your liability coverage to this timeshare unit.** This will cost you approximately $15 more per year.

- ✔ **If you rent the unit to others, endorse your homeowner's policy to cover that rental.** This will cost you about $25 per year.

If you swap units with someone else, your use of their unit is covered automatically by your homeowner's liability coverage.

Protecting your property when you're back home

If you aren't renting your property and you only occasionally use it, you can reduce the chance of both burglary and fire by installing a central burglar and fire alarm system. After installation, this kind of system costs only about $20 a month to monitor. You can even add an option for temperature monitoring if the condominium is in a cold weather climate — the alarm company will be alerted if your temperature drops below a certain temperature, so that if the furnace has failed, your pipes won't freeze and cause massive water damage.

Chapter 13

Running a Home Business without Losing Your Shirt

I've worked with scores of home business owners over the years, and most of them have one thing in common: little or no business insurance. And yet these businesses have risks that could cause financial ruin if they were to occur.

Home businesses are inadequately insured for two reasons:

✔ The homeowner's policy, even with the optional business endorsements, falls far short of meeting the coverage needs of most home-business owners.

✔ Many home-business owners are unaware of all the risks arising from their business and that their homeowner's policy doesn't cover many of the risks that they do know about.

If you own a home business, or you're thinking about starting one, this chapter is for you. Here, I fill you in on the many different property and liability risks you face and show you how best to protect yourself, using both insurance and non-insurance strategies.

If you don't own and operate a business from your home, but you do work from home (even occasionally) as someone else's employee, see Chapter 11 to find out how to avoid the property and liability coverage gaps in your homeowner's policy.

Considering the Risks of a Home Business

Perhaps the most important part of managing home business risks is knowing what those risks are. You can't manage what you don't know about.

If you currently own, or are even considering owning, a home business, make a list as you read through this chapter, identifying the unique risks your business faces.

The typical homeowner's policy has the following business limitations:

- ✔ **Zero business liability coverage of any kind:** No premises liability, no products liability, no professional liability, no workers' compensation, and so on.

- ✔ **Minimal coverage on business personal property:** Typically $2,500 on-premises and only $250 off-premises.

- ✔ **Zero coverage for any detached structures used even in part for business purposes, other than garaging cars.**

In the next sections, I show you how to manage these risks so that your home business — and you! — are protected.

Measuring Your Property Risks

Home businesses almost always involve some property risks — _structural_ (a building), _personal_ (stuff), or maybe both. Consultants have offices complete with office furniture. Wholesalers and retailers have inventory. Even piano teachers have pianos.

To properly cover your home-based business assets, you need to consider replacement cost totals for five types of business property:

- ✔ The rebuilding costs of the home office or work area that is located in your residence

- ✔ The rebuilding costs of any detached structures used even partially for business

- ✔ The cost to replace your business personal property at home

- ✔ The cost to replace your business personal property away from home
- ✔ The labor costs to reproduce valuable papers, like customer files, maps, and so on

When determining your business property values in this chapter, use the current replacement cost for a new item — you'll be consistent with how most small-business policies value property.

Structural property risks

Sometimes, having a home business requires you to build a place to operate from. This place may be part of the residence itself, like a finished office, or it may be located in all or part of a separate, detached structure.

If your office is part of your home

If your business space is built into your residence, you just need to make sure that your homeowner's coverage (Coverage A) on your home is high enough to rebuild a new house, including the cost to rebuild the business environment. You won't need any special business endorsements.

Why? Because the homeowner's policy has no restrictions or limitations for any part of your primary residence structure used for business purposes. There are limitations on business personal property but not on the building itself.

If your office is in a detached structure

If your business operates from a detached structure, the entire structure — not just the part used for business — is excluded from many insurance companies' homeowner's coverage. Here's what you need to do to fix the problem:

- ✔ Buy an endorsement allowing the business use of the structure.
- ✔ Raise your detached structure coverage (Coverage B) high enough to rebuild all detached structures on your lot.

Business personal property risks

Many home business owners have offices full of computers and equipment. If you operate a franchise out of your home, you may have a garage or basement full of inventory. If you're an attorney, you have client files that contain vital information.

What kinds of business property does your business have? Make up an inventory of your equipment as I take you through the following checklist. Next to each item, list your best guess as to its current replacement cost, if you had to buy it new today.

- **Office furniture and equipment:** The majority of home businesses have at least some office equipment. Besides the usual desk, chair, and telephone, you may have a filing cabinet, a copy machine, a fax machine, or a scanner.

- **Computers:** Almost all home businesses have computers. But be sure to include on your list not just the computer but also all peripherals — mouse, keyboard, printer, modem, wireless router, cables, and other hardware. Include software on your list if you don't keep off-site duplicates.

- **Inventory — owned and non-owned:** If you keep inventory on your premises — either in your house or in a detached structure — you need to add it to your list of risks. Set the value on your list at your peak inventory limit.

  Even if you don't own the inventory but you're holding it on consignment, you still may be responsible for it. Check your supplier contract to see whose responsibility it is. If it's yours, add the peak values to your list under non-owned inventory.

- **Supplies:** Supplies are easy to overlook. They include things like business cards, business stationery, staplers, computer paper, and, of course, the caffeine tablets you take to help you stay conscious during your 80-hour workweek. I recommend setting this value at $2,000 (at a minimum).

- **Accounts receivable:** This risk represents the estimated lost revenue from your inability to collect old receivables when your records are destroyed. Put this on your list only if you aren't willing to store backups, made at least weekly, off-premises.

- **Away from home — in transit, in storage, and shipping:** Because homeowner's policies cover business property away from home for much less (typically a $250 limit) than they cover items when the items are at your home, having a separate category on your list for property away from home is important.

  In transit means items you take with you, such as laptop computers, attaché cases, or sales samples. *In storage* means stuff like the old files and excess equipment I keep in off-site storage; you may keep inventory or other items in storage. *Shipping* can be incoming, outgoing, or both.

If both, have a separate value for each on your list. Even if you're currently arranging insurance through the shipper, enter a value here anyway. You may be able to reduce your shipping insurance costs by arranging the insurance on a bulk basis if you do a lot of shipping.

Assessing Your Liability Risks

Don't risk more than you can afford to lose. (See Chapter 2 for more such guiding principles.)

Most lawsuits cost $40,000 to $100,000 (or more) to defend, and judgments or jury awards can add hundreds of thousands of dollars to that amount. Being uninsured for any potential business liability is probably risking more than you can afford to lose, and puts your personal assets in jeopardy.

If you can't afford to buy the liability insurance your business needs to protect itself or find a way to avoid uninsured risks, close the business.

Injuries at home: From employees to clients to delivery people

If you have a home business, you're suable for injuries that occur on your home premises if they're business related. "But," you protest, "I never have clients or customers come to my home!" Maybe so. But almost any business gets an occasional package delivered. If that delivery person falls and is injured, your homeowner's policy has zero coverage for you or the business.

Regardless of whether you have employees or clients in your home, I recommend you include this risk on your list and buy coverage for it. The cost to insure this risk can be as little as $15 a year!

Injuries and property damage away from home

If you venture outside your home for business purposes, you could injure someone or damage someone's property. Depending on the nature of your business, this risk may be great — for example, if you're a personal trainer who trains clients in their homes, or you sell cosmetics at parties held in other people's homes.

If you sell a product or perform a service: Products liability

If you sell any kind of product or perform any kind of service (such as the building trades, computer or equipment repair, and so on), add this risk to your list.

The essence of the risk is that it involves your liability for injuries or property damage after the product or completed service is being used by the customer. So, for example, a customer's carpet was ruined by cleaning products that you sold him, or an eyeliner you sold caused a client a serious eye injury, or a computer starts crashing the day after you performed a tune-up, or a deck you built collapses and people are seriously injured. These are all examples in which you would be liable, and you need insurance to protect you.

Independent contractors: Their mistakes are yours

Whether you like it or not, when you subcontract some of your work to others, you're suable for their mistakes. You can avoid that risk by having the customer buy directly from the contractor. If you act as the front person with the customer, however, you need to add this risk to your list.

Here's an example: I'm an insurance agent. If I recommend a roofer to a client to fix storm damage and, two months later, the roof leaks, I have no liability — just a customer not too happy with the quality of my referrals. If, however, I tell the customer that I'll send someone out to fix the roof and subcontract a roofer to do it, the client pays me, and I take a cut and pay the roofer, I'm liable, along with the roofer, for the water damage caused by the roofer's defective work.

Employee risks: From workers' compensation to discrimination and more

If your business requires you to hire one or more employees, you face some additional risks, most of which can be insured. These risks include those related to state-mandated workers' compensation benefits. Less-obvious employee-related risks include the possibility of being sued for discrimination when you don't hire or fire someone. In this section, I cover employee-related risks and give you my recommendations on handling them.

While you're at it, make sure that you know the difference between an employee and an independent contractor. You can face serious penalties and liabilities if you try to get away with treating an employee as an independent contractor. (Check out the nearby sidebar for more information.)

Workers' compensation

In most jurisdictions, if you have an employee, you're required by law to provide workers' compensation insurance to cover medical bills and lost wages for your employee if she suffers an occupational injury or certain occupation-related diseases. If your business has even one employee, add this risk to your list.

Check with your agent or state department of labor to find out if you can exempt yourself, and family members who are employees, from coverage.

Employee benefit liability

The *employee benefit liability* risk is applicable to you if you employ someone and provide her any kind of group benefits — health, disability, or life insurance. It represents your risk arising from errors in administering the group insurance program, such as not adding newly hired employees properly to the coverage or not notifying terminated employees properly of government-mandated continuation rights that they have when they leave.

Never the twain shall meet: Independent contractors and employees

I see a lot of small-business owners — especially building-trade contractors and one-person shops — try to reduce their employee costs by treating workers who should be employees as independent contractors. By employing these people as independent contractors, the business avoids paying workers' compensation premiums, the employer's share of Social Security taxes, unemployment compensation taxes, group benefits, retirement plan contributions, and so on. All together, this is a substantial savings — usually from 25 percent to 50 percent of the total compensation. That's a ton of money saved for a small-business owner.

But some real downsides to this exist besides the ethical issues — primarily with the risk you take by not buying workers' compensation insurance and then having to pay workers' compensation benefits out of your own pocket if your worker gets injured on the job. The IRS has really cracked down on this practice. By IRS standards, someone is your employee if he works almost exclusively for you, often on the business premises; an independent contractor earns money from other sources in addition to you.

If you have a group program covering your employees, add employee benefit liability coverage to your risk list and to your business insurance coverage. The annual cost is as little as $150 a year!

Don't risk a lot for a little.

Professional errors

If you sell a professional service, add this risk to your list. Some of the professionals who should be concerned are insurance agents, accountants, lawyers, virtually every kind of consultant, architects, engineers, beauty consultants, doctors, dentists, veterinarians, real estate agents, real estate appraisers, and morticians.

A professional liability policy covers you if a mistake you make on the job hurts your client. Here are some examples:

- ✔ A surgeon who leaves the scalpel in her patient
- ✔ An insurance agent who forgets to add a client's car to an auto policy prior to an accident
- ✔ A lawyer who loses a client's case because he forgot to file the suit on time

Buying a separate professional liability policy (also known as errors and omissions insurance) is important because, without it, you have no coverage elsewhere. Business liability policies almost always exclude coverage for professional errors. And homeowner's policies exclude liability coverage for anything business related.

When you buy professional liability coverage, be sure that:

- ✔ **It covers what you do.** I recently had a very successful business client, who did management consulting, buy a less expensive errors and omissions policy from another agent. When I reviewed the new policy, it covered computer consulting but specifically did not cover — you guessed it — management consulting!
- ✔ **It covers your defense costs and any legal judgment stemming from your responsibility for the errors of independent contractors who do work for you.** Be careful: *Many policies do not cover defense costs or your liability for errors involving your independent contractors.* You want a policy that does.

Vehicle risks

Don't skip this section, even if you have no business vehicles! There are several ways you and your business can be at risk regarding vehicles:

- ✔ **If the business owns or leases vehicles:** The tricky part of this risk is to make sure that both you as an individual and your business as owner or lessee are *both* properly protected. Here is the secret to avoiding problems: If you own or lease the vehicle in your personal name, buy a personal auto policy. If you own or lease a vehicle in your business name, buy a business auto policy. (See the sidebar "Practicing monogamy: Why you should only have one insurance agent at a time" for an example of someone who did it the wrong way.)

- ✔ **If you occasionally borrow or rent vehicles for the benefit of the business:** If your business *is* incorporated and occasionally borrows or rents vehicles, even if it has no owned or leased vehicles, the business will need hired auto liability coverage.

- ✔ **If you have employees or independent contractors who even occasionally run an errand for your business with their vehicles:** If your business, whether incorporated or not, has even one employee or independent contractor, you can pretty much count on the fact that the employee will at least occasionally run a business errand. And if that's the case, your business will need non-owned auto liability coverage. Both hired and non-owned coverages are inexpensive — only $60 to $75 each per year.

It's pretty hard to be in business and not have at least *one* of those exposures. Add to your list the ones that apply to your business.

Practicing monogamy: Why you should only have one insurance agent at a time

I've been the business insurance agent for a small company for about eight years. I review the company's insurance program every year with the company's owner, Elmer, who has his personal insurance through a different agent. One year in our review, I discovered that he had purchased two company-owned vehicles for his and his wife's use, but he never told me because he chose to insure them through his personal insurance agent. This decision created some serious gaps in his coverage.

The corporation — which, as owner of the vehicles, would be named in every lawsuit involving the vehicles — had *no* liability coverage as an owner under Elmer's personal auto policy. The corporation, which was the sole owner of both cars, had *no* collision and comprehensive coverage. Worse yet, because Elmer had no personal ownership interest in either car, his personal auto policy would have owed nothing at all if either car had been damaged, totaled, or stolen! Unbelievable, but true.

Managing Your Human Risks

When I refer to human risks, I'm talking about your life, health, and disability risks — all three of which can be substantial. If you worked for someone else, things like major medical bills, loss of income from a long-term disability, and life insurance for your loved ones would normally be covered. But these risks are your responsibility when you own a home business.

When you're working for yourself, make sure that your benefits are at least as good as, if not better than, whatever benefits you'd receive as an employee for someone else. You should have an equally good retirement plan and vacation package, too. If you can't provide these things for yourself, are you doing what's best for yourself by being self-employed?

You can buy life, health, and disability coverages privately if you qualify medically, or you can buy it under a company group plan if you have employees. It doesn't matter where or how you get these vital coverages. Just get them, and add them to your list of risks.

If you don't have employees and you can't qualify for private health insurance because of a preexisting condition, you may be able to get into a group plan with an association. (See "Association programs," later in this chapter, for more information.)

See Part V for specific information and recommendations on life, health, and disability insurance.

Reducing Your Home-Business Risks without Insurance

Avoiding, reducing, retaining, and transferring (ARRT) are the four non-insurance methods of treating risk. (For more information, see Chapter 3.) In this section, I tell you how you can use all four of these non-insurance methods in reducing your home-business risks.

Avoiding risk

When it comes to risks related to a home business, you can completely avoid the risk in two ways:

✔ **By not starting the business or closing your existing business:** Odds are, you aren't willing to get out of business just to avoid risk — after all, if you're considering a home business, you're already not as risk averse as most people are, so you're willing to take some chances to reap the rewards.

✔ **By making prudent business decisions:** For example, you may decide, if you're a manufacturer's representative, to stop offering a line of home trampolines because your projected annual profit on the line is $3,000 and the cost of the product's liability premium is $10,000.

Reducing risk

You can reduce the risk to both yourself and your company in a variety of ways:

✔ **Reduce the risk of lawsuits threatening your personal assets by incorporating your company.** Incorporating isn't for everyone, but I think every home business should consider it — with the help of a good small-business attorney. For more on incorporating, check out *Incorporating Your Business For Dummies,* by The Company Corporation (Wiley).

✔ **Reduce the inventory you keep on premises.** Have the manufacturer ship orders directly to your customer.

Retaining risk: Paying for the loss yourself

Retention amounts to paying for the loss yourself. This strategy works well in two situations:

✔ **When you want to reduce your premium by opting for larger deductibles:** For example, you may be able to save 40 percent on your health insurance bill by choosing a $2,000 deductible.

✔ **When you reduce the risk as much as you can and self-insure what remains:** For example, you may back up your accounts receivable data weekly and self-insure any losses that occur between the two backups.

There are two other ways to retain losses — neither of which I can recommend:

✔ **Declining critical insurance:** One of my former clients declined long-term disability on himself. Two years later, he was seriously injured and out of work for two years. But with no income and no insurance, he lost both his home and his business. Not a good decision.

✔ **Having a coverage gap without realizing it:** Another bad use of retention is accidental retention, where you have a major uninsured gap in your coverage that you don't know about and a serious loss happens with no coverage. That's the *worst* kind of retention, and it can easily occur if you don't work with an insurance expert. (See Chapter 4 for tips on how to find an insurance agent, and turn to the nearby sidebar for information on hiring a risk manager.)

TIP

If your needs are complex, choose an agent who is an insurance expert in the area of home-business insurance as well as personal insurance.

Hiring a risk manager: The ultimate strategy

If you want expert help with everything covered in this chapter — insurance plan design, advice on non-insurance strategies, advice on business contracts, and even help with insurance you buy elsewhere (such as through professional associations) — then this is the very best advice I can give you:

Promote the best insurance agent you can find to the role of *risk manager*.

If your state law allows, pay a negotiated annual fee — probably ranging from $300 to $600 a year — to provide the following value-added services to better manage and coordinate your business and personal risks. Most of these services aren't paid for by sales commissions (hence, the need for an added fee). Your risk manager will help you:

- ✔ **Place whatever insurance he is able to place for you *competitively* through the insurance company or companies he represents (including your personal insurance; your home-business insurance; and your health, life, and disability insurance).** Why? Because he has more leverage to help you get the coverages you need with insurers he already has relationships with. Also, the insurers send him copies of your policies so he can more easily monitor your program. And, as an insurance agent, he's empowered to make the changes to your insurance program directly, so *you* won't have to.

- ✔ **Come up with creative non-insurance strategies for avoiding, reducing, retaining, and transferring risks to help you minimize your insurance purchases.** Insurance companies don't pay agents anything to help you lower your insurance costs. The annual fee you're paying him makes it possible for him to do this for you.

- ✔ **Design coverage specifications for your entire personal and business insurance program, help oversee the policies you buy elsewhere, and coordinate them and reduce gaps between them.**

- ✔ **Help you read your business contracts and make recommendations that your attorney can use to reduce risks in the language before you sign them.** Also, modify your insurance program as needed to keep your insurance coverage in full compliance with the insurance recommendations you make.

- ✔ **Do a complete review of your entire insurance and non-insurance program about once a year and help you implement any changes.**

I know this is possible because I have been acting as a risk manager and insurance agent for my small business and personal clients for over 20 years. I do all of these things and more for them. But I caution you: Even though having a risk manager is the ideal solution to managing everything that you're doing, this is an emerging field, so finding someone won't be easy.

Transferring risk to someone else

Transferring occurs when someone else agrees to pay your claims so you don't have to. The most common way of transferring risk is buying insurance, but transferring can also be used in non-insurance ways.

Here's a good example of a non-insurance use of the transfer strategy: I have a client who designed high-end bicycle pedals, sold them on the Internet, assembled them himself, and bought an expensive product liability policy. As orders grew for the pedals, he subcontracted the production and assembly to a local manufacturer, which agreed to do 100 percent of the assembly and packaging and, in writing, agreed to add my client as an additional insured on its product liability policy. My client thus successfully transferred the risk and insurance to a third party (the manufacturer) and significantly reduced his insurance costs in the process.

Sources for Home Business Insurance

You can choose from several sources for home-business insurance. Most home business owners, at a significant risk to them, mix and match. You may be getting your property, liability, and workers' compensation insurance through your insurance agent. Your professional liability insurance may come from an association that you're a member of. Your product liability insurance may come from your franchiser. And your life, health, and disability may come from a second insurance agent. I cover the pros and cons of each source in this section.

Having an expert agent who serves as your personal risk manager is by far and away the best choice for you. You're considerably less likely to get caught in a major claim that isn't covered properly. If that's not available to you, your next best choice is to work with as few agents as possible — again for the same reason.

Homeowner's business endorsements

As a general rule, homeowner's policy endorsements are inadequate for most home businesses — they typically cover only sole proprietorships and often can't cover an incorporated business. They can provide on-premises liability coverages, but few provide off-premises liability, products liability, or several other kinds of business liability covered in this chapter. Homeowner's policy endorsements can cover business property at home, but most don't offer much coverage away from home.

In my experience, most homeowner's home-business endorsements provide incomplete coverage, full of gaps.

A home-business endorsement is often a great idea for employees of companies who do a lot of their work at home. If this is your situation, you'll be glad to know that the endorsement typically does a good job of covering your two major concerns:

- ✔ Liability coverage for people getting injured on their premises making deliveries
- ✔ Personal property coverage on your home office furniture and equipment

See Chapter 11 for more information on how to protect yourself if you're someone else's employee but you do some work from home.

Business owners' policies

A business owner's policy is my recommended insurance policy for the majority of home businesses. Business owner's policies are reasonably priced — starting at about $500 per year. (As of this writing, a few policies were even available for as little as $300 a year!)

The great thing about business owners' policies is that they're designed for small businesses. Most of the property and liability coverages you'll need as a home-business owner are either included automatically or available for a nominal extra charge. I always prefer business owner's policies to homeowner's home-business endorsements — you get far better coverage for not much more money.

Not all home businesses, however, qualify for a business owner's policy. Insurance companies differ greatly as to what kinds of home businesses they will insure under a business owner's policy. Some insurers restrict eligibility to offices and small retail stores; others are willing to insure nearly every type of home business, including building contractors, software developers, Web site designers, and franchises like Amway or Mary Kay.

If you're told your business won't qualify for a business owner's policy, you can still get your business insured under a more expensive commercial insurance policy. But before you shell out the extra cash, check around with other insurance companies — your business may easily qualify for a business owner's policy somewhere else.

Insurance from franchisers

If your home business is a franchise — whether you sell cleaning products, environmental products, cosmetics, or anything else — you can get some of your insurance through the franchiser. Franchisers offer franchisees (that's you!) two major advantages with their insurance programs:

- ✔ A great price for what they offer
- ✔ Access to specialty coverages that would be hard for you to find elsewhere

But they also have two major disadvantages:

- ✔ **The coverage is often not comprehensive for the franchisee.** Usually a number of holes exist in the coverage. I've found large coverage gaps in every one of these policies that I've reviewed.
- ✔ **You don't get any professional advice to help you set up the right coverage for your particular needs.** Having expert advice is extremely important when buying any insurance, especially business insurance.

Finally, most franchisees buying the coverage believe that if the franchiser is offering them the coverage, it must be wonderful — and I've never found that to be completely true. For the coverages that you're offered, the price is great. But if you work with a good insurance adviser locally who acts as your risk manager, you can get the expert help you need to overcome both the disadvantages I outline and supplement the franchise insurance program with the other insurance coverages you'll need. You can end up with both a comprehensive plan and a very good price, if you have good professional help.

If you're considering getting involved in a franchise, I recommend that you first gather all the contracts you will be required to sign, as well as a detailed summary of the different insurances available from the franchiser, and take them to the insurance professional you've chosen to be your risk manager. She'll help you identify the hidden risks of the contracts and the insurance gaps in the program the franchiser is offering and help you design strategies to avoid both.

Association programs

Professionals in a particular trade often band together to form associations. Benefits of belonging include access to information, the chance to network with others in your field, ongoing education, lobbying power, and the availability of insurance (which is discounted because of mass purchasing power). For example, the Freelancers Union (www.freelancersunion.org) and Avant Guild (www.mediabistro.com/avantguild) both offer group insurance for their members, and many other associations and unions do the same thing. Look for one related to your line of work.

Associations are also often a good place to buy professional liability insurance at up to 50 percent off market rates. They're also a good place to buy specialty coverages unique to a particular industry that are unavailable or quite expensive in the open market, such as insurance protection against unintentional alleged sexual or physical abuse of children (necessary if you operate a daycare, for example).

Chambers of commerce

If you're a home-business owner and you don't have the leverage to get great pricing on your own, your local Chamber of Commerce may be a good source for small-business group insurance — life, health, and disability products, in particular. Often the annual cost of chamber membership is returned many times over in premium savings on chamber insurance programs.

Chapter 14

Getting What You Deserve for Your Homeowner's Claims

In This Chapter

▶ Avoiding depreciation deductions on structural damage claims

▶ Discovering five steps to a great claims settlement

▶ Getting the most for your personal property claims

▶ Collecting faster and better

*F*ires, tornadoes, hurricanes, hail, burglaries. The only thing harder than having a claim for loss or damage to your home or belongings is having a claim and having a fight on your hands trying to collect.

In this chapter, I show you what you can expect from your insurance company when you have a homeowner's claim and arm you with the tools you need to collect everything you're covered for as smoothly and painlessly as possible.

Too often, claims are denied or underpaid because you didn't have the right advice or the right coverage in place. Even the best insurance companies don't pay you for something you didn't have insured. (See Chapters 9 through 12 for more on how to get the right homeowner's coverage and Chapter 4 for help in choosing a highly skilled agent.)

Structural Damage: Collecting What You Deserve

When structural damage is done to your home, your idea of a great insurance settlement would go something like this: You close your eyes, turn around three times, and open your eyes to a home without damages and with all the repairs paid for.

Unfortunately, the reality typically goes a bit more like this: The adjuster inspects the damage, writes a repair estimate, and sends you the estimate and check, minus the deductible. You may be pleased to have the claim settled so quickly . . . until you try to find a contractor who will do the work for the adjuster's price — especially difficult after a storm has pushed up the costs of labor and materials. You can't find anyone who will agree to do the repairs for the amount of money that your insurance has provided. Unfortunately, this problem occurs far too often.

What can you do if you're in a situation like this, where the adjuster's estimate and check are well below what a contractor wants for the job? How do you get the contractor to bend? How do you get the adjuster to pay more?

Knowing your rights

The "full cost to repair or replace the damage" — that's what your policy says the insurance company has to pay you. Not the amount an insurance adjuster *thinks* the repair should cost. Not what a contractor would *like* to charge. You're owed the *actual* repair or replacement cost. The insurance adjuster and the contractor who will be doing the repairs need to agree on what that price is — these two parties need to meet at the site and hammer out a price that they both can agree to.

When you settle a home structural damage claim, be sure that your preferred contractor agrees, beforehand, to do the repairs for the amount the insurance company is offering.

Doing your part to make your claim go smoothly

If you just sit back and hope that your insurance company takes care of you, you'll likely be disappointed. Although you have certain rights, you often have to fight for them — or at least be assertive enough to make sure that you get what you're paying for.

Here are five tips you can follow to ensure a fast and fair settlement, and to stay out of disputes on home structural claims:

> ✔ **If you don't already have a contractor you know and trust, get repair estimates from at least two contractors who have been recommended to you by friends and family.** Interview the contractors. You're not necessarily looking for the lowest bid — you want the best workmanship.

(You can often tell a lot about the quality of the contractor by the quality and professionalism of the estimate.)

Use a reputable, local contractor. Watch out for out-of-town journeymen who flock to storms in hopes of a good payday. The locals are much more likely to be around to stand behind their work if a problem arises later.

Check references. Get proof of liability insurance and workers' compensation insurance. Don't work with a contractor who doesn't have both coverages. (If a contractor doesn't show you written proof that he has both coverages, you're more vulnerable to claims brought against you for job-site injuries. Plus, if a repair fails and later causes injuries or property damage to your home or your family, you can go after the contractor's liability insurance company.)

Listen to your gut and pick the contractor who feels the most comfortable. It doesn't have to be the contractor with the lowest bid. After all, you have to live with the repairs. Most adjusters will work with the contractor you prefer, as long as the prices are reasonable.

✔ **Don't allow solo inspections or estimates.** Don't agree to your insurance adjuster inspecting your home alone. Don't agree to the adjuster writing his own estimate. Without an agreed-upon price, the estimate is worthless, so don't allow him to waste his time — or yours.

✔ **Connect the two parties.** Tell the adjuster the name and cellphone number of your contractor. Also share the adjuster's name and cellphone number, as well as the claim number, with the contractor. Then insist that they call each other to arrange a meeting at your home for the purpose of jointly agreeing on the amount of damage and on an acceptable repair cost.

✔ **Don't sweat the dollar amount.** Don't worry if the agreed price is less — even significantly less — than the contractor's initial bid. That's why adjusters have jobs — to make sure that repair costs stay reasonable and to keep contractors from writing themselves blank checks.

✔ **Control additional damage problems upfront.** Make sure that when the parties meet initially and agree on a price, they also agree to work with each other directly if additional damage is discovered — and to keep you out of the middle. Then hold them to that commitment. Don't let them suck you in. If your contractor calls needing an okay for additional repairs, insist that he work out permission directly with the adjuster.

If you encounter roadblocks or are in danger of pulling your hair out, call on your agent for help. Part of your agent's job is to go to bat for you at claim time to help you collect what you deserve.

Getting paid for your sweat

Whether a toilet overflows, a storm damages the roof, or a fire destroys the kitchen, you'll personally do some cleanup work — often extensive work. In these situations, most homeowners spend personal time doing whatever they can to protect their property from further damage. In fact, the policy even *requires* homeowners to protect their property. If you don't do so, the insurance company doesn't owe you for the additional damage you could have prevented.

Keep track of your time. The insurance company owes you fair compensation for it, up to the amount it would have had to pay a laborer to do the same work. Rarely do adjusters tell homeowners to keep track of the time they spend cleaning up after minor incidents or disasters — and a lot of homeowners unknowingly lose out on justifiable compensation.

Jumping over some common pitfalls

Despite your best efforts, you may face one or more common structural damage pitfalls. In this section, I help you navigate this sometimes treacherous territory.

But my house is worth more than that! Contesting depreciation deductions

Most people think their homeowner's policy pays to rebuild structural damage, regardless of the age or condition of the damaged structural parts. But the truth is, you only get paid the full replacement cost of partial damage to your home if you insure your home for 80 percent or more of its replacement cost. Otherwise, your insurer pays only the *depreciated* value of the damage, up to the insurance limit for your home structure. Essentially, the usual homeowner's policy says, "We'll pay you in the same manner you insure your home. If you insure for the replacement cost, we'll pay replacement. If you insure based on its used value, we'll pay for the used value of the damage — the value after depreciation."

Homeowner's policies allow you to *under*-insure your home by up to 20 percent, and they still pay the full replacement cost of the claim for partial damage to your structure. If you're off by more than 20 percent, you risk facing depreciation deductions.

What about when you, in good faith, honestly tried to insure for the replacement cost new and the adjuster, at claim time, says that you fell short and wants to deduct depreciation from your claim offer? For example, suppose your home is damaged by a fire, and the full replacement cost of the damaged area is $100,000. And suppose you had, in good faith, talked to a real estate agent or a builder who estimated the cost to rebuild — when you bought the house — at $350,000, so you insured it for that amount. Now, suppose that the claims adjuster estimates the *actual* cost to rebuild — at the time of loss — at $500,000. Because the difference between the amount for which you've insured the house and the amount to rebuild it is more than 20 percent, the adjuster is offering less than the $100,000 replacement cost of your claim. What can you do?

You can avoid the penalty in the following ways:

✔ **Contest the adjuster's replacement estimate.** Adjusters are human — they make mistakes. Request a copy of the computation and check it for accuracy. Sometimes all that's needed is a simple correction of the data in order to lower the adjuster's replacement estimate to within the acceptable range.

✔ **If contesting the estimate fails, put together a credible replacement cost estimate of your own.** Your agent may be able to do one for you, or you can pay a credible builder to do one. (You can also do one on the Web at sites such as www.building-cost.net. This online estimator is credible because it uses data from the "National Building Cost Manual". I found this site relatively easy to use and probably best of all it's free!)

Don't ever accept a depreciation penalty for under-insuring your home. Always contest.

Mismatched mishmash: Coping with the matching problem for shingles and siding

In 1998, the Minneapolis/St. Paul area was hit with the worst hail storm ever recorded there. In fact, it was the worst storm of any on record for the state of Minnesota. It lasted only 15 minutes, but it caused $500 million in damage to cars and homes.

The hail typically damaged half a roof, or two of the four walls of a house. But, especially for older homes, the new shingles that were available often didn't match an old, discontinued color. And siding from ten years ago wasn't made anymore, so the new, replacement siding didn't match the color or design of the siding on the undamaged walls.

Homeowner's policies require insurance companies to repair or replace only the damaged area. Period. (It's not an insurance company's fault that a type of roof tile or siding isn't made anymore — and if they had to pay for an entire roof or re-side an entire house every time a few shingles blew off or a few siding panels were dented, homeowner's insurance rates would sky-rocket.) Most insurance companies didn't pay for replacing the undamaged areas just so it all matched.

Insurance policies are supposed to make the customer whole. Having a hodgepodge of different roof tiles or two different sets of siding hardly restored all those homes to what they were before the storm. There was no joy in Mudville.

If you ever have a structural damage claim where the repaired area won't match the rest of the house, here's how I suggest you proceed.

There is a little-known, seldom-used clause in the back pages of every homeowner's policy called the *pair and set clause*. It's used primarily to help settle personal property claims involving damage to one or more of a set of items (one shoe, one stereo speaker, one diamond earring, and so on) where the remaining item of the set is worth less because of the loss of the other item. The clause recognizes the unfairness of paying for just one shoe or one earring — the other shoe or other earring loses value, too, without a mate.

The pair and set clause says that if the damaged or lost item cannot be replaced exactly, making the set, as a whole, lower in value, the insurance company must pay the difference. So, let's say you have a set of ten collectible dishes worth $6,000. You prominently display just one dish, and keep the other nine safely stored away. The dish you display is stolen. The exact dish can't be replaced and, without the dish, the set of nine is now worth only $3,000. Applying the pair and set clause, the insurance company owes you the $3,000 drop in the total value of the set, even though the lost plate itself may have been worth only $600 if you had tried to sell it.

Roof shingles are part of a set, as are siding panels. Using the pair and set clause, if some pieces of the set of roofing or siding panels are damaged and can't be matched, the insurance company owes more than just replacing the damaged area with something that doesn't match the undamaged area. It owes the difference in value, before and after the loss. It's not any more fair to put on mismatched shingles than it is to pay for a new plate that doesn't match the rest of the set.

So how do you determine the value of a set of roof shingles before and after a loss? The policy doesn't define that. Here's my suggestion if you have a roof or siding matching problem that you can't agree on with the adjuster. Using the pair and set clause, ask your adjuster to pay the replacement cost of the damaged areas and the depreciated value of the undamaged areas.

You don't have to remember the details of pair and set computations. But do remember that a clause in your homeowner's policy may help you collect more than just the replacement cost of your damaged roof or siding if the new materials don't match the old materials.

Collecting for your additional living expenses

One of the nice features of homeowner's insurance is that it pays not only for damage to your home and personal property but also for the additional living expenses that you have to incur if you can't live in the house.

The key word here is *additional*. The additional living expense (ALE) coverage pays reasonable costs for temporary living facilities, moving, furniture and appliance rentals, and meals out as needed. It can even pay for extra gasoline costs. It pays for almost any living expense that truly is additional — it pays for any expense that you wouldn't have had to pay if your home hadn't been damaged. It won't pay your house payment, because that's not an expense you've incurred because of the damage to your home. Any amounts paid are offset against living expenses that are lower, such as the heating and cooling bill being $75 less a month because the house is empty.

ALE pays the difference between your costs that go up and any costs that go down. The goal is to keep your bank account the same as it would have been if the claim had never occurred.

One of the best things about ALE coverage is the impact it has on an adjuster. The adjuster wants to keep ALE expenses low. To do that, she has to get your house repaired and livable again, and soon!

Getting Paid for Your Stuff

The most important ingredient of a good claims settlement is getting the right advice and having the proper coverage. Assuming that your claim is, in fact, covered by your homeowner's policy, here are some tips to help you collect the most for your stuff.

Understanding how replacement cost coverage works

Most off-the-shelf homeowner's policies pay for the used or depreciated value of your damaged or stolen belongings. But they also offer an additional cost option called *replacement cost coverage,* which will pay for the cost — new — of all items you actually replace. The thing to know about replacement cost coverage is that, in order to get a payment based on cost new, you have to actually replace the item with something comparable. (You can upgrade to a big-screen TV, for example, but you have to pay the cost difference yourself — your insurance will only cover the cost of your "little" 26-inch TV if that's what was stolen.)

If you opted, wisely, to buy replacement cost coverage, you'll usually end up getting paid two or more times by the insurance company:

- ✔ The first check pays you for the used or depreciated value of your property.
- ✔ When you replace what you lost, you get an additional check for the difference between the used value and the replacement cost.

Don't let the adjuster forget to add sales tax to all payments in states that charge sales tax. It's easy to overlook, but you're definitely entitled to it.

Improving the settlement with your photographic inventory

If you've spent the half-hour it takes to photograph or videotape all your belongings and then stored the photos or video away from home, you'll have three major benefits at claim time, especially following a burglary or serious fire:

- ✔ **You'll be able to jog your own memory.** You don't get paid for something you don't remember to claim. Imagine returning to your home after a burglary. Rooms ransacked. Stuff missing. Some you remember (the TV, the stereo); some you don't (the jewelry box, the guitar, the baseball card collection, some items of clothing). You're traumatized and not thinking clearly, and then the police and the insurance adjuster ask you to list everything that was stolen. I guarantee you that you won't remember everything, and that's when your photographic record will be a huge help.

- ✔ **You'll have a documentation of your loss.** Sometimes a property claim can be a hassle if the adjuster starts asking for proof of purchase, like a receipt or a cancelled check. At best, the experience will be frustrating. At worst, you won't get paid for what you lost. Photos help solve this problem. Most adjusters accept a photo of the item in your home as proof of ownership. Imagine having to prove that you owned a $5,000 antique cherry desk. Having a picture of the desk in your home, covered with your papers, sure would help.

✔ **You'll get fully paid for treasures.** If your special treasure is destroyed or stolen, the burden of proof rests on you to prove what you lost. For example, you have to prove that the $20,000 painting that was stolen was indeed an original — not just a $1,500 print. (Imagine the potential fraud if adjusters paid these claims without proof!) Pulling out the photos and the original receipt or appraisal enables the adjuster to easily pay you the full value. (In fact, when you have the photos and bill of sale/appraisal, the adjuster will even pay for a current value appraisal and pay you that value.) Documentation is everything at claim time!

See Chapter 9 for tips on making a good photographic inventory.

Collecting faster and better with your own inventory form

Here's how a typical personal property claim goes: The adjuster asks you to list what you lost and provide photos, cancelled checks, or receipts. Then the adjuster shops around (which can take weeks) and comes back to you with an offer. It's up to you to either accept the offer or contest it. You may want to contest the offer if he's pricing the wrong model of TV, computer, or camera; if the clothing prices he uses are from a discount store and you bought all your clothes from high-end department stores; or if he's depreciating your clothing based on a five-year life, when your high-quality clothes had a much longer life.

Most people unhappily take the adjuster's offer, though possibly getting him to bend in a few areas. They don't know they have rights or how to contest the offer. But they *do* know that after an experienced, knowledgeable adjuster has done his homework, it's difficult to move him from his position. Trust me: There's a better way.

Be in charge of your own claim. Do the research yourself. Request the amount you want and have solid evidence to support it. Use your own inventory form. (The one provided by most insurance companies, if they even provide one, is not at all user-friendly, nor is it complete.)

Using either a manual or automated spreadsheet, here are the columns to include on your inventory form:

✔ Property description

✔ Quantity

✔ Age (in years)

- Replacement cost source (name of the store or Web site)
- Telephone number or Web address of store
- Expected life (in years)
- Today's replacement cost (tax included)
- Depreciation percentage (age ÷ expected life)
- Depreciation amount (today's replacement cost × depreciation percentage)
- Depreciated value (today's replacement cost – depreciation amount)

Making up your own inventory and calculating what is due to you before the adjuster does any of his own research is critical. If you've already done the legwork, he's less likely to contest your data. All any adjuster needs in order to justify paying you what you want for your claim is good documentation from you for his file. The adjuster needs documentation so that when his supervisor wants to know why he paid you those amounts, he has all the information in writing.

The adjuster, upon reviewing your data, will usually do one of two things:

- Pay what you're asking.
- Call you to dicker about a few items. ("You've used a 15-year life for clothing. We don't ever allow more than 10 years.")

There will be some give and take, but no matter how far he moves you from your position, it won't ever be as far as the offer he would have made to you if he had done the work himself.

Part IV

Singin' in the Rain: Umbrella Policies and More

The 5th Wave   By Rich Tennant

"Does our insurance cover a visit from *60 Minutes?*"

In this part . . .

Most people are way under-insured when it comes to lawsuit protection. They buy only $100,000 or $300,000 of coverage, which won't begin to cover the value of a serious injury or death they cause. And that's where an umbrella policy comes into play. In this part, I explain the three advantages of an umbrella policy, how umbrella policies differ dramatically in the scope of their coverage, and how to choose an umbrella that covers the risks that are unique to your lifestyle.

When there are big changes in your life, your insurance should change, too. In this part, I show you what changes to make to your insurance program so you stay fully protected, from the cradle to the grave.

Chapter 15

Introducing the Personal Umbrella Policy

You don't have enough liability insurance. Period. No one does. In over 2,000 insurance reviews I've done for prospective clients, I've seen that at least 80 percent to 90 percent of them were grossly under-insured for injury lawsuits. The most common liability limits on auto and home policies I see are either $100,000 per person or $300,000 per accident. That's not much for a human life — not enough to pay for all the medical expenses of the person you severely injure, plus a possible lifetime of lost wages and compensation for pain and suffering.

If you don't have nearly enough protection, what can you do? Here's some really good news: You can buy a second layer of liability coverage, called a *personal umbrella policy,* that sits on top of your other personal liability coverages for your car, home, boat, and so on. It defends you and pays legal judgments against you when a covered lawsuit exceeds your primary liability insurance limits.

Best of all, an umbrella policy is amazingly inexpensive — usually about $150 to $200 per year for $1 million of coverage. And about $75 to $100 per year for each additional $1 million of coverage. ***Note:*** This is not a typo. These costs are truly per *year* — not per month!

Buying an umbrella policy is flat-out the best value in the insurance business. It includes some of the broadest coverage in the insurance business at an incredibly low price. Buying an umbrella policy also satisfies two guiding principles from Chapter 2: not risking more than you can afford to lose and not risking a lot for a little.

Affording an umbrella is easy. You don't even have to increase your insurance bill — just shift dollars away from less important coverages. For example, you can save a few hundred dollars by raising the deductible on your car insurance and homeowner's insurance by $500, or by dropping collision coverage on an older car. Use that savings to more than pay for an umbrella policy.

In this chapter, I introduce you to the basics of umbrella policies, fill you in on how an umbrella meshes with your other insurance policies, and help you determine how much coverage you need.

Discovering the Umbrella Policy's Major Coverage Advantages

If you decide to buy an umbrella policy, you gain more than just higher coverage limits for injuries and property damage you cause — although the higher limits are a great advantage. You also receive

- ✔ Additional coverage for defense costs when the defense coverage under your primary policies runs out
- ✔ Coverage for many types of lawsuits not covered by your other policies (those famous coverage gaps everyone complains about)

Additional coverage to defend yourself

What actually happens when you're sued for a dollar amount greater than your primary liability insurance limits? You receive, from your insurance company, a piece of mail — probably registered mail — that looks something like this:

We Care About You Mutual Insurance Company

Re: Your June 19, 2010 Accident

Dear Mr. Soon-To-Be-Very-Poor:

You are being sued by Mr. James Johnson, the injured party in the above-referenced accident, for $650,000. Your automobile liability insurance limit with us is only $250,000. We will pay your defense costs for the first $250,000 of this lawsuit. You will be responsible for your own defense costs beyond that amount.

We strongly suggest you hire your own attorney right now to protect you for that part of the lawsuit not covered by our policy.

Yours truly,

Grumpy Corporate Attorney

We Care About You Mutual Insurance Company

Why do they send you this letter? Because each of your primary insurance policies defends you only for lawsuit amounts up to your liability policy limit. If you're sued for more than your liability limit, you're personally responsible for the amount of any lawsuit that exceeds your primary liability limit, including the cost of defense for that difference. Those added defense costs often run $75,000 or more. One huge advantage of an umbrella policy is that it pays for those added defense costs.

Gap coverage

My client Mike and several of his friends were all turning 50 at about the same time, so they decided it would be fun to have a jumbo group 50th birthday party. They rented a big barn at an empty local fairground. And they decided to make beer and wine available, at no charge, which added a potential liability for alcohol-related car accidents.

Mike called me because the fairgrounds required the friends to carry $1 million of liability insurance for the one-day event that also had to include the fairgrounds as an insured party. I asked him if he was signing the rental contract personally. He said no, it was in the name of two of his friends. I advised Mike that a one-day, special-event policy would cost about $500. But I also advised him that if either of his friends had an umbrella policy, the friend might be covered automatically. Neither one of them did. Mike signed the contract because he had an umbrella policy that fully covered him for $2 million of liability for this type of rental contract. His umbrella also was broad enough to automatically protect the fairgrounds, as he had contractually agreed to do, and was broad enough to cover the risk of liability for alcohol-related car accidents.

To briefly explore the insurance issues involved in a little more detail, the exposures that Mike faced were

- ✔ Liability for his own actions that caused injuries
- ✔ Liability he assumed in the contract, agreeing to be responsible for the actions of everyone else at the event
- ✔ Liability if any partygoer drank too much and caused an auto accident, resulting in a lawsuit — a lawsuit that any provider of alcoholic beverages at a social event may face
- ✔ The costs to defend and protect the fairgrounds for any lawsuit brought against it
- ✔ Liability for damage caused by anyone to the rented barn, such as a fire caused by a guest's carelessly thrown-away cigarette

Many of these risks were not covered by any other policy, at least not for the amount required by the fairgrounds. Mike's umbrella covered every single risk, automatically. His group saved the $500 cost of a one-day policy that may not have even covered all five of the risks I just listed. I sent the fairgrounds proof of insurance, and everybody was happy!

But one little problem remained: On the remote chance that a lawsuit exceeded Mike's $2 million umbrella policy limit, by contract, Mike would have been solely responsible for that excess amount. Therefore, each of his fellow birthday celebrants separately signed a legal agreement to share equally in all losses not covered by the umbrella. By the way, the party was a great success!

What's the point of the story? To illustrate a little-known, major advantage of a good umbrella policy. It not only provides a second layer of liability coverage on top of your other liability policies, but it also fills a lot of the gaps — the gaps between the policies.

A really good umbrella policy covers many of the lawsuits against you that aren't covered by your auto, home, or other personal policies. (See Chapter 16 for more information on how to determine what your coverage gaps are and how to find a good umbrella policy that covers them.)

In fact, the only real difference between a poor umbrella policy and a great one is how well it covers the cracks.

Coordinating an Umbrella with Your Other Insurance

The coverage under an umbrella policy can be triggered when you're sued for more than your primary liability limits. It also can be triggered when you're sued for something covered only by your umbrella and not by your primary policies (in other words, the gaps). When the latter happens, the umbrella "steps down" and defends and protects you as if it were primary coverage, subject only to a modest deductible, called a *self-insured retention* (SIR) — typically, $250 or $500.

In the fairgrounds story (see "Gap coverage," earlier in this chapter), four of the five risks that Mike assumed — the last four risks — were gaps and were covered only by the umbrella policy. If any of those four risks occurred, Mike would have paid only the $500 umbrella deductible, or SIR.

In this part, I fill you in on how you might need to change your primary insurance to meet umbrella requirements and give you tips for avoiding gaps between your primary and umbrella coverage.

One reason that umbrella policies are so inexpensive is that they generally don't cover small lawsuits. An umbrella policy requires that your automobile, homeowner's, and other personal policy liability limits (also known as *primary liability limits*) meet certain minimum requirements. Depending on the insurance company, the minimums vary from about $100,000 to $500,000. To get an Umbrella, you must first raise your primary liability limits to these minimums and guarantee that you'll always maintain them. If you violate this guarantee and fail to meet these minimum requirements, you'll be personally liable for the difference between what you've guaranteed your coverages will be and what they actually are.

For example, say that the minimum auto liability coverage needed to obtain the umbrella that you have is $500,000, but you've allowed your coverage to slip to $250,000. If you're found liable for $700,000 in damages, the umbrella policy still kicks in after the first $500,000 has been paid — $250,000 by your auto insurance company, and $250,000 by you. (You promised to maintain $500,000 of coverage. You broke that promise by carrying only $250,000. You owe out of your own pocket the $250,000 shortfall.)

Insurance companies offering umbrella policies are not consistent in the amount of primary liability coverage that they require. Talk to your agent to be sure that your primary coverage always meets your umbrella requirements.

Because an umbrella policy requires you to maintain specific primary liability insurance limits, you must be aware of very serious dangers:

- ✔ **Don't let any primary policy cancel for nonpayment.** If you do and you're sued, you'll have to pay the loss out of your own pocket, a loss that otherwise would have been covered.

- ✔ **Pay attention to all notices that come from your umbrella insurer.** They often require you to raise one or more of your primary coverage limits as a condition of keeping the umbrella. If you don't see or don't read the notice and don't raise your limits as required, you'll be personally responsible for the gap.

Determining How Many Millions to Buy

Here's my bottom-line recommendation (for those of you who read the ending of a novel first): Buy $1 million more umbrella coverage than you think you need. If you think you don't need an umbrella at all, buy a policy with $1 million of coverage; if $1 million sounds right, buy a $2 million policy; and so on.

Most people underestimate the economic value of a serious injury, as determined by a court of law. Also, an extra million of coverage costs so little — around $75 a year. When it comes to catastrophic lawsuits, you're better off erring on the high side. No one ever went bankrupt over a $75 premium.

Reviewing available limits

Personal umbrella policies are sold in million-dollar increments. Most insurers offer a maximum available coverage limit from $2 million to $5 million — several up to $10 million. Beyond $10 million, the choices are limited and the cost per million escalates because those buying more than $10 million of umbrella coverage are generally quite wealthy and highly vulnerable to lawsuits.

Assessing how likely you are to be sued

In addition to the seriousness of an injury, there are several factors that influence not only the likelihood of your being sued for more than the amount your policy covers you for, but also the dollar amount of the lawsuit.

Your current financial status factor

The size of your current income and/or current assets, particularly liquid assets like investments, affects the probability of your being sued for an amount that's greater than your automobile or homeowner's liability limits. If you have a high income and/or a high net worth, congratulations! You're very suable.

I often see people who have only one of the two — a high income or a high net worth — overlooking how suable they really are. People like new doctors or lawyers in their first year of practice, making almost six figures, but with no money in the bank — yet. Or seniors on a modest retirement income but with a large, mostly liquid, portfolio. Both types of people are highly suable and definitely should have an umbrella policy — probably with limits of $2 million or more.

Your future financial status factor

If you get a large judgment against you today, for more than your liability insurance limits, it sits out there in limbo waiting for your financial situation to improve. Most people easily overlook their future suability when they're assessing their need for an umbrella policy. If you're a medical student, a law student, a computer engineer — anyone training for a high-paying career — keep this in mind. If you think you may have a lot more money in the future than you have today, you need an umbrella policy to cover your liability risks.

The exceptional risk factor

Lawsuits can occur from either activities (such as hunting, fishing, or playing sports) or exposures (such as cars, homes, boats, and animals). The exceptional risk factor recognizes that one or more of the activities or exposures in your life has a greater potential of causing serious injuries or death and, thus, more substantial lawsuits. Examples include owning a pit bull, operating a day-care center, having a swimming pool (especially one with a diving board), and having a trampoline in your yard.

If you have these or other exceptional risks in your life that have large lawsuit potential, you're a candidate for an umbrella, even if you're only of modest means.

The legal environment factor

The legal climate in your geographic area is definitely a factor in the size of legal judgments and jury awards. In California, where there are a zillion lawsuits for substantial amounts of money, you need a larger umbrella policy limit. In rural Arkansas, where the pace is slow, people don't lock their doors, and lawsuits are rare, you may still need an umbrella, but the legal environment is probably not a factor in how large it needs to be.

Your personal comfort factor

Insurance is all about peace of mind. When you decide on an umbrella policy limit, do a gut check. If you still feel fearful of possibly not having enough insurance, spend an extra $75 and buy another $1 million of coverage.

I'm a good example of this recommendation: I'm your typical middle-class American. My income, assets, and other factors suggest that a $1 million umbrella policy is about right, but my gut disagrees. I feel a lot better getting $2 million of coverage, especially when the extra million only cost me $5 a month.

Your moral responsibility factor

Every once is a while, clients remind me of that golden rule about caring for your fellow men and women. They're often of modest means and not necessarily very suable. They may not really need an umbrella. I'll suggest a liability limit on their automobile, homeowner's, and other policies — say, $300,000 — and they'll say, "Oh, no, I want more than that. If I seriously hurt someone, I want to make sure he's fully cared for — that I can provide for him by paying all his medical bills, all his lost wages, and pay him something extra for all the pain and suffering I put him through. I can't undo the hurt I've caused in his life. But at least I can help take care of his financial burden." Such people are rare and wonderful.

Setting your limits: My bottom-line recommendations

So you've thought long and hard about your own lifestyle, considered all the factors that go into deciding to buy an umbrella policy, and now you just want a dollar figure. Here are my recommendations for umbrella policies:

- ✔ Buy a personal umbrella policy of at least $1 million.
- ✔ Buy at least $2 million in coverage if you have some affluence.
- ✔ Buy at least $5 to $10 million in coverage, or more, if you're very affluent.
- ✔ Buy $1 million more than you think you need.
- ✔ Buy a policy that covers the major liability gaps in your primary insurance program (see Chapter 16).

Chapter 16

Choosing the Right Umbrella for Your Lifestyle

In This Chapter

▶ Identifying the coverage gaps in your liability insurance program

▶ Using an umbrella checklist to plug those gaps

▶ Buying the umbrella policy that's right for you

A few years ago, my clients Jon and Mimi did something I've often fantasized about: They rented a houseboat with some friends and their kids for a ten-day vacation on gigantic Rainy Lake on the Minnesota-Canada border. It was a 40-foot floating luxury cabin, propelled by two 125-horsepower outboard motors, and worth about $300,000.

Jon signed the rental agreement on behalf of the group and was offered insurance for $10 a day from the rental agency, Happy Houseboats. He called me to see if his auto or homeowner's policy covered him. I assured him they did not. His auto policy didn't cover boats (no surprise there). And although homeowner's policies do provide some liability coverage for small, rented boats (see Chapter 7), they definitely don't provide coverage for 40-foot houseboats with 250-horsepower motors, nor do they provide coverage for damage to the boat itself, regardless of the boat's size. Jon and Mimi did not have a personal umbrella policy at the time.

Jon faxed me a copy of the rental contract and a copy of Happy Houseboats's optional insurance coverage. The risks that Jon and Mimi were facing that were *completely uninsured anywhere* were:

✔ Injuries they caused to others (including drownings)

✔ Damage they caused to the houseboat itself (up to the $300,000 replacement cost)

✔ Damage they caused to all the houseboat furnishings, valued at $50,000 to $100,000

✔ Lost rental income while the damage they caused to the houseboat was being repaired

In addition, the contract with Happy Houseboats made them responsible for:

✔ Injuries, property damage, damage to the boat, damage to the furnishings, and loss of rental income caused by their friends' careless driving. Scary, isn't it?

✔ All other damage to the houseboat no matter *how* it was caused, even acts of God (meaning that if a tornado tore the boat to shreds, Jon and Mimi needed to ante up over $300,000!).

As horrible and unfair as this contract is, similar language and obligations are found in almost every rental contract you sign. Read your rental agreements and make sure you've arranged full insurance somehow. Otherwise, avoid the risk and don't rent. Don't risk more than you can afford to lose (a guiding principle from Chapter 2).

Just how good was the Happy Houseboats insurance coverage? The good news is that it covered any damage to the boat, no matter how it was caused, subject to a $500 deductible. The really bad news is that the most the policy would pay was $2,500. (No, that's not a typo — it was a $2,500 coverage limit on a $300,000 boat!) Even the guy behind the counter selling the insurance didn't know it had a $2,500 limit.

Even if the insurance covered damage to the boat without any dollar limit, I wouldn't have advised Jon and Mimi to buy the insurance — because it covered only the damage to the houseboat. It provided zero coverage for all the other liability risks for injuries and property damage to the public. Besides, my clients had a far better option — the right personal umbrella policy.

The rotten insurance coverage from Happy Houseboats would have cost Jon and Mimi $100 ($10 a day for ten days). I found them a $2 million umbrella policy covering all the otherwise uninsured risks for an annual cost of $150. Then I did what I recommend you or your agent do in this type of high-risk circumstance — I got the interpretation confirmed by the claims department of the insurance company. All the risks were indeed covered, subject to a $1,000 deductible.

It's important to know that many umbrellas won't cover all the risks my clients assumed in renting the houseboat. Some, in fact, wouldn't cover any. Helping you identify an umbrella policy that covers the special risks in *your* life is the goal of this chapter.

Covering the Gaps

A personal umbrella policy has three advantages: higher liability limits, extended coverage for defense costs, and gap coverage — coverage for many of the lawsuits excluded by primary policies (like the gaps in coverage in the houseboat example, earlier in this chapter).

Virtually all umbrella policies are identical in providing higher limits and extended defense costs. Where they differ — hugely — is how well they cover the gaps in your primary coverage.

The worst umbrella policies don't cover any gaps. I've looked at umbrella policies from about 30 insurance companies. Two major insurance companies — both household names — offer umbrellas that have no gap coverage at all. Selling an umbrella without any gap coverage is like selling a car with three wheels.

On the flip side, some of the best umbrella policies, with the highest ratings, cover all kinds of gaps but may not cover your unique coverage gap. For example, you may have a pilot's license and occasionally rent planes. Because you don't own a plane, you don't have aircraft liability coverage. This is a big gap. You also have no liability for damage you cause to the rented planes. With the price of planes, that is a second huge gap. When you select your umbrella policy then, you should be looking for an umbrella that covers both of those gaps. Only a few do.

Again, by *gaps* I mean the liability risks in your life that are not covered by your primary insurance policies. Here are just a few possible examples of activities you may engage in that aren't often covered by auto or homeowner's policies.

- ✔ Renting "toys" of all kinds, such as snowmobiles, boats, all-terrain vehicles (ATVs)
- ✔ Renting cars outside the United States and Canada
- ✔ Racing sailboats
- ✔ Employing a nurse or nanny
- ✔ Assuming liability when you sign a contract
- ✔ Serving on nonprofit boards of directors
- ✔ Having underground fuel tanks and septic systems

A closer look at these gaps follows, along with the reasons why it's so important to get an umbrella that covers them.

The renting "toys" gap

When you rent "toys" — boats, snowmobiles, ATVs — you're liable for any injuries and property damage you cause to other people and their possessions. You're also responsible for damage you cause to the rental item, sometimes even when the damage wasn't caused by you, if the rental contract requires it. If you occasionally rent these items, you want to make sure that your umbrella policy covers all these risks.

Watch out for umbrella coverage on rented boats. Many have length or horsepower limitations and don't cover the type of boat you may rent. For example, I occasionally rent sailboats that are up to 30 feet in length. My homeowner's policy covers boats I rent only if they're under 26 feet, for liability, and it completely excludes all damage to the boats in my care. So, I have an umbrella policy without any length restrictions. If I rent the *Queen Mary* for the afternoon, I'm fully covered — up to my umbrella policy limit, that is. (See Chapter 7 for much more on insuring owned, borrowed, or rented boats and recreational vehicles.)

The car rental gap

Like rented toys, when you rent a car, you're liable for injuries and property damage you cause to others, and all damage to the rental car, whether you caused it or not.

If you rent a car in the United States or Canada, your personal auto policy covers you for the first risk — your liability for injuries and damage to the public — and sometimes the second risk — damage to the rental car — depending on whether you have collision and comprehensive coverage on at least one of your cars.

If you rent cars even rarely, don't consider an umbrella that doesn't cover both of these risks (see Chapter 6 for more information on managing car rental risks). Most umbrellas do.

When you rent a car in Mexico or abroad, you have the same two liability risks as you do in the United States and Canada. The difference is that 99 percent of personal auto policies don't cover any automobile usage outside the United States and Canada. If you'll ever rent a car outside the United States or Canada, make sure that your umbrella policy covers both of these risks worldwide.

Even if your umbrella covers you, I recommend that, when you're outside the United States or Canada, you buy the optional coverage for damage to the rental car from the rental agency and keep your umbrella as a backup. Why?

So you're not tied up with claim hassles when you return a damaged car. Domestic insurance companies are not set up to provide immediate claim service in foreign countries.

Make sure you have true worldwide coverage. I recently reviewed a "worldwide" umbrella that excluded lawsuits not filed in the United States! If you need worldwide coverage, make sure that's what your policy gives you.

The contracts gap

Are you aware of how many times you've signed a personal contract? Sure, car rentals are fairly common, and you may have signed a contract for a vacation residence. But what about all the others?

For example, when you rent tools and equipment for household projects (like the chainsaw you rented to cut up the dead tree in your yard), you sign a contract in which you agree not only to be responsible for damage to the tool but to pay for an attorney and pay any judgment against the rental company for injuries caused while you're using the tool.

Here's another example: If you rent facilities for special occasions (like the reception hall you rented for your daughter's wedding), you sign a contract agreeing to be responsible for anything that happens, even injuries or damage caused by one of the guests, and you have to defend and pay any judgment against the facility owner.

I wouldn't even consider an umbrella that doesn't cover the liability you take on when you sign an equipment or event rental contract.

The nonprofit board gap

Suppose you're caring enough to serve on the board of directors for your child's youth hockey association. Further suppose that, with the potential for head injuries in that sport, the board took on the responsibility of the selection of the hockey helmet to be worn by the kids. If a child using the helmet suffers a head injury because the helmet has a design flaw, everyone would be sued — certainly the helmet manufacturer and, most likely, you, personally, and the entire board. Even if you won, you'd be responsible for legal fees, which could run into the tens of thousands of dollars. And if you lost, you'd also be responsible for your share of the judgment. Your automobile, homeowner's, and other primary liability policies won't pay a dime. But many umbrella policies would completely defend you and, if you lost, pay the full judgment against you, subject only to a small deductible.

The wedding reception contract

My client Kathleen was getting married and was busy with the planning. She negotiated with a restaurant to host the wedding reception. After they agreed to the terms, the restaurant asked her to sign their standard contract, which she faxed to me to see if her home and umbrella policies covered her. The contract had the usual terms that you can expect: She would agree to be responsible for injuries or property damage she caused, as well as those caused by guests. In addition, she would agree, in the event of the restaurant being sued, to protect, defend, and pay any judgment against the restaurant, *no matter what the cause!*

In short, by signing the contract, she would be agreeing to be responsible for injuries caused by the restaurant or its employees. If several guests got sick or died, caused entirely by food poisoning from the restaurant's contaminated food, she would be agreeing to take the fall for the whole thing. Even if her umbrella would cover this unjust provision, her $1 million limit wouldn't be enough for that type of multiple-injury claim.

I advised her to remove that requirement from the contract or withdraw from the deal. The restaurant's reaction? It refused to alter the contract. It scoffed and said, "People have been signing this same contract for years and no one has *ever* complained before." (Very scary!) My client wisely withdrew from the deal, much to the restaurant's amazement. Two days later, the restaurant called her and agreed to add the phrase, "except for the negligence of the restaurant and its employees," which solved the problem.

This true story has two points:

✔ Don't sign a contract — especially for something with as much risk as a wedding reception — without reading the contract. Preventing the claim is far better than being liable for it, even if the claim is covered by insurance.

✔ Own a personal umbrella policy. Many of them cover the numerous obligations you take on through the everyday contracts you sign.

If you serve without compensation on a nonprofit board, one of your criteria in selecting a personal umbrella policy should be coverage for your board activities. The umbrella coverage isn't comprehensive — it covers primarily injuries or property damage stemming from your activities or decisions. It won't cover other types of lawsuits such as failure to buy the right insurance coverage, sexual harassment, wrongful termination, discrimination, and so on. But at least you have partial coverage.

If you receive any compensation or serve on a for-profit board, the umbrella won't apply. The only way I'd serve on these boards is if the organization had in place adequate amounts of *directors' and officers'* (D&O) liability coverage and if, in writing, the company agreed to defend me in court and pay any judgment against me for any of my activities stemming from my involvement with the board and not covered by the D&O insurance.

The company-furnished car gap

If your employer furnishes you with a company car, be aware of two possible gaps in your liability insurance protection: One has to do with co-workers who are injured riding with you; the other has to do with drive-other-cars coverage.

Co-worker injuries

The majority of business auto policies covering your company car exclude coverage for you if you injure a co-worker riding with you. The co-worker, who was injured on the job, in most cases receives workers' compensation benefits for medical bills and lost wages. But, unless local laws prohibit such suits, in addition to the workers' comp benefits, the co-worker can also sue you. The really bad news is that most of the time you have no insurance protection. If you have a company car, make sure the umbrella you buy provides coverage for this serious risk in order to close the gap. (**Note:** You may also need to add *extended non-owned* coverage to your personal auto policy. Check with your agent.)

Drive-other-cars gap

When you're furnished a company car by your employer, you're covered to drive the car by the employer's business auto policy. But you're not covered under the business auto policy for cars you borrow or rent personally.

If you have a personal automobile in addition to the company car, skip this section. Your personal auto policy already provides coverage when you drive borrowed or rented vehicles.

If, however, you have no personal vehicles and, thus, no personal auto policy, you'll have no drive-other-cars coverage. Have your employer add the coverage for all family members to her business auto policy, if she's agreeable. Most employers will. The small additional cost may be your responsibility, however.

If your employer won't add the coverage, the right umbrella policy will cover you for two risks you face driving borrowed or rented cars:

- ✔ Your liability for injuries and property damage you cause to the public
- ✔ Your liability for damaging the car itself

If you have a company car, make very sure that your umbrella covers both of these risks.

The employer's liability gap

Workers' compensation insurance pays an employee who is injured on the job her medical bills and lost wages in such amounts as required by state law, regardless of fault. A second coverage in a workers' compensation policy is *employer's liability coverage,* which defends and pays any judgments against the employer if the employer is sued for a work-related injury by others, such as an employee's husband who is suing for his loss of his wife's companionship after her on-the-job death.

It isn't just the wealthy, with their maids and gardeners, who have domestic help and need to buy workers' compensation and employer's liability insurance. For example, many elderly or disabled people hire personal-care attendants. And it's not just the wealthy who hire nannies these days.

What if you're sued as a result of causing an employee's injury, for more than your employer's liability coverage limit? You'll want additional coverage from an umbrella policy. The majority of umbrella policies do not include additional employer's liability coverage. A few, however, do.

If you have an employee or if you have a workers' comp policy for whatever reason, employer's liability coverage should be in the umbrella you choose.

The pollution gap

Most liability policies these days exclude coverage for your liability for pollution. Two types of pollution can result in a lawsuit against you — immediate, accidental pollution (such as your underground fuel tank springing a leak and emptying into the surrounding soil), and gradual pollution (such as seepage from that tank over months or years).

The consequences of either can be severe — having to pay all cleanup costs, which can run into the tens of thousands of dollars, as well as potentially massive fines and penalties. So this is a pretty serious risk. (See the sidebar "The underground heating oil disappearing act" for an example of how this gap may affect you.)

To the best of my knowledge, no umbrella covers the seepage kind of pollution. The good news is that some do cover pollution that's both sudden and accidental.

If you have pollutants stored on your premises, especially underground, add pollution coverage to your umbrella shopping list.

The underground heating oil disappearing act

My clients Desi and Lucy called one day quite upset. They had no heat in their home even though, the day before, they had their underground heating oil tank filled to the top. They had no way of quickly proving it, but they guessed that their tank had sprung a leak and 150 gallons of heating oil had spilled into the ground. Being good citizens, they immediately reported it to the local pollution control people who, instead of expressing their gratitude for Lucy and Desi's good behavior and immediately beginning a cleanup, told them that they were financially responsible to pay all cleanup costs, which could become massive if the oil reached underground waters.

Homeowner's policies almost universally exclude pollution liability. And my clients had declined umbrella coverage. Desi and Lucy were lucky this time. The oil never reached water. But they were out a few thousand dollars in legal fees and excavation and cleanup costs. Some umbrella policies would have paid all costs, subject to a small deductible.

The moral: If you have a fuel tank on-premises, especially underground, get an umbrella with pollution spill coverage. And if possible, reduce the risk significantly by not putting the tank underground. Keep it above ground, where leaks and seepage can be noticed and fixed immediately.

Creating Your Own Gap Checklist

Before you can go in search of the umbrella policy that best fills the gaps in your primary coverage, you need to be able to intelligently communicate your needs to an insurance agent or company.

To help you do that, I've created a checklist (see Table 16-1). I guarantee you that it does *not* include every conceivable gap in liability insurance coverage. But if you use the checklist, it'll lead you to an umbrella policy that covers all or most of the gaps on the list for which you're currently uninsured.

Table 16-1	Personal Umbrella Coverage Checklist	
	Mandatory Coverages	
Gap Description	*What Coverage You Need*	*Comments*
Territory of coverage	Worldwide	Make sure lawsuits outside the U.S. and Canada are covered.
Personal injury liability	Libel, slander, false arrest, and so on	Underlying insurance may be required. Be careful.

(continued)

Table 16-1 *(continued)*

	Mandatory Coverages	
Coverage of newly acquired vehicles, boats, and so on	Automatic; no notice required	Poor policies require notification in 30 days or no coverage. Dangerous!
Liability assumed in contracts	Weddings, parties, rentals of all kinds	Poor policies limit coverage to residential contracts only.
Punitive damages	Allowed in some states	You could travel in a state that allows them.

	Optional Coverages	
Gap Description	*What You Need*	*Remarks*
Damage to rented or borrowed property	Cars, boats, snowmobiles, rented residences, and so on	Coverage usually won't apply if you're required to insure the item.
Renting boats	No length or horsepower limitation	If there is a limit, it needs to be much larger than any boat you'd ever rent.
Renting snowmobiles	No engine size limit	
Renting other motorized vehicles	ATVs, go-karts, trail bikes, golf carts, and so on	No restrictions.
Renting cars outside the U.S. and Canada	Worldwide	No requirement that the suit be filed in U.S. or Canada only.
Renting vacation property	Worldwide	
Service on nonprofit boards	Usually limited to bodily injury and property damage only	Usually no coverage if any compensation is paid to you.
Employer-furnished car	Coverage for injured co-workers	Careful. Primary coverage may be required.
Coverage to drive other cars	Only needed if you have no personal auto policy	
Employer's liability	Covering your domestic help (nannies, contractors, and so on)	Requires that you have a primary policy.

Optional Coverages		
Incidental office	Coverage for work-related injuries on your premises — usually an optional coverage	May require primary coverage under your homeowner's policy.
Pollution liability	For fuel storage leaks and other sudden spills	Covers only sudden and accidental; no coverage for seepage.
Sailboat racing	A crew member	Often excluded in primary homeowner's or boat coverage.
Aircraft liability	Including liability for damaging the aircraft, if rented	If you own the plane, you'll need a primary coverage policy. If you rent the plane, you may not require primary coverage.
Excess uninsured and under-insured motorist	Additional coverage for your injuries in an accident; optional coverage under some umbrella policies	Caused by drivers with less injury liability coverage than you have. Buy if it's available and reasonably priced.

Considering your coverage: Mandatory versus optional

The mandatory portion of Table 16-1 includes exposures that are so common that each of them should be covered even in the most basic umbrella policy. Some insurance companies argue that coverage for *punitive damages* — extra damages awarded by a jury for gross negligence (like driving drunk even after your license has been suspended for drunk driving) — aren't important if you live in a state banning punitive damage awards. I disagree because people travel to other states. The state you're traveling in may allow punitive damages, so you need that coverage.

Umbrella policies differ the most in the area of optional coverages. For example, many provide poor coverage on rented boats, extending coverage to only small boats and boats with small motors. In the land of 10,000 lakes, that's a very undesirable restriction. If you live in Minnesota, or any other state with a lot of boating, or if you occasionally rent boats no matter where you live, I recommend that unrestricted boat liability using non-owned or rental boats be a mandatory part of your umbrella coverage.

Another example: If you take some work home and have a home office, your homeowner's policy should include an incidental office endorsement (see Chapter 11 for the reasons why). Your umbrella must also be amended to include incidental office liability coverage or you'll have a gap.

Finally, some companies offer excess uninsured and under-insured motorist coverage (see Chapter 5). This protection covers medical costs that you and your passengers incur from a car accident caused by a driver with less liability coverage than the economic value of your injury. It's extra coverage that pays only if the value of your injuries exceeds the uninsured and under-insured motorists coverage on your auto insurance policy. It's great coverage to have if you're seriously hurt, but give it less priority than your uninsured lawsuit gaps. If you can cover all your uninsured gaps in an umbrella, that also makes uninsured and under-insured motorist coverage available — and if your budget can handle it, I recommend you take it.

Using the checklist

If you're going to buy an umbrella policy, you want one that covers the activities you actually engage in, right? You would never buy an auto policy that covered you Monday through Friday and excluded weekends. But that's exactly the type of umbrella policy that most consumers buy and agents sell — a policy that may leave you high and dry at claim time.

This chapter is all about getting those weekends covered. Here's how the umbrella checklist can help. Check off any of the optional coverage areas (gaps) that apply to you and begin the hunt for the right policy. Be fore-warned — the insurance marketplace won't be prepared for you. When you hand out your checklist to prospective agents, most will be surprised. No one has ever bought an umbrella policy from them in this fashion before. All agents, including me, don't know off the top of their heads how their umbrella policies will fill those gaps you've checked, so you probably will need to leave a copy of the checklist with them. That's reasonable. This is a complex issue to be handled with care.

By the way, how your agent deals with your request is, in my opinion, one of the best tools to help you select a great agent. Pay attention to how knowledgeable prospective agents are in discussing your particular gaps. If an agent seems annoyed at the request, appears confused by it, or is clearly not knowledgeable about the gaps, find another agent. (See Chapter 4 for tips on selecting a good agent.)

Buying the Policy

Here are the three most common mistakes people make when buying a personal umbrella policy:

- ✔ **They buy their auto and home policies first and then buy the umbrella from the same insurance company.** In short, the mistake is settling for whatever umbrella comes with the auto and home policies, no matter how poor it may be. *Note:* Buying your policies from the same *agent* is usually a good idea, but automatically buying them from the same *company* is a bad idea if you want the best umbrella policy (as the next bullet points out).

- ✔ **They buy their umbrella policy from a different agent than the one who sold them auto and home insurance.** The damage occurs because the two agents don't communicate, leaving you very vulnerable to gaps between your primary and umbrella coverages.

- ✔ **They buy their umbrella on price and ignore coverage.** This usually happens because they think all umbrellas are the same and because they don't realize the importance of gap coverage. They're unaware that they even have gaps.

The three antidotes to these mistakes are building your insurance program starting with the umbrella policy first, keeping your primary and umbrella coverages with the same agent, and considering price last rather than first. Here's more information on each one of these three.

Buying your umbrella policy first

If your only reason for having an umbrella policy is to get higher liability limits on your automobile and homeowner's policies, and if you don't have any concerns about gap coverage, taking the umbrella that comes from the insurer of your auto and home is fine. Taking that umbrella is also fine if it covers all the gaps in your umbrella checklist (unlikely but possible).

But if you want an umbrella that plugs as many of your liability insurance gaps as possible, the best way to build your insurance program is to start at the top with the umbrella policy and decide on that policy first, *before* you buy auto or home insurance. Here's why: Due to the small premiums and increased risk, many insurers don't even offer an umbrella policy unless they insure your home and auto, too. If your home and auto insurance is already set up with Company A, but that company has an umbrella that doesn't suit your needs, and you discover that Company B and Company C both have umbrella policies that cover all your gaps but they require your car and home insurance, you'll have to cancel and move your auto and home insurance — a lot of unnecessary work to get the umbrella you need.

If, on the other hand, you compare umbrellas first, you'll logically narrow down your choices to either Company B or Company C. You can then compare the prices of each company's auto and home policies and go with whichever of the two has the best total price. You may pay a little more for the whole program than you would have paid if you used Company A, but when you're navigating across the ocean of life, how much more will you pay for a boat that won't leak or sink?

Pick an agent, any agent

For the record, there are two types of insurance agents:

- Those who represent one insurance company only — often referred to as *exclusive agents, captive agents,* or *direct-writer agents*

- Those who are free to represent more than one company — usually referred to as *independent agents*

Exclusive agents include those who represent insurance companies like State Farm, Farmers Insurance Group, or Liberty Mutual. Independent-agent insurance companies include national insurers like Safeco, Hartford, and Chubb, and most regional insurance companies (such as Harleysville, Auto-Owners, and Cincinnati).

Which type of agent is better for you? The best insurance agent you can find is the one who can get you the coverage you need. Whether he's independent or exclusive makes no difference. The only real difference when trying to buy the right umbrella is convenience. If the exclusive agent you prefer offers only one umbrella choice that excludes coverage for a lot of activities you're exposed to, you'll be forced to buy your umbrella policy elsewhere. In contrast, the independent agent, by having more than one umbrella option, increases your chances that you won't have to seek another agent to get the coverage you want. But even the independent agent may not have in his portfolio the best umbrella policy for your needs.

Great advice. Great coverage. That's all that matters.

Buying your insurance from the same agent or company

If you buy your primary and umbrella liability coverage from the same insurer, your insurance coverage fits together better with less chance of a gap (Legos and Legos versus Legos and Tinkertoys) than if you split your policies between two or more insurance companies.

If you do buy all your polices from different insurers but at least from the same professional agent, whatever gaps could exist between your policies can be reduced or prevented with the help of the agent. For example, suppose that you have auto and home insurance through Company A and your umbrella through Company B but all your policies are through the same agent. Now suppose you add an incidental office at home and add the appropriate homeowner's endorsement to cover injuries to delivery people. Your astute agent will know that your umbrella won't extend to that office without a special amendment. She will then add that amendment and, thus, avoid a potentially serious gap. If you had the umbrella with a different agent, the umbrella agent would never have been notified, and you'd have that gap.

To reduce the chance of gaps between policies, keep your auto, home, umbrella, and other personal liability policies together — ideally, with the same agent and the same insurance company.

Placing coverage and financial strength before price

Do not make your umbrella decision on the price of the umbrella alone. You could end up comparing a Hyundai to a Hummer.

Start with selecting the umbrella policies that best cover the gaps you listed on your checklist (see "Creating Your Own Gap Checklist," earlier in this chapter). Then make sure the insurer is strong financially (see the sidebar "Measuring insurer strength"). You don't want them going belly-up in the middle of a lawsuit against you. Then and only then look at the umbrella pricing — but only as a part of the pricing of the whole insurance program.

Measuring insurer strength

Why is insurer strength so important when purchasing a personal umbrella policy? Don't states have an insurance guarantee fund protecting consumers against insolvency? Yes, most states do have such a consumer protection fund. But few such funds go as high as $1 million or more. Minnesota's limit, for example, is $300,000. But even if the fund limit were high enough, collecting from it is a long, drawn-out process — hardly the kind of stress you want in the middle of a lawsuit against you.

Several organizations rate insurance companies. The one with the longest track record — and a great reputation — is A. M. Best, which assigns insurers a strength rating from A++ to C, much like school grades. (See www. ambest/ratings/definition.html for an explanation of the ratings.) If you want more information on an insurer you're considering, go to www.ambest.com and click Ratings & Analysis); there, you can get a wealth of information on any company. I don't recommend buying an umbrella from any insurance company with an A. M. Best rating below A (in other words, a B+ or worse) unless it's unavoidable.

Chapter 17

Changing Your Insurance When Your Life Changes

In This Chapter

▶ Getting married

▶ Building, remodeling, and moving

▶ Hiring a nanny

▶ Transferring your home to a trust

*W*hen you experience a major life change, you need to change your insurance coverage. The insurance plan you had before the change often won't cover some of the new risks you've taken on during and after the change. Under the standard homeowner's policy, you have no coverage for any of the following incidents:

✔ You're sued for $350,000 for injuries to three guests at a party your son hosted in his apartment — the apartment you helped him qualify for by cosigning the lease.

✔ You're remodeling your home, and a carpenter is injured when his own scaffolding collapses. The accident is no fault of yours, whatsoever. But you're sued for workers' compensation benefits of $200,000 — $120,000 for medical bills and $80,000 for lost wages.

✔ In the same remodeling job, $25,000 of heating and air-conditioning equipment, sitting in your yard and about to be installed, is stolen in the middle of the night.

✔ You're sued for $75,000 for damage to the furnishings of the condominium below your aging mother's condo, caused by water overflowing from a tub she was filling and forgot about. Your mother, on her attorney's advice, had just transferred ownership of her condominium to you.

These scenarios are just a few examples of possible serious, uninsured claims, all of which originate as the result of a significant change in your life. In this chapter, I show you how to manage the insurance risks of life's more common changes — from the cradle to the grave.

Goin' to the Chapel: Getting Married

From getting engaged up to the wedding ceremony, you face special risks. In this section, I give you some strategies to help you manage them.

Getting engaged

If a valuable ring is involved in the engagement and you want it insured in case it's lost or stolen, you should schedule it as an addendum to a homeowner's or renter's policy. A basic homeowner's policy provides little or no jewelry coverage, especially for the loss of a diamond or other gem, so the ring must be scheduled. If you already have the wedding rings and if they have any value, you may want to schedule them as well. (See Chapter 10 for more information on scheduling jewelry.)

Generally, the ring should be insured under the policy of its owner. If the owner still lives with her parents, add the ring to her parents' homeowner's policy. If the owner rents but has no renter's policy, it's time to get one (see Chapter 9).

Living together before marriage

Set up a homeowner's or renters policy in *both* names. If you buy the insurance under only your name, your partner has no personal liability coverage under your policy for activities — such as injuring someone while playing racquetball. Plus, your partner's personal belongings won't be covered. Both of your names need to be on the policy in order for both of you to be protected.

Move both your car insurance policies to the same insurance company and buy the same liability limits on each policy. Why? Because your personal auto policy won't cover you while you're driving your partner's car. (It excludes coverage on cars you have regular access to.) Being insured with the same company assures you that your policy terms will be identical, no matter which car you drive — which will also make for a far easier claim experience. Buying the same liability limits assures that the same amount of money will be available to each of you for lawsuits regardless of which car you're driving. If you buy $300,000 of coverage and your partner has $50,000 of coverage, when you drive your partner's car the only coverage you have is his $50,000. The only way you can get $300,000 of coverage, when you live together, is for him to have the same $300,000 liability coverage as you have. If your partner won't agree to the same coverage, don't *ever* drive his car.

Some auto insurance companies offer an optional coverage called *extended non-owned liability coverage,* which extends your coverage to his vehicle, and vice versa. If your insurer offers it, add it to both policies. It's not expensive.

Tying the knot

After you get married, set up homeowner's or renter's insurance in both names (see Chapter 5). Make sure the property limit is high enough to cover your belongings as well as your wedding gifts. Also, combine your vehicles on one car insurance policy (see Chapter 5 on buying car insurance and Chapter 9 on buying homeowner's or renter's insurance.).

If you're both working, continue your group health coverage if it's provided to you by your employers. If one of you doesn't have health coverage through work, add the uninsured spouse to the insured spouse's group policy. You generally have 30 days from the wedding date to do so without having to *qualify medically* (prove that you're in good health). After 30 days, you can be declined due to poor health. (See Chapter 18 for advice on buying individual health insurance.)

Make sure you have enough life insurance to pay for a funeral and other final expenses. Most jobs include enough free life insurance to cover these costs. If one of you has life insurance through work and the other one doesn't, add the uninsured spouse onto the insured spouse's group policy. You can also buy an individual policy. (See Chapter 23 for tips on estimating your life insurance needs.)

Be sure to change the beneficiaries on all life insurance policies — individual or group — to each other.

Don't overlook long-term disability insurance, especially if you need two incomes to make ends meet (see Chapter 22).

Be careful of contracts you're asked to sign related to the wedding reception. Make sure the terms are reasonable. I had one client show me a restaurant rental contract where the wedding party had to agree to be responsible not only for injuries they caused, but also for injuries the restaurant caused — like food poisoning. Sign something like that, and you'll be in deep trouble — with the possibility of no insurance — if a guest is injured at the reception! It's a good idea to have an attorney review contracts like this, before you sign them, where there are substantial risks. You're better off changing the location of the reception than paying thousands of dollars to defend and pay judgments against the restaurant for its negligence. Check with your agent to make sure that your personal liability coverage — home and/or umbrella — will protect you if you do get sued for injuries or property damage at the reception.

Measure Twice, Cut Once: Building or Remodeling a Home

Whether you're building your dream home or remodeling your current one, you've taken on a lot of additional risks, many of which are not automatically insured. Enjoy the excitement, but make sure that your insurance is adequate for the new risks in your life.

Here's a list of some of those risks and how I recommend you handle them:

- ✔ **Property damage to new construction from fire, wind, vandalism, and so on:** If you're building a new home, have a clear understanding with the builder, in writing, as to who is responsible for the property insurance. Make it a requirement that the party who buys the insurance also names the other party as loss payee. Require that proof of the insurance be provided prior to the start of construction. If you, as the homeowner, are responsible for the insurance, buy a homeowner's policy rather than a builder's risk policy. Homeowner's coverage is much more comprehensive and includes, at no extra charge, liability coverage for job-site injuries.

  If you're remodeling, increase your homeowner's building-coverage limit, at the time the work starts, to the revised cost to replace your home with the improvements.

- ✔ **Theft of building materials:** Normally materials aren't covered until they're installed in your home. Either contractually require the contractor to be responsible for all materials until they're installed, or add a theft of building materials endorsement to your homeowner's policy and delete the endorsement when everything is installed.

- ✔ **Lawsuits from job-site injuries:** These are usually covered by your homeowner's policy, but this is a good time to reevaluate your personal liability limits. Consider adding an umbrella policy if you don't already have one (see Chapter 15). Also, in your construction contract, require the contractor to defend you and pay any judgment against you for injuries or property damage he or his crew cause. Request proof of the contractor's general liability insurance before work starts. If he doesn't have insurance, you're much more apt to be sued yourself if someone gets hurt.

- ✔ **Workers' compensation claims filed against you for medical bills and lost wages from any worker injured on the job:** This risk is *not* covered by your homeowner's policy. Require written proof from your contractor that he has workers' compensation insurance covering all workers before any work starts. Run all labor costs — even if you're paying your friends to chip in — through the contractor, so that you're not at risk for anyone's injuries.

Another option is to buy your own workers' compensation policy for the period of construction, especially if you're acting as your own general contractor.

Don't start new construction without someone — you or the contractor — having workers' compensation insurance in place.

✔ **Injuries and property damage that happen to you or your home after the work is completed:** For example, the furnace blows soot through the house, a defective fireplace causes a major building fire, or the roof leaks from a defective installation. Require in your construction contract that the contractor provide you proof of general liability insurance, including completed operations coverage, which covers this kind of claim. If there are injuries or damages later, you may have a source of insurance to collect from.

✔ **The contractor skipping out and not paying subcontractors, who then file liens against your property:** Require the contractor to get lien waivers signed by all subcontractors prior to your paying for the work. Or, if he's not agreeable to that, pay the subcontractors directly.

✔ **Misunderstandings between you and the contractor, causing significant frustration and financial loss:** Always work with a contract and a good attorney. Incorporate into the contract the issues addressed in this list!

And Baby Makes Three: Becoming a New Parent

When you're expecting the birth of your first child, it's time to revisit three types of insurance that may need to be changed:

✔ **Health insurance:** Under many health plans, newborns cease to be covered 30 days after birth unless you notify your health insurance company within that 30-day period requesting that your child be added to your coverage — so call the insurance company. And don't wait 30 days — call immediately. If you're married, you may have a choice between the mother's policy and the father's policy. If you do, compare costs, features, and the freedom to choose doctors. (See Chapter 18 for the most important elements of a great health insurance plan.)

✔ **Life insurance:** This may surprise you, but insuring your child isn't the most important issue. Instead, when a child is born, you have to buy or significantly raise your *own* life insurance protection to make sure that the baby will be protected if you die. Don't forget to insure the homemaker if one of you will be staying home. This is also a good time to reassess life insurance beneficiaries and change your contingent beneficiary to "all surviving children" instead of "my brother Ralph." (See Chapter 23 on how to determine life insurance needs.)

✔ **Disability insurance:** If you've put off buying this coverage, now is a good time to rethink your decision. The loss of a paycheck would be a bigger hardship now that you have a new baby. (See Chapter 22 for more on disability insurance.)

A Spoonful of Sugar Helps the Medicine Go Down: Hiring a Nanny

You've recently become proud parents. As soon as you found out you were expecting, you probably started considering your child-care options. Do you put the baby in daycare, or do you hire a nanny to care for your child in your home?

If you go the nanny route, you have a couple options: You can hire a nanny through a professional nanny service, which costs quite a bit more but has a number of advantages:

✔ The agency screens candidates and checks references for you.

✔ The agency provides temporary nannies to fill in when your nanny is ill or takes a vacation or simply doesn't show up.

✔ The agency carries liability insurance in case one of your children is injured in the nanny's care. (Most self-employed nannies don't have any liability insurance.)

✔ The agency carries workers' compensation insurance covering the nanny if she's injured on the job, regardless of fault. This significantly reduces the chance of the nanny suing you for a job-related injury.

✔ The agency does all the withholding, pays all the payroll taxes, and issues the paychecks to the nanny so you don't have to.

Not all nanny services provide all these benefits, so make sure you understand what you're getting into before you sign on the dotted line.

A second option is to hire your own nanny. You can hire her as an independent contractor, a common approach but one that has liability and potential tax consequences that aren't, in my opinion, worth taking. A better and safer choice is to hire your nanny as an employee. Yes, you'll need to cut her a paycheck and do some withholding. And, depending on what state you're in, you may need to buy workers' compensation insurance for her. (Check with your state's department of labor for information on workers' compensation requirements for domestic employees. Many states exempt you from having to provide the coverage for a single employee.)

If you're required to buy workers' compensation insurance, you benefit in two ways:

✔ The nanny is prohibited by law from suing you if she gets hurt on the job.

✔ The nanny can collect for her medical bills and lost wages from your workers' compensation policy, regardless of how it happened.

For more information on household employees and the IRS rules, go to `www. irs.gov/publications/p926/index.html` or call 800-829-3676 and request Publication 926: Household Employer's Tax Guide.

If your nanny will be driving your child or picking them up as part of her duties, your child could be injured in a car accident caused by the nanny's negligence. Here are some steps you can take to protect yourself and your child *before you hire the nanny:*

✔ **Get her signed permission to check her driving record**. Request her driver's license number and vehicle plate number. Then provide both numbers and her signed permission to your auto insurance agent and request her driving and accident records. If her record isn't clear for at least three years, look into other candidates.

✔ **Get proof of her automobile insurance liability coverage if she uses her own car.** Make sure both her liability coverage and uninsured/under-insured motorists coverage are at least $300,000. If not, ask her to increase them to at least that level. Offer to pay the additional cost if need be. The cost for extra liability coverage is very small — $50 to $100 a year tops.

✔ **Add her as an occasional operator to your car insurance if she'll be using your car regularly.**

For more information on hiring a nanny, go to `www.nannyjobs.com/ ResourceEmployers.aspx`. There you can find an article that I co-wrote in 2004 with the then–Nanny of the Year, Michelle LaRowe, called "Finding and Hiring a Nanny."

Go West (or East or North or South), Young Man! Moving

Moving is nearly always a huge undertaking, full of heavy lifting, hard work, and a year's worth of stress. The last thing you want to think about when you're planning a move is insurance, but if you overlook insurance, your move may be even more stressful than it already is. When you move, your belongings may be in storage or in transit for some period of time. If your new home is ready for move-in right away, your belongings will, at the very least, be in transit on the moving truck for however long it takes to get from your old home to your new one. And if your new home isn't ready yet, your stuff may be in storage for days, weeks, or even months. If your things are in storage, you may have to live in a motel with some of your belongings.

Here's what I recommend: First, to cover your personal property that's in transit and/or in storage, don't cancel the homeowner's or renter's policy insuring your old home. Then, manage your risks as follows:

- ✔ **Property being moved while in transit:** Basic homeowner's insurance covers only specific losses like collision and theft. It won't cover all losses, such as breakage of furniture and electronics from load shifting. So add special perils contents coverage to your homeowner's policy, insuring the contents in the home you're leaving. This special form covers almost any loss outside of a few exclusions such as breakage of fragile items (dishes, crystal, and so on). If you want fragile items covered for breakage, you'll need to schedule them. (Or pay the movers to do the packing and buy breakage coverage from them.)

- ✔ **Property in storage:** Basic homeowner's policies do cover, in full, all personal property in a locked storage facility up to the contents policy limit. But the types of losses covered are limited to fire, wind, vandalism, theft, and so on. No coverage exists, for example, for water damage from roof leaks or groundwater damage of any kind. To cover yourself, add special perils contents coverage, which covers almost all losses, including water damage from roof leaks. Although it excludes groundwater damage at home, it covers groundwater damage *away* from home, such as for items in storage.

- ✔ **Property at your temporary location:** Your homeowner's policy covers any property you have with you in a temporary location up to the contents policy limit for up to 30 days. Beyond 30 days, coverage drops to 10 percent of the policy limit on contents. If you're going to be in that location longer than 30 days, you don't need to make special insurance arrangements to cover your stuff if you're okay with the 10 percent limit.

If you're not, ask your agent to negotiate an extension for the time you need. Or, if that fails, buy renter's insurance. (If you're storing most of your stuff, the 10 percent limitation is usually plenty for whatever you have with you.)

✔ **Damage to the moving truck, if you decide to move yourself.** In the rental contract you sign, you're liable for anything — even storm damage. Coverage is available from the rental agency, but it's expensive. My suggestion is to decline coverage from the rental agency, if you have both collision and comprehensive coverage on at least one of your cars. The coverage you have on your own car will transfer to the truck. If you don't have the coverage, either have your agent add the coverages to your car insurance policy or buy the coverage from the rental agency.

Many car insurance policies limit this coverage to trucks with a gross vehicle weight rating not exceeding 10,000 pounds. Ask the rental agency how much the truck weighs, and if it exceeds 10,000 pounds, call your agent to see if your policy has that 10,000-pound limitation. If it does, buy the coverage from the rental agency.

✔ **Liability when operating the rental truck for injuries and property damage to the public:** As long as you have personal auto insurance, no additional coverage is necessary. Personal auto insurance fully covers this risk up to your policy limit. (It may be a good time, though, to reevaluate your auto liability limits. Should they be increased? Or is it time to buy a personal umbrella policy?) If you don't have personal auto insurance, you can usually get the liability insurance from the rental agency where you'll also have to get your collision damage coverage.

Whenever you're between homes and having to make temporary living and storage arrangements, you need personal property and liability coverage at multiple locations. Do not cancel the homeowner's or renter's policy on the property you're moving from until coverage at the new, permanent location begins. That way, the contents and liability coverage from the homeowner's or renter's policy will continue to cover your needs while you're in transition.

A fairly common twist to the previous moving example occurs when, instead of doing all the moving yourself, you hire a moving and storage company to move your stuff to their warehouse, store it for you, and then move it again to the new home. Aren't the movers liable for anything that happens, including breakage, damage, and even water damage in storage?

It depends. If you don't make special arrangements, the fine print in your moving contract limits the moving company's liability for damage to your stuff to a fraction of its value, typically 50¢ per pound! (For your $2,000 big-screen TV that weighs 80 pounds, they would owe you only $80 \times 0.5 = \$40$.) The contract usually also exempts the movers from damage they didn't cause, such as flood damage to the property in storage.

Beware of moving contracts. They are usually very anti-consumer. Read them carefully, or have your insurance agent read them, so that you know what you're responsible for before a claim happens. The moving company may insure the full value of your property if you pay them a little extra, but still not for every kind of loss — many still exclude acts of God or groundwater, and they usually won't cover breakage unless you pay them to do the packing.

Before buying the optional insurance from the moving company, fax a copy of the coverage to your agent or attorney to make sure that there aren't any nasty surprises. I still prefer adding the special perils contents endorsement to your homeowner's or renter's policy, if you don't already have it. It's less expensive than the moving company's optional insurance and usually is far better coverage, except for the fact that it excludes breakage of dishes, china, and the like. If you want these items covered, get the mover's insurance.

Emptying Your Nest: Sending a Child to College

When you're getting ready to send your kid to college, your insurance needs may change. Here's a quick list of the types of insurance you'll want to look at and potentially alter:

- ✔ **Health insurance:** Most colleges offer optional student health coverage — buy it if it's inexpensive. This coverage enables your college student to access convenient care at the student health center. (Let's face it: The more convenient the care is, the more likely he'll be to get the care he needs right away.)

Don't rely on student health insurance exclusively, though — it's usually not that strong. Continue major medical coverage on your child as well, for the big stuff.

- ✔ **Car insurance:** Most insurance companies give a 10 percent to 25 percent discount for a B average or better, and another 30 percent to 40 percent (or more) discount if the student is attending college over 100 miles from home and has no car at school. Ask for the good student and distant student discounts.

You can eliminate all charges for your student while she's at school if she surrenders her driver's license. Just get a receipt and send it to your agent. This idea is especially good if your child has recent tickets or accidents that are driving your insurance rates sky high. If she comes home for the summer, she can then reactivate her license for three months. You'll have saved a bundle on insurance costs in the interim.

✔ **Personal property:** Most homeowner's policies extend your homeowner's contents coverage to your child's belongings at school. Most policies stop coverage after 45 days without occupancy (meaning, your kid can't leave the stuff unattended for the summer and still have it covered by insurance, but he can leave it over Christmas break). If he isn't spending the summer at school, bring the stuff home or store it.

If your kid has expensive valuables or an expensive laptop computer, those items can be scheduled on your homeowner's policy for the best possible insurance — covering everything from breakage to soda spilled on the keyboard.

✔ **Your liability for your kid's apartment:** Many college students, especially after a year or two, opt for an apartment off-campus rather than a dorm.

Do not cosign a lease to help your kid qualify for the apartment. Sign a rent guarantee instead, which guarantees that you'll make the rent payment if your student doesn't. Being a cosigner makes you potentially suable for everything that goes on in that apartment (like serious injuries at college parties).

If you've already made the mistake of cosigning the lease for your college student's apartment, buy some liability coverage for yourself. Adding the apartment to your homeowner's and umbrella liability policies should only cost about $20 a year.

It's Not Me, It's You: Divorcing

Ending a marriage is tough enough without the additional stress of insurance disputes. Here's my advice to help you minimize problems.

Before the divorce

Because the divorce process takes a long time (sometimes a very long time), spouses often live separately while still being legally married. Before your divorce is finalized, you need to address a couple insurance issues:

✔ **As soon as you both agree to start divorce proceedings, separate your cars onto separate policies.** Still list both names, if the vehicle titles are in both names, but your name should be first on your own policy; use your address on your own policy, too, so that the bills are mailed to you. This strategy gives you the best possible coverage and it keeps you from being victimized if your soon-to-be ex (intentionally or unintentionally) fails to pay the premium.

✔ **Cover yourself and your property if you move out of the house.** If you rented a new place, the primary homeowner's policy on the house you shared with your soon-to-be-ex provides no theft coverage and no liability coverage at your new apartment.

At the very least, get liability coverage for injuries and property damage at the apartment. The least expensive way to do that is through a policy endorsement added to the primary homeowner's policy (and umbrella policy if you have one), at a cost of about $20 a year.

If theft is a concern, buy a renter's policy covering the apartment — in both your name and your spouse's name until the divorce is final. Costs for these policies start at $150 a year and up.

In a separation and pending the divorce, don't remove the person who moved out of the house from the homeowner's insurance, even if the insurance company requests it. Both parties must remain as co-named insureds on the face sheet of the policy. Why? Because until the divorce is final, both parties still equally own the home, both have an interest in the house if it is damaged or destroyed, and both need worldwide personal liability coverage.

After the divorce

If you haven't already split up the car insurance, do so now. Do not remove either spouse from the homeowner's policy until the deed has been changed.

Be careful: Many times, following a divorce, the home is put up for sale and both parties continue to own it until it's sold. If that's the case, don't remove either party's name from the policy until the sale is finalized.

If either spouse has been covered under the other's group health insurance policy, that spouse will lose health insurance coverage when the divorce is final. If you're the one losing coverage, here are my suggestions:

✔ **If you have group coverage available on your job, request coverage from your employer right away, to start the date your coverage ends under your ex's policy.** If you do so within 30 days of the divorce, you're usually guaranteed coverage without having to qualify medically.

✔ **If you don't have coverage available through your job, exercise your COBRA right to continue coverage under your ex's group policy (if you're eligible) while applying for your own individual health policy.** (See Chapter 19 for more information on COBRA and HIPAA rights. See Chapter 18 for tips on buying individual health insurance.)

Rear-ended and blindsided

Cassandra called me one day to report that she was in a serious car accident. She was rear-ended. Her medical bills totaled over $40,000, and she ended up being away from work for about a year. She had, much to her surprise and anger, no car insurance to cover the accident. Why? About a year earlier, she and her husband separated and filed for a divorce. Her husband insured only his car and never told her that she wasn't covered, even though he had verbally agreed to continue insuring both cars.

Cassandra was unnecessarily victimized. Had she followed the advice here and split up the insurance as soon as they separated, her own personal auto policy would have covered her injuries and lost wages. Luckily, her health insurance covered her medical bills. But the rest of her loss she had to pay for out of her own pocket.

Make sure that you're the owner of your life insurance policy. Have the billing address changed to your address. And change the beneficiaries from your ex to your children or another person. Reevaluate your life insurance needs. You may need less or, if you're a single parent, you may need substantially more. (See Chapter 23 for tips on estimating your life insurance needs.)

If you declined disability insurance coverage in the past because your spouse's income more than covered the bills, buy it now. If your paycheck stops because of a disability, you'll be hurting if you don't have this vital coverage. (See Chapter 22 for tips on buying long-term-disability insurance.)

Hand Me My Gold Watch: Retiring

When you're retiring, you need to address some specific and unique insurance issues. To start, change the use of your car to pleasure use — you'll save about 15 percent to 20 percent on your car insurance. Also, make sure you're getting any senior discounts the insurance company offers.

Take the approved defensive driver course if your insurance company gives you enough credit off your premium. In Minnesota for example, seniors get a 10 percent credit off their rates for three years. Every state is different, so check with your agent.

What to do about your health insurance depends on your age and whether you qualify under the federal COBRA law (turn to Chapter 19 for more on COBRA continuation rights):

- ✔ **If you (or your spouse) are less than 62 years old or if you're not eligible for COBRA,** apply for guaranteed individual coverage under federal HIPAA laws for you and/or your spouse, and keep it until you're both 65 years old and qualify for Medicare. If you're healthy enough to qualify for an individual plan in the open market, and if the rates and/or coverage are better than your HIPAA plan, go that route instead.

- ✔ **If you're between 62 and 65 years old and you do qualify for COBRA,** exercise your right to continue your health insurance through your previous employer for up to 36 months, or until you qualify for Medicare. However, if you're healthy enough to qualify for an individual plan that is less expensive or offers better coverage than your COBRA plan, apply for that plan and, if approved, keep the individual plan to age 65 and drop the COBRA coverage.

- ✔ **If you're 65 or older,** apply for both Part A and Part B of Medicare directly from Medicare. Once approved, apply for a good Medicare supplement policy to plug the many shortcomings of Medicare. At that time, also apply for Medicare Part D (prescription drug coverage). I recommend that you buy both the supplement and Part D coverage from a knowledgeable agent because of their complexity.

   If you apply for a Medicare supplement policy and Part D within six months of turning 65 or losing your group coverage, whichever is later, there are no health questions — coverage is guaranteed. (See Chapter 20 for my tips on buying a good Medicare supplement and Part D. See Chapter 19 for more on your COBRA and HIPAA rights.)

Also, reassess your needs relative to life insurance. With less income, you may need less life insurance. If you still need life insurance and your health is poor, consider converting the group life insurance you had at work to a permanent, personally owned policy. Most group life insurance policies give you that option if you apply within 30 days of retirement.

Trust Me: Transferring Property to Trusts

Attorneys are increasingly recommending to their older clients that they transfer ownership of their home (and sometimes their personal property such as cars and boats) to a trust or to their adult children — usually for tax reasons. Although these transfers may save on taxes, they result in some serious insurance gaps if changes aren't made to the insurance program of the old and the new owner to cover the ownership change.

For example, Betty, age 68, follows her attorney's advice and transfers owner-ship of her $400,000 home and all its contents to a trust, with a provision that gives Betty the right to continue to live in the house for as long as she wants. If Betty has a $400,000 homeowner's policy on the house and a tornado destroys it, how much will the policy pay Betty? Not much. She's no longer the owner. And the trust has lost a $400,000 asset because the trust had no insurance on the home. Betty's policy wouldn't pay the trust because the trust isn't named on the policy.

If you transfer ownership of your home to anyone else — to a trust or to one or more of your adult children — you no longer can collect under your policy as the owner. And the new owners cannot collect under your policy either. You must make some changes to your homeowner's insurance at the moment ownership is transferred, covering the new owner's ownership interest.

The former owner of the property should co-name the new owner — the trust or the adult children — as co-named insureds on the declarations page (the coverage summary page) of the policy. This way, the old and new owners are equally protected against damage if they're both named and, as a bonus, the old and new owners are also equally protected for lawsuits. List any trust as a co-named insured on the umbrella liability policy as well.

If adult children, rather than a trust, receive the property, I recommend, in addition to being a co-named insured on the parent's policy, that the adult children extend their home and umbrella liability policies to the new loca-tion. This extension should cost about $20 a year.

Coping with the Death of a Loved One, and Caring for Your Loved Ones after You're Gone

One of the greatest acts of love is buying more life insurance than your sur-vivors will need. And make sure they know about it, as well as where you keep the policies. One of the saddest things I see survivors go through after a loved one dies is the hunt for the life insurance policies. If they can't be found, they'll never be collected on. Even if they eventually are found, search-ing for them is an unnecessary and traumatic experience for the survivors.

Make a list of every life insurance policy you have, make several copies of the list, and give the copies to two or more people. Include on the list the following:

✔ The insurance company name and address

✔ The policy number

✔ The effective date

✔ The death benefit amount

✔ The beneficiary

✔ The agent's name and phone number

✔ The location of the original policies

Here's a checklist for the survivors:

✔ Gather the original life policies (or the inventory form, if you have one). Ask the insurance companies to fax or mail you their claim forms. Have certified copies of the death certificate and copies of the newspaper obituary to file with each claim form.

✔ Don't take the deceased off any insurance policy, including the personal umbrella policy, until the deceased's ownership interests have been properly transferred. Otherwise, the estate is exposed, with no insurance.

✔ If a vehicle is involved, notify the auto insurance company of any new drivers.

If the deceased is not married, add the executor as a co-named insured onto the deceased's auto policy until the estate is settled. Otherwise, the car (for most uses) will be uninsured.

✔ If you've been covered as a family member under the deceased's group health insurance policy, you may have the right to continue coverage for up to 36 months under COBRA. You're also guaranteed the right, under federal HIPAA law, to apply for and receive an individual policy. If you're in good health, apply for an individual health policy.

✔ If the deceased had disability insurance, cancel it. There may be a refund due you on prepaid premiums.

Part V
Managing Life, Health, and Disability Risks

The 5th Wave   By Rich Tennant

"It's the strangest rider to a health insurance policy I've ever seen, but she was covered in the event she ever melted."

In this part . . .

Sometimes it seems as if there could be nothing more catastrophic than losing a home or a family heirloom, but there is. Keeping yourself and your loved ones safe and healthy is the most important thing in the world. Yet serious illnesses, injuries, and even death occur to everyone at some point. The only thing worse than having a serious health problem is having it without the proper insurance coverage in place. If you suffer an injury and you aren't prepared, your financial health can be destroyed in an instant.

In this part, I show you how to avoid suffering such catastrophic financial losses. I tell what you need to know to make good choices about individual and group health insurance. I also fill you in on long-term-disability and long-term-care insurance. I tell you about Medicare, including prescription drug coverage. Finally, I cover life insurance, so that you can still look after your loved ones, even when you're no longer around.

Chapter 18

Buying Individual Health Insurance

Most people are able to get the health insurance they need through their jobs. Lucky for them! But many people have to buy their own health insurance, for a variety of reasons (for example, they're self-employed, they work for a small company that doesn't provide health insurance, they retired before the age of 65, and so on). If you're in the market for individual health insurance, this chapter shows you what you need to know and what you need to do.

Chapter 19, on group coverage, contains lots of great information. Even if you're shopping for individual coverage, you may want to take a quick glance through it.

Discovering What Makes a Great Health Insurance Plan

Facing serious, life-threatening illness is traumatic. I know, I've been there. Everything else you're worrying about in life suddenly becomes unimportant. The only thing that could make it worse is fear. Fear about your health insurance coverage. Fear that the escalating bills will exhaust your coverage limit. Fear that the specialist you want to see for your illness isn't approved by your insurance company. Fear that holes in the coverage will leave you personally responsible for huge bills that could wipe out all your savings — and even put you in serious debt. That's why a solid health insurance plan is so important.

An excellent health insurance plan must include five key ingredients:

- ✔ **A coverage limit high enough that it won't likely ever be exhausted, even for the most catastrophic medical expenses.**

- ✔ **An annual dollar limit you can live with on your out-of-pocket maximum.** (The _out-of-pocket maximum_ is an important feature of health insurance policies that limits your annual responsibility for your health insurance policy copayments and deductibles.)

- ✔ **No dollar limits on types of expenses, such as dollar limits on daily room charges or dollar limits for types of surgical procedures.**

- ✔ **Freedom to see specialists without a referral.**

- ✔ **Worldwide coverage.**

Do most plans meet all five criteria? Nope. I estimate that less than half of the individual and group health plans sold in the United States include all five elements that make a great health insurance plan.

Why do these five elements matter? Because you want a plan that won't, even in the worst case, cause you major financial hardship — and a plan that lets you choose the most skilled care provider, especially in serious or life-threatening situations, such as treating your 6-year-old's leukemia, surgically removing your spouse's brain tumor, or performing skin grafting operations after you've been badly burned.

Setting a high enough coverage maximum

When I started selling insurance in the 1970s, health insurance policy limits were just $10,000 per claim. Policies were available that provided up to an additional $25,000 in coverage. My clients could sleep well with $35,000 in total coverage. Today, that same peace of mind requires at least a $3 million in coverage limit.

Policy limits come in two varieties:

- ✔ **A dollar maximum _per claim:_** The per-claim maximum is the most the insurance company will spend for any single illness or injury. If your limit is $1 million, for example, your policy will pay up to $1 million for your injuries in a recent car accident, and then up to another million for next year's cancer, and another million for the following year's Parkinson's disease.

> ✔ **A dollar maximum *per lifetime:*** Lifetime limits, where every dollar spent this year reduces the limit available for future years, are more common. If your lifetime limit is $1 million, your $225,000 car accident bill reduces your lifetime limit to $775,000. Then your $150,000 cancer bill reduces the $775,000 lifetime limit to $625,000, and so on.

When buying health insurance, I *strongly* recommend a maximum policy limit of at least $1 million *per claim* or $3 million *per lifetime* (or a policy with no limits at all, if you can find one).

Capping your out-of-pocket costs

Most health insurance plans require some kind of copayment on your part. (A *copayment* is the dollar amount your policy requires you to pay toward your bills.) You may have a copay per visit (such as $25 for each office visit or $75 if you go to the emergency room). Perhaps you have a deductible of $500 a year before your coverage kicks in (meaning that you pay the first $500 of your medical expenses each year). Or maybe your policy pays 80 percent of all covered medical bills, with you responsible for the other 20 percent.

Paying the per-visit copays or the deductible usually isn't a hardship. But paying 20 percent of all your major medical bills in one year, without any limit on the possible amount of your contribution, *can* be. If you have a baby who's born three months premature and who needs pediatric intensive care for a long time, your bill could run $400,000 — and your 20 percent copay would be $80,000! If your baby needs surgeries, your bill could jump to $750,000, and your 20 percent copay would be $150,000! That's too big a risk for almost anyone to assume.

Avoiding internal policy limits

A good health insurance policy has only one policy limit — either a limit per claim or a limit per lifetime. It contains no other dollar limitations. Many mediocre policies contain internal limits such as $200 a day for room and board, $400 a day for intensive care, or dollar limits on specific surgeries ($4,000 for an appendectomy, $35,000 for quadruple bypass surgery, and so on).

Even if the limits are adequate today (and most aren't), in four to five years, given the rapid pace of medical cost inflation, you may end up getting only half your bill paid.

Avoid like the plague any health insurance policy that contains internal policy limits on room and board, surgeries, or anything else.

If you have a group plan with internal limits from your employer, buy an excess major medical policy with a large deductible that has no internal limits, to pick up most of the shortcomings of the group plan.

Making sure you don't have to beg to see specialists

Many healthcare plans (such as many HMOs or PPOs) offer lower costs but take away your right to decide what kind of treatment you can get and whom you can get it from:

- Usually, you agree to get all your primary care from a small list of approved clinics where costs can be controlled more easily.

- You agree to seeing a specialist only if your primary physician will refer you out (which means "referral begging" to you).

- You agree to give the insurance company the final say on what type of procedure or treatment you can have.

That's a lot to give up for a savings of about 15 percent on your premiums.

If your employer-provided group plan doesn't offer choice, you can buy an individual major medical policy with a moderately high deductible. If you don't like your choices under managed care, you go see whomever you want and pay just your deductible.

Managed care worth considering

In recent years, a managed care hybrid plan has emerged. It's a two-tiered system. The first tier is managed care. When you go to your chosen primary doctor, you get almost 100 percent coverage — even if you see a specialist, if it's a referral from your primary doctor. The second tier is freedom of choice: You can go to almost anyone — any specialist — no referrals needed. You just have to chip in on the extra cost (for example, a $300 deductible, plus 20 percent of the bill). When something serious is going on, the extra out-of-pocket expenses for the freedom of choice are worth every penny.

Ensuring that you're covered away from home

Many managed care plans don't cover you outside your home territory, except for emergencies. Here are two stories from my own client files:

✔ Lee just bought a winter vacation condo in Arizona. (Why anyone would want to flee Minnesota's winter wonderland of ice, snow, and subzero temperatures is beyond me.) Checking the Medicare supplement policy he owned from a local HMO, he discovered that there was no coverage for anything but emergency care outside Minnesota — a real problem for someone living five months of each year outside the state. Luckily, we moved his coverage to another Medicare supplement policy that gave him greater freedom of choice before anything serious happened.

✔ Jim and Jane's daughter, Angela, was attending college out east. She fell and injured a knee. The emergency care was covered by their HMO policy, but follow-up care with physical therapists was not covered at all. It turns out that their otherwise excellent insurance has one major flaw: For anyone residing out-of-state part of the year, nonemergency care isn't covered!

Should you buy travel medical insurance? No way, no how

Travel medical insurance pays medical bills you incur through travel, within a certain date range and up to a dollar limit (such as $5,000). It's Las Vegas insurance, plain and simple. You're gambling that you'll get sick while you travel. Not a smart gamble — it violates almost all the rules for buying insurance that I introduce in Chapter 2. Plus, it often duplicates, unnecessarily, your existing health insurance. The only time that travel medical insurance may be of value is if you have a very large deductible on your health plan and you're buying travel medical insurance to cover the deductible while traveling.

If you're traveling abroad, call your health insurance company before you leave to find out its preferred method of handling claims incurred abroad. Is there a 24-hour toll-free phone number you can call? Are there any coverage restrictions abroad?

Warning: Be very careful if you do buy travel medical insurance. Read the policy carefully. Many are very restricted, so you may as well throw money down a rat hole.

Medical evacuation insurance: A potentially good idea

If you travel much, especially if you travel abroad, and you get seriously ill, the hospital or treatment facility you end up in may not be state-of-the-art in terms of doctors, equipment, or both. *Medical evacuation insurance* covers the costs of airlifting you from a remote area, in a medically equipped and staffed aircraft, to a top hospital.

Medical evacuation insurance does not duplicate any other insurance you have. A good policy covers the cost (about $35,000 to $75,000) of bringing an intensive-care jet, fully staffed and medically equipped, to wherever you are in the world and flying you to a preferred treatment facility. Coverage is available from travel agents, tours, and credit card companies on a per-trip basis, and from travel assistance companies who sell the coverage on an annual basis for people who travel frequently.

If the coverage and the company are good, medical evacuation insurance is a good idea, especially if you travel a lot or have a health condition (like a heart problem) that places you at greater risk for being in a medical emergency abroad.

If you buy medical evacuation insurance, try to find a policy that:

✔ Pays for you to be transported to your home hospital or another hospital of your choice — not their choice.

✔ Lets you (not a doctor, not a plan representative) make the call to evacuate or not — a huge advantage!

✔ Has no dollar limits on costs. (The cost to evacuate you from China may be $100,000!)

✔ Covers preexisting conditions. (This is very important — many plans do not.)

✔ Transports you at your option, regardless of medical necessity.

✔ Covers you while traveling within your home country — not just abroad.

✔ Provides a full medical staff.

The best company I've encountered is Med Jet Assist (phone: 800-963-3538; Web: www. medjetassist.com). It meets all the criteria I just listed. Plus, the policy is underwritten by the highly trusted Lloyds of London, and it's reasonably priced — $225 a year for individuals and $350 for families — no matter how often you travel.

Make sure that your policy covers you worldwide for nonemergency care. If it doesn't, either replace it or buy a supplemental policy that provides the coverage. Higher copayments for care given out of state are fine, as long as you have coverage.

Saving Money on Individual Coverage

You can cut costs on individual plans in three ways:

- ✔ You can reduce your coverage and the insurance company will give you a direct premium credit.

- ✔ You can put money into a health savings account (HSA) combined with an approved high-deductible health plan (HDHP). A HDHP is a high-deductible major medical policy that meets the requirements of the IRS for use in conjunction with an HSA. (See "Saving with health savings accounts," later in this chapter, for more information).

- ✔ You can opt for a higher deductible when your health and self-care are exceptional but when the insurance company has no way of lowering your premiums.

Changing your coverage

You can save money on your insurance by cutting out unneeded coverage. For example, if your individual policy currently includes coverage for maternity, and you know you're not going to need it, you can drop that coverage and save money on your insurance premium.

You can also cut back on doctor choice — by switching to an HMO from a PPO, for example.

Socking away money in a health savings account

An HSA operates like an individual retirement account (IRA) coordinated with an IRS-approved high-deductible major medical health insurance plan (HDHP). The big advantage of an HSA is that it allows you to pay for your major medical deductible as well as elective medical and dental expenses with pretax dollars. For most people, that's equal to a 25 percent to 30 percent savings on their medical and dental bills!

Here's how an HSA works:

✔ **As with an IRA, contributions are income tax deductible.**

✔ **Earnings on the account are tax sheltered.**

✔ **The maximum contribution per year is set annually by the government.** For each person age 55 and older, an additional "catch-up" contribution is allowed. To find out what the current allowable amounts are, as well as anything else you want to know about health savings accounts, go to www.ustreas.gov and click on the Health Savings Account link.

✔ **In order for the HSA contributions to be tax-deductible, you must also have an IRS-approved high-deductible health plan (HDHP).** The HDHP must include options for a minimum deductible and a maximum deductible set by the government each year. There usually is a cumulative family deductible amount for policies insuring two or more people in the family. There is no coverage under the policy until the entire family reaches the family deductible in a calendar year. (Be careful when choosing your family deductible!) There generally is an option for 80 percent coverage as well as 100 percent coverage after the deductible is satisfied.

Choose the 100 percent option. After you've satisfied the high deductible in a calendar year, you'll have peace of mind knowing that all covered expenses will be 100 percent paid, for the rest of the year.

✔ **From the HSA, you can pay your deductibles and most other medical and dental expenses that your health plan doesn't cover (such as laser eye surgery, glasses, contact lenses, hearing aids, and dental work).** Because the HSA money has never been taxed, you're paying those bills with pretax dollars — a huge advantage.

✔ **If you've stayed reasonably healthy, you can leave unused funds on deposit and either use them in future years or save them as supplemental retirement dollars.** If you don't use them for medical bills, withdrawals are taxed much like traditional IRAs when you do retire.

You can set up an HSA wherever you can establish an IRA — banks, savings and loans, investment houses, insurance companies, and so on. Because of the need to write checks to pay doctors and buy prescription drugs, I've found that banks work best — that way, you can have an account with both checks and a debit card.

You can make your life a lot easier when using an HSA to pay deductible expenses and other expenses by following these simple suggestions:

> ✔ Don't pay any medical bill or pharmacy charge until your insurance company has reduced the cost to its negotiated discount pricing.
>
> ✔ Fund the account early in the year so you have plenty of cash available if medical bills are sizable in the first quarter of the year.
>
> ✔ Keep all your receipts for all services you've paid through your HSA (medical bills, pharmaceutical bills, dental bills, and so forth) in a medical folder in case you ever get audited. For a complete and current list of IRS-approved medical and dental expenses, go to www.irs.gov and search for Publication 502, or call 800-829-3676 to have it mailed to you.)

Taking care of yourself and opting for higher deductibles

The best way to save money on an individual policy, without cutting back on coverage, is to quit smoking. Unlike group policies, almost all individual policies differentiate smokers from nonsmokers — significantly — because the claims costs for smokers are much higher.

Insurance companies don't offer individual health insurance to people who are high-risk medically. So, everyone else — from the super-fit and super-healthy to the average or below-average health risk — pays the same rate and shares the losses.

If you're healthy and take good care of yourself (through exercise, diet, stress management, rest, and personal safety), how can you get credit if insurance companies don't offer any? The answer: Opt for higher deductibles.

The difference in cost between a $300 deductible and a $1,000 deductible with some insurers is a whopping 45 percent! As the size of your family or age increases, that 45 percent can save you a *fortune* — especially when you consider that you're assuming only $700 more risk per person each year. If you're paying $4,000 a year for just yourself, 45 percent would save you $1,800 in premiums!

Pricing for each level of deductible is based on *average* risk. If you're much fitter and healthier than average, you're paying more than your share, no matter what level of coverage you buy. But the higher your deductibles, the more you'll save. Being above average in terms of health, your chances of having to spend that higher deductible are much less.

Getting paid to work out

How would you like to get paid cold hard cash to work out regularly? It would certainly be a little easier to crawl out of the sack at 5:30 a.m. on those cold winter mornings, wouldn't it?

Many health insurance companies are starting to give monthly credits of around $20 per month toward your health club membership if you can document that you work out at least 12 times a month. Check with your insurance company and see if it offers this deal, or just check with your club to see if your insurance company participates.

When deciding between two deductibles, choose the lower deductible if you're in doubt. You can raise your deductible later, anytime you want. But to lower it, the whole family must qualify medically — not likely if you've just incurred some big medical bills.

Coping with Health Insurance Problems

Throughout your life, you'll undoubtedly face tough decisions regarding health insurance. You'll be turned down because of a preexisting condition, your kid will go off to college and be offered insurance through school, your group coverage will end because you've lost your job. . . . These are just a few of the challenges I cover in this section.

When you can't get insurance

If you or a family member for whom you're responsible has a health condition for which you can't get insurance (in other words, you've been rejected for individual coverage), you need to broaden your way of looking at the problem. Very few people can't get health insurance for a medically uninsurable condition if they're willing to make some life changes.

Over the years, I've read numerous horror stories about families who have suffered financial ruin because of one family member's medical expenses. I remember one story in particular about a family who lost their insurance because of a job change. The new job didn't offer group insurance, and their son was uninsurable. He had an ongoing condition that required years of treatment and thousands of dollars of expenses. According to the story, this family sat helplessly while their life savings dwindled to nothing. You want to know the truly sad part? I believe that their financial ruin could have been prevented if they had considered some other choices.

If you're willing to take one or more of the following actions, you can prevent a financial catastrophe from happening to you because of an uninsured family member:

- ✔ **If your employer doesn't offer group coverage, talk to them about starting to offer a group plan.** Enlist the support of your coworkers. The Health Insurance Portability and Accountability Act of 1996 (HIPAA) requires insurance companies to accept all members of a group, regardless of health. If your employer adds group health insurance coverage, the worst-case scenario is that the condition won't be covered for the first 12 months. (See Chapter 19 for more information on preexisting conditions.)

- ✔ **Change employers.** Get a job with a company that offers group medical coverage to its employees and their families.

- ✔ **If you're in a state that has a major medical insurance plan for uninsurable people, sign up immediately.** Call your state insurance department to find out.

- ✔ **Move to a state that offers catastrophic individual major medical coverage for uninsurable citizens.** Minnesota, where I live, has such a plan, and so do many other states.

You may balk at the idea of doing something as seemingly drastic as changing jobs or moving to a different state in order to get health insurance for yourself or a sick family member. But from my perspective, those are far better alternatives than complete financial ruin.

Dread disease insurance: Just say no

We all have fears of one kind or another, and many of our fears have to do with getting sick with an awful disease. Some parts of the insurance industry have responded to those fears with policies that cover specific diseases — for example, policies that cover only cancer.

If you have a high-limit ($3 million to $5 million), high-quality major medical policy that already covers cancer, buying another $1 million of coverage just for cancer is throwing money out the window. However, if you have a poor medical policy (such as one with a $250,000 lifetime limit), buying an extra $1 million of coverage is a good idea — but not coverage just for cancer.

If you're considering buying a dread disease insurance policy (a policy that covers only specific illnesses) because your health insurance isn't very good, don't. Save your money and use it instead to get a top health insurance policy or an excess major medical supplement to the policy you have that covers all illnesses and injuries — not just the ones you fear.

If this story happened today instead of a few years ago, the new HIPAA law would have guaranteed this family — at the time the group coverage at the prior job was ending — the right to an individual policy regardless of health. And if certain conditions were met, the insurance would have covered their son's preexisting medical condition immediately. (See Chapter 19 for more on qualifying for HIPAA.)

When you're broke

If you're in a financial crisis — temporary or permanent — and you just don't have enough money available for health insurance, you can still protect yourself somewhat by managing your medical risks in advance.

If you don't develop a game plan for handling medical costs before you're faced with them, you may end up being personally responsible for the entire cost of any emergency care that you need.

Look into various assistance programs in which medical care is provided either at no cost or at a nominal cost. In my community, for example, programs are available through Lutheran Social Services or Catholic Charities. In exchange for a very small amount of money per month, all family members receive the medical care they need. Participants are limited to designated medical facilities, but they get medical care now, without facing a huge debt later. Also check in your area for free clinics.

If you or a family member is in economic distress, research what's available in your community now and have an emergency plan so that you know where you're going for care if and when you need it. A medical emergency isn't the time to figure out what your options are.

When your kids outgrow your policy

Depending on your particular insurance policy terms, your children are only covered under your family plan to a certain age — usually age 19 or, for full-time students, until 25. Insurance polices are very inconsistent on this.

Whether you have group or individual coverage, before your kid turns 18, check with your insurance company or agent and find out what your insurance company's rules are for maintaining coverage for your child. Find out how many credits your kid must carry per school semester to stay eligible. Will she be eligible in the summer if she hasn't registered yet for the fall semester? What if she drops out of school for a while? Get clear on all this beforehand. Claim time is not the time to find out that your child isn't insured.

School accident insurance: To buy or not to buy?

Most elementary and secondary schools send information home with students about insurance for injuries that occur on school grounds or at school events. It's most commonly offered to student-athletes.

Here's what I recommend you do:

✔ Assuming there aren't any exclusions to worry about and that it's reasonably priced, buy it if you have a high deductible on your health insurance plan.

✔ If you have minimal deductibles or copayments, don't buy it. It just duplicates coverage you already have.

When you have a kid in college

Should you buy the optional student health insurance available from your kid's college? If the insurance is provided automatically as part of tuition costs, should you drop your kid from your family health policy and rely exclusively on the school coverage?

When my clients come to me with these questions, I always ask them to send me a full copy of the college's student insurance policy. What I discover, in almost every case, is that the policy has

✔ Excellent preventive care — coverage for physicals, eye exams, and so on — at the student health center on campus

✔ Excellent coverage for other doctor care, if the care is provided at the student health center

✔ Hospitalization coverage at the university's hospital, but usually only for a limited time (such as 30 days)

✔ Poor medical coverage away from school — both hospital and doctor

✔ Poor coverage for substantial medical bills

✔ Often, no coverage during the summers

 My advice: Keep your student insured on the family health plan and buy the student health coverage, too. The school's coverage is usually pretty inexpensive. Plus, many family heath plans don't cover expenses incurred at your student's college health center anyway, and the student health insurance plans available from colleges always cover these expenses. If your kid can just drop by the campus health center, she's a lot more likely to get the care she needs than if she has to trek to the nearest hospital or doctor whom your plan covers. So buying the student health plan can help keep your student healthier.

The revolving-door college student

If you have a kid who can't seem to make up his mind about going to college (he's in for a semester, out for a semester, back in for a semester, and so on), and you're covered by a group policy that is eligible for COBRA continuation rights (see Chapter 19 more on COBRA), here are my recommendations:

1. **When he drops out, notify your employer to exercise the 36-month COBRA continuation option.**

   This way, your kid stays insured under your group insurance. The only difference is that you'll foot 100 percent of his premium costs (if you weren't already) while he's out of school.

2. **When he returns to school (and is taking the required number of credits), cancel COBRA and add him back onto your coverage as a dependent.**

   Each time he drops out and then returns, follow these same steps, until he reaches

the maximum age for students to be covered under your policy — usually age 25. If he's still in school when he reaches the maximum age for students to be insured on your policy, or if he's without insurance for any other reason, exercise his 36-month COBRA option until he can arrange coverage on his own individual health policy.

If he's not eligible for COBRA (in other words, if you have an individual policy or your employer has too few employees to qualify for COBRA), set him up with his own individual policy the first time he drops out of school. Then just keep his individual policy in force during the revolving-door period.

Remember: If he were turned down for health insurance because of health history issues, he would have the guaranteed right to an individual policy under HIPAA. (See Chapter 19 for more on HIPAA.)

Never drop your college student from your family health insurance plan, even if you buy the student health insurance offered by the college. You'll need your family plan for any serious claims.

When you need temporary health insurance

Many states allow health insurance companies to offer the public temporary health coverage to meet short-term needs (such as covering a person who's between jobs or a college student who isn't covered by student health insurance during the summer). Coverage is usually available in increments of 30, 60, 90, 120, and sometimes 180 days, and it's usually quite good — typically, temporary policies have a coverage limit of $1 million or more, and they usually include freedom of choice and a maximum amount on out-of-pocket expenses.

The biggest advantage to a temporary policy is that you can qualify with almost no medical questions asked. Coverage can be immediate, if needed.

But temporary coverage has several disadvantages:

- ✔ Preexisting conditions aren't covered. If you've ever been treated for a condition in the past, you won't be covered if the condition flares up again.

- ✔ The insurance is usually not renewable.

- ✔ When the coverage period you've chosen ends, so does the coverage — often, even if you're lying seriously ill in the hospital.

- ✔ Claim payments are often delayed.

- ✔ Coverage outside the country is often excluded.

Because of these major limitations, you generally want to avoid buying temporary insurance unless you have no other option. If you're between jobs, continue your group coverage from your prior employer under COBRA if you can. And for summer coverage for college students, keep them continuously insured all year round under your family plan.

In one situation, temporary coverage makes sense — when you're applying for individual coverage and you currently have no insurance. You complete an application and pay a premium to apply for individual coverage. If the insurance company approves you, it'll generally issue your policy retroactively, if you desire, effective on the date you applied. If, while your application was pending, you were hospitalized or incurred other medical bills, those bills would be covered. But what if the company declines your application? You would be uninsured for any bills that you'd accumulated since you applied, even if the medical conditions were new.

Even after you apply for individual coverage and pay the initial premium, you're not necessarily covered. Only if the company later approves you — a process that normally takes 30 to 60 days — will you have been covered since the date of your application. That's a long time to risk being uninsured.

Here's how you can use short-term coverage to protect yourself when you have no insurance and while your application for long-term coverage is being considered:

1. **Buy a 60-day short-term policy to be assured of insurance coverage for any new medical condition or injury that occurs while your long-term application is being considered.**

2. **Apply simultaneously for long-term coverage, requesting an effective date, if approved, for 60 days from now to coincide perfectly with the expiration of your short-term policy.**

Then, if your long-term policy application is rejected, you at least had coverage for new conditions while your application was being reviewed. Without the short-term coverage, the new medical problems would have been totally uninsured.

When you're getting a divorce

Because about 50 percent of the marriages in the United States end in divorce, the problem of continuing health insurance after a divorce is significant. Your options depend on which spouse has insurance and through whom:

- ✔ **If both spouses are employed full-time and have their own group health insurance coverages,** health insurance isn't a problem.

- ✔ **If both spouses have group coverage available through their employers, but one spouse has declined employer-based coverage and opted to be covered under the other spouse's policy,** all he needs to do is apply for coverage at his own place of work within 30 days of being dropped from his ex's policy, to avoid having to qualify medically.

- ✔ **If only one spouse has group coverage available through his employer and the other spouse doesn't have group coverage available at work,** the one being dropped from the group coverage should obtain an individual policy through an agent. Coverage may be guaranteed under federal HIPAA laws (see Chapter 19 for more on HIPAA rights).

If you have kids, things can get more complicated. When both parents are employed and each has coverage at work, the best thing to do is normally to continue the children's coverage through the parent whose coverage is best for the children.

But what if one parent is required in the divorce decree to pay for the children's coverage and the children are currently not on that parent's policy? Here's an example: Sue and Tom divorce. The court orders Tom to pay the children's health insurance costs to age 19. But Sue has them insured under her plan. Their options are as follows:

- ✔ Sue can continue having them on her plan with Tom reimbursing her — but getting that reimbursement sometimes can be a source of conflict.

- ✔ Tom can move them to his plan, usually without the children having to qualify medically if the move is done within 30 days of the divorce. But transferring coverage is a problem if Sue doesn't like Tom's policy or his plan won't cover the children's doctors.

✔ Sue can set up an individual policy covering just the children, with the bills sent to Tom (assuming that the children can qualify medically).

I like the option of setting up an individual policy, especially if Tom has the premiums paid electronically from his checking account and Sue's mailing address is on the policy. This way, the premiums are always paid on time, so the chances of a cancelled policy and a resulting uninsured claim are reduced. By having Sue's mailing address listed on the policy, Sue gets copies of the policies and changes, as well as any late premium notices if the electronic payment isn't made for whatever reason.

An individual plan also gives the parents more flexibility to determine the coverage they want for their children. And the coverage won't end if Tom or Sue's job ends, which is safer for the children's welfare and much less stressful for their parents. (See Chapter 19 for information on how the children's application for individual coverage may be guaranteed, regardless of any pre-existing health problems.)

When you become self-employed

If you're leaving your job to become self-employed, don't continue your COBRA option for the entire 18 months before applying for individual coverage. The problem with continuing COBRA this long is that it risks future insurability — during those 18 months, your health may go bad, and when the 18 months are over, you'll be stuck with less-than-desirable choices.

Here's a three-point plan I recommend that reduces the risks of coming up short on COBRA:

1. **When you leave your job, continue your group coverage under COBRA, if you're eligible, so that you'll have uninterrupted health insurance coverage.**

2. **Stay with COBRA while you test the self-employment waters.**

   If you don't like self-employment, just continue COBRA until you're back working for another company and are covered by its group plan.

3. **The moment you decide to stay self-employed, apply for a good individual health plan, keeping COBRA while your application is being evaluated.**

   If you're approved, drop COBRA. If you're declined, keep COBRA until you've located replacement insurance (see "When you can't get insurance," earlier in this chapter).

Chapter 19

Making the Best Group Health Insurance Decisions

In This Chapter

▶ Choosing among group health insurance options

▶ Continuing coverage when you leave your job

*T*he good news about group health insurance is that somebody else is paying part of the premium. The bad news is that your plan choices are somewhat restricted, and the coverage stays with the job when you leave. In this chapter, I help you make good choices about group health insurance while you're employed and offer my recommendations about continuing your coverage after you leave.

Picking the Best Group Health Insurance

Having to make group health insurance decisions can be difficult. There's no agent in your corner who can coach you. The insurance company or your employer can answer questions, but they can't give advice. Without good information, it's easy to make a serious mistake.

These are just a few of the kinds of questions I get from my clients about their group health insurance programs:

✔ Should I cover my spouse under my group insurance even though she's covered on her own policy at her job?

✔ How can I, as a single parent, avoid paying for a nonexistent spouse under the group family rate?

✔ Should I insure my college daughter on my group plan if she buys the school health insurance coverage?

✔ I have three different group plans to choose from at work. Which is best for me?

The following sections give you some tips on making good decisions on these and other issues.

Choosing between two or more plans

I often get calls from clients who want help choosing among group insurance options offered to them at work. Having multiple options is especially common with large employers or the government. If your employer offers more than one group health insurance option, I recommend that you do the following:

✔ **Consider price last.** The only exception to this rule is if your finances are in poor condition. Otherwise, set aside cost for now.

✔ **Look at the five ingredients of a good health insurance plan (see Chapter 18) and see how the insurance options you have to choose from compare.** With any luck, at least one of the available plans includes all five ingredients. If it does, take that one.

If two or more plans include all five ingredients, choose the one that also has paperless claims (meaning the doctors and hospitals file the claims directly to the insurance company). If two or more plans also offer paperless claims, then, and only then, decide on price.

Suppose your employer offers these three choices for group health plans for your family of four:

✔ Option A is a true freedom-of-choice plan where you can go anywhere you want for care. The only drawback is that you have to file your own claims. Your monthly cost is $750.

✔ Option B is a limited-choice managed-care plan. It meets only one of the five key criteria of a good plan — it has a limit on annual out-of-pocket expenses. Its only advantage is low cost — $475 per month.

✔ Option C is a hybrid of A and B. You can get care anywhere without a referral. Its only drawback is that if you go outside the rather substantial primary-care network (86 percent of the doctors in the state), you'll face a $300 deductible and probably will have to file your own claim. Your cost is $650 per month.

If these were your choices, you'd choose Option B only if, due to poor finances, price was all-important. It meets only one of the five criteria of a good plan.

You'd choose Option A if access to any doctor anywhere was worth the extra $1,200 a year and you could stand to file your own claims.

Personally, I would choose Option C. (In fact, these were my choices, and I did choose C.) It meets all five criteria of a good plan, and claims are paperless. I'm comfortable with the doctors who are available to me, and I can actually go to any other doctor if I'm okay with higher copays and filing my own claims.

To help you make a good decision, if you're still unclear about what choice to make, consider spending $100 to $200 to consult with a good insurance agent you know who is an expert on health insurance — maybe the agent who helped you with your life insurance. Bring in your group insurance options. You shouldn't need to buy more than one hour of the agent's time.

Covering your spouse and dependents

The following list includes some of the issues I'm asked about regarding how best to cover family members, along with my recommendations:

- ✔ **Double-covering a spouse:** The question of whether to cover a spouse under your plan as well as under your spouse's plan comes up most often when each spouse has coverage paid entirely by the employer and one of the two employers also pays all or most of the spouse's and dependents' coverage.

    Don't double-cover yourself or your spouse. When two companies insure the same person, you can't collect twice, so claims are shared or fought over. It becomes a claims nightmare. Instead, choose the plan that best meets the five criteria of a good health insurance plan.

- ✔ **Covering children when both spouses have a group plan:** Where should you cover the children — under your plan or your spouse's? In this situation, you weigh out-of-pocket costs in premiums, copayments, and deductibles against the coverage of each plan. These out-of-pocket costs can be dramatically different. But again, choose the plan that best covers the five criteria. Price should be the least important part of the decision.

    When choosing which plan is best, don't minimize how important the ability to choose top specialists will be if one of your precious ones is facing a serious illness or injury.

✔ **Avoiding the single-parent penalty:** The most equitable group plans charge a price per head. So if you're a single parent, you don't pay for a nonexistent spouse. Or if you're childless, you don't pay for nonexistent children. But it doesn't always work that way. Sometimes group insurance offers only two choices — individual and family. Family includes husband, wife, and all children for one price. But family also includes single-parent families and childless families. If your family is small, you pay the same amount as a person with a very large family.

Here's how you can avoid paying for nonexistent family members, assuming that your dependents are in good health:

- Accept the group coverage on yourself because the employer is footing at least part of the cost.

- Buy a quality individual policy for your dependents.

If even one of your dependents has a health problem that would make him ineligible for individual coverage, bite the bullet and pay the family rate at work to get your dependent covered.

Continuing Coverage When You Leave Your Job

Since 1985, the federal government has taken steps to allow employees and dependents to continue their health insurance when they would otherwise have lost it due to terminated employment, divorce, or other life events. The government's goal has been to try to make group health insurance portable, especially for those whose medical history would not allow them to qualify for individual health policies. In this section, I fill you in on two federal laws that may give you some insurance continuation rights when you lose your group health coverage, and I offer advice on when to exercise those rights.

Understanding COBRA

The Consolidated Omnibus Budget Reduction Act (COBRA) gives employees of companies that employ 20 or more people the right to continue group medical coverage at their expense when their coverage under an employer's plan ends, for a period of time — usually 18 months or 36 months.

Generally, COBRA applies only to employers with 20 or more employees. But several states have enacted laws requiring COBRA to apply to smaller employers, too. Check with your state insurance department or click on your state on the National Association of Insurance Commissioners Web site (www.naic.org/state_web_map.htm) to see what the laws are where you live.

Discovering what triggers eligibility

You're eligible for COBRA if any of the following occurs:

- Your employment ends for any reason other than gross misconduct.

- You, as a covered spouse, and the covered employee get divorced or legally separated.

- Your hours are reduced below the minimum necessary to qualify for group coverage.

- You become eligible for Medicare.

- You become totally disabled.

- You cannot continue your children's coverage after their age disqualifies them from continuing under your group plan — the cutoff age is typically 19 (or up to 25 for a full-time student).

- The covered employee dies, if you're the spouse or child of the employee.

Understanding your rights when a COBRA event is triggered

You've lost your job. Your health coverage is ending on the last day of this month. Your boss has handed you a form to sign with your decision on whether you want to continue your health insurance under the company's group policy. You're wondering, "Do I have to decide right away? How long do I have to make payments if I do elect COBRA?"

Here are some answers to those and other questions:

- **Required notices:** Your employer must notify you of your COBRA rights in writing when you're first hired and at the time of a triggering event. And when the triggering event happens, you have 60 days from the *later* of the day the notice was sent to you or the day your group health coverage ends to elect your COBRA continuation option.

- **Payment of premiums:** You have 45 days from the date you officially elect to continue your group coverage to pay the employer the first premium. You must pay retroactively back to the date your group coverage ended. So if your group coverage ended on June 30 and you elect to continue under COBRA on August 29, you have until approximately mid-October before the first premium is due. But if the premium is $700 a month for your family, you would need to remit $2,800 for July, August, September, and October, plus another $700 by October 31!

  After you've elected the coverage, all future monthly premiums for each month are due by the first of that month, although, by law, you can be up to 30 days late and not lose your coverage.

The employer is not required to, and generally will not, bill you. So if you forget to send a payment within 30 days of the due date, you're uninsured retroactively on the due date and you lose all further COBRA continuation rights.

If you know that you'll need the coverage for only a short time (for example, you're eligible for coverage from your new employer in 120 days), eliminate the risk of accidentally missing a payment due date. Pay your ex-employer the full four months of premium payments in advance.

✔ **Termination:** COBRA continuation coverage ends when:

• You voluntary terminate it.

• Premiums aren't paid within 30 days of the monthly due date.

• A covered person becomes covered under another plan.

• A covered person becomes covered by Medicare.

• The employer discontinues offering group health insurance to all employees.

• The COBRA continuation maximum period has ended.

To find out more about COBRA rights in your state, check with your state insurance department.

Making your COBRA election decision

If you're not sure whether to exercise your COBRA rights, here are a few general guidelines to help you with your decisions:

✔ **Don't go even a day without major medical insurance.** Remember the rule from Chapter 2: Don't risk more than you can afford to lose.

✔ **Don't use temporary health insurance when you're between jobs, if you qualify for COBRA.** Always exercise your COBRA continuation option instead. Yes, it's more costly, but unlike temporary policies, it covers preexisting conditions.

✔ **Do exercise your COBRA continuation options anytime your maximum possible need for coverage won't exceed the maximum period of your COBRA option.** The COBRA option is seamless, and it allows you to continue using the same doctors in the transition period.

✔ **If the maximum possible need for coverage exceeds the length of your COBRA options, do continue COBRA for the short term while applying for individual coverage.** Then drop the COBRA option when the individual policy is approved and all preexisting conditions are fully covered. (See Chapter 18 for your rights to an individual policy under HIPAA.)

Understanding HIPAA

The goal of the Health Insurance Portability and Accountability Act of 1996 (HIPAA) is to make it possible for you to move from one job to another when you or family members have health problems that otherwise would keep you trapped in your current job because either you would be turned down for health insurance at a new job or your preexisting medical problems would be excluded. (See the sidebar "Hip-HIPAA-hooray!" for an example of how HIPAA makes it possible to change jobs.)

HIPAA rules also entitle a person losing group insurance at an employer, after COBRA options expire, to apply for individual coverage with no preexisting condition exclusion if they meet certain conditions.

A *preexisting condition* generally means any physical or mental health problem diagnosed, cared for, or treated in the six months prior to the enrollment date on your new group plan.

The HIPAA law makes it possible for you to change jobs even if you have a preexisting medical condition by

✔ Requiring that all insurers of groups of two or more employees cannot decline coverage on a new applicant for group insurance solely for health reasons.

✔ Limiting the length of time a preexisting condition can apply to a newly hired employee to 12 months (18 months for late entrants).

✔ Giving credit for any prior group or individual coverage during the 12 months prior to the effective date of the new group coverage. (For example, if you had coverage for 9 of the past 12 months, you would have only a 3-month exclusion on preexisting conditions.)

✔ Banning pregnancy and prenatal problems from being considered preexisting conditions.

Be sure to check for the most current information on HIPAA before acting. Laws can and do change.

HIPAA rules apply to any application for group health insurance offered by a company that has two or more employees. It also applies to applications for individual health insurance plans but only if your prior coverage was group coverage.

HIPAA rules don't apply to changes from one individual health policy to another individual or group health policy. You can still be declined because of preexisting problems or have preexisting health problems excluded from the coverage. Therefore, don't ever drop an existing individual plan for another individual plan if you have preexisting conditions that won't be covered under the new plan.

Whenever individual or group health coverage you have is terminated (by you or by the employer), HIPAA rules require that the insurer provide you with a *certificate of credible coverage.* Give the certificate to your employer when you start your new job, and apply for the new company's group coverage. Likewise, give the certificate to your health insurer when you apply for an individual policy. As long as you've had health coverage for at least 12 months, with no lapse of 63 days or more, you can't be turned down for coverage or be subject to any unique limitations on account of preexisting conditions.

Hip-HIPAA-hooray!

Before HIPAA

Bill, a bright 43-year-old engineer, is stuck in a dead-end job doing work he loathes. He knows about some much better-paying jobs doing work he would be perfect for, but he can't take them. He's stuck. Why? Because he has an 8-year-old son with an enlarged heart — a condition that has already required two surgeries with at least two more scheduled in the next five years. If Bill takes a new job, either his son will be turned down for coverage or the heart condition will be excluded. So Bill's hands are tied. He can't make the job change he would love to make.

After HIPAA

Bill can take the best job he can find without any insurance concerns. Because he's had continuous coverage for more than the past 12 months, HIPAA guarantees that he can't be turned down, nor can there be a preexisting condition applied for his son's heart condition. Bill is a happy camper.

But suppose Bill wanted a break. He takes a six-month sabbatical between the old job and the new. How can he keep all the protection of HIPAA? Simple. He just has to elect to continue his prior group coverage, under COBRA, during the sabbatical.

Chapter 20

Buying Medicare and Supplements

. . . .

In This Chapter

▶ Understanding the four parts of Medicare

▶ Recognizing Medicare's shortcomings

▶ Discovering what makes a good Medigap policy

▶ Saving money with lower-cost options

. . . .

*1*f you're approaching 65 years old, you're about to enter a new dimension — a dimension of time and space unlike any place you've ever been. You're about to become eligible for America's national health insurance program for seniors — Medicare.

Remember when you were a kid, going to an amusement park? Remember the fun house with all the funny mirrors, barrels, slides, and trap doors that surprised you? That, for most people, is the Medicare experience. In fact, for many seniors, dealing with Medicare choices is a lot more like a haunted house: scary, eerie, overwhelming, full of surprises and bad outcomes. And those bad outcomes can be financially disastrous for you.

There is no shortage of Medicare information available to seniors — excellent information, in fact. However, the amount of the information — no matter how excellent — is overwhelming to most people. Don't feel bad: Medicare — with all its options, enrollment periods, supplements, and more — has been one of the most difficult insurance programs I've had to learn and keep up with.

I have one goal in this chapter: to empower you to make excellent choices regarding your Medicare options in a series of several steps. These are the exact recommendations I give to my clients who are becoming eligible for Medicare.

In this chapter, I deviate from the norm by sharing my bottom-line recommendations first. Follow that advice, and you'll be in good shape — you'll have great coverage and the easiest path. If you want the rest of the story, you can read on. If you don't, skip it!

Cutting to the Chase

As you turn 65, you're in one of three situations:

- ✔ You're still being covered by an employer's group health plan (yours or your spouse's).
- ✔ You're still covered by an individual plan, which will end when you turn 65.
- ✔ You're completely uninsured.

Regardless of your current situation, make sure you find an agent you can work with who is an expert on Medicare plans and supplements in your geographic area. The cost of the expertise is usually zero. You'll have a better-designed plan with much less frustration. (See Chapter 4 for more information on buying insurance the right way — with professional help.)

I refer to Medicare eligibility starting at age 65 but, in fact, it can start for anyone on a Social Security Disability Insurance (SSDI) claim who has been receiving benefits for 24 months. It also can start with anyone who has been diagnosed with end-stage rental disease (ESRD). My comments in the rest of the chapter apply to all three groups of people.

If you're covered by a group health policy at age 65

If you're covered by a group health policy either by your employer or a spouse's employer, you're fortunate. In addition to identifying an expert agent you can work with, you have two simple steps to follow:

1. **Sign up for Medicare Part A hospital coverage only, three months before you turn 65.**

2. **Decline all other Medicare options and Medicare supplement options until three months before you're losing your group coverage.**

   Then follow the advice in the next section.

If you aren't covered by a group health policy at age 65

The vast majority of retirees fall into this category. If you're in this group, start by identifying an expert agent to help you with your process. I guarantee you that your path will be so much easier for you if you take this advice.

In this scenario, there are three steps:

1. **Three months before you turn 65, sign up for Medicare Part A hospitalization and Medicare Part B medical coverage.**

   Ask that your start date be the first day of the month in which you turn 65.

2. **Prepare a list of all your current medications.**

3. **When you get your Medicare card, showing that you have both Part A and Part B coverage, make an appointment with your insurance agent to talk about Medicare Part D prescription drug coverage and a Medicare supplement policy.**

   Bring your list of current medications and your Medicare card with you to your appointment. Work with your agent to find a Part D plan that covers all your current medications.

If you don't take any medications now and you're inclined not to buy the Part D coverage yet, buy it anyway to avoid late-enrollment penalties later. Just buy the cheapest plan you can find — don't worry about choosing the perfect Part D coverage plan. You can change plans between November 15 and December 31 every year, to start January 1, regardless of your health or the number of medications you take.

With your agent's help, also buy a good Medicare supplement (also known as a Medigap policy) to cover most of what Medicare doesn't cover.

Choose your Medigap policy carefully because you can't change plans later on usually without medically qualifying. (See the "Determining what makes a good Medicare supplement" section, later in this chapter, for information on what makes a good Medicare supplement policy.)

Understanding Medicare Basics

Medicare has four components:

- ✔ **Part A:** Part A covers hospital bills. It's free to you if you've worked at least ten years in Medicare-covered employment. And it's a good thing it's free, because Part A is mandatory. You set it up through Medicare.

  Part A has a deductible that you must pay before coverage kicks in. It doesn't offer coverage outside the United States.

  In addition to the deductible, Part A has significant copayments, set up by Uncle Sam, for each day of hospitalization beyond 60 days. It has a maximum of 90 days of hospital coverage per illness, with an additional 60 days that can be used only once in your lifetime.

- ✔ **Part B:** Part B covers non-hospital bills (doctor and related bills). Part B has an income-adjusted monthly cost. For your Part B costs, call 800-633-4227 or go to `www.medicare.gov`. Part B is optional, and you set it up through Medicare.

  Part B has a deductible that you must pay before coverage kicks in. It doesn't offer coverage outside the United States.

  Part B has a front-end deductible when you visit a doctor, have lab tests, or incur other medical bills. Then Medicare pays 80 percent of *approved* medical and doctor bills, without limit. You're responsible for the other 20 percent of approved bills, plus 100 percent of any excess charges beyond what Medicare allows. If you have a $100,000 open-heart surgery bill, Medicare may, for example, approve $60,000 and pay $48,000 (80 percent), leaving you owing $52,000!

- ✔ **Part C:** Part C, a managed-care option, is called Medicare Advantage. Part C is optional. (See "Saving Money on Medicare Costs," later in this chapter, for more information on Part C.)

- ✔ **Part D:** Part D covers prescription drugs. Part D is optional. You purchase it directly from an insurance company, ideally with the help of an expert agent.

Most people sign up for parts A, B, and D right away when they become eligible — usually at age 65. Some people who are still employed and have group coverage at work delay buying parts B and D until they retire or lose their coverage — which is a good idea, by the way.

Discovering Medicare's pitfalls

In the beginning of Chapter 18, I lay out the five crucial components of a good health insurance plan. See Table 20-1 for how Medicare stacks up.

Table 20-1	Evaluating Medicare
Health Insurance Criteria	*How Medicare Measures Up*
High coverage maximum	Room and board are limited to 90 days maximum per illness, plus 60 extra days to be used once in your life.
Cap on out-of-pocket expenses	Your 20 percent Part B copay has no cap. And, of course, Medicare doesn't pay for any expenses that are unapproved by them.
No internal coverage limits	Medicare sets limits on doctor charges at their discretion.
Freedom of choice of doctors	There are no restrictions on doctors — unless you opt for managed care, which I don't recommend you do.
Worldwide coverage	Medicare provides coverage in the United States and U.S. territories only.

Would you buy Medicare if it were sold in the marketplace? No way! It meets only one of the five criteria of a good plan — there are no restrictions on the doctors you see. In fact, most states wouldn't even approve the product to be sold. Fortunately, the insurance industry has responded to the shortcomings of Medicare with Medicare supplement policies (known as *Medigap* policies) that plug many of Medicare's coverage gaps.

Don't have original Medicare parts A and B without a good Medicare supplement policy. Period.

Determining what makes a good Medicare supplement

A good Medicare supplement should:

- ✔ Pay all of Part A hospital costs, for at least one year beyond what Medicare pays for (90 to 150 days).

- ✔ Pay all of the 20 percent of Part B doctors' charges that Medicare allows but doesn't pay, plus at least 80 percent of the charges Medicare disallows.

- ✔ Include immediate medical coverage outside the United States — worldwide — with either no limit or a very high limit.

- ✔ Include coverage for nonemergency medical care, without penalty, when the care is provided in a state other than your home state.

- ✔ Include the freedom to choose doctors and hospitals countrywide.

Note: I intentionally left payment of the Part A and Part B deductibles off the list of criteria for a good supplement because even the worst Medicare supplement usually pays those. Plus, neither of the deductibles will cause you major financial hardship if you have to pay them yourself.

The majority of Medicare supplements fail to meet all the criteria I just listed.

The two most common shortcomings of a poor Medicare supplement are the following:

- ✔ It doesn't provide extra days of hospital coverage.
- ✔ It doesn't pay anything toward the portion of doctors' charges that Medicare disallows.

Federal law gives you a six-month open enrollment period for a Medigap policy of your choice — three months before and three months after the start date of your Part B coverage. (If you are still employed and/or are covered by group insurance, you should wait to sign up for Part B until your group coverage ends.) During the open enrollment period, you can get any Medicare supplement you choose, guaranteed, with no medical questions asked. After that six-month period ends, you have to medically qualify to get a supplement.

Some new changes to Medicare laws also allow you to get any Medicare supplement, regardless of health, if you move out of state, if your plan is canceled, or if your benefits are reduced.

Start shopping for a supplement about three months before the month of your 65th birthday. Apply for a Medigap policy about one month before you turn 65 so that coverage coincides with your Medicare start date. You'll need to show a Medicare ID card proving that you have both Part A and Part B before you can apply.

Never, under any circumstances, buy more than one Medicare supplement. If you currently have a poor one, don't buy another poor one to supplement your first poor policy. Instead, replace the existing, poor policy with a good one.

A very small percentage of unscrupulous insurance salespeople have, over the years, sold seniors — worried that major medical costs could wipe out their savings — multiple policies. If you're one of those seniors, find someone to help you choose the best policy to keep, and cancel the rest. You can also lodge a complaint with your state insurance department — it may prosecute the insurance agent.

Choosing your Medigap policy

Comparing Medigap policies used to be a horrendous job. Separating the handful of good policies from the scores of mediocre ones was a supreme challenge even for an insurance expert. But not anymore. The job of comparing Medigap polices has become much easier. In fact, in every state except Minnesota, Wisconsin, and Massachusetts, Medigap policies must be one of 12 flavors — plans A through L.

Plans F, G, I, and J meet all the requirements of a good Medicare supplement. They're the only plans that cover the excess charges that Medicare disallows. Plans G, I, and J do provide at-home recovery care as well as meeting all the other criteria.

For a comparison of the 12 plans, as well as other information on Medigap policies, go to www.medicare.gov/medigap/default.asp and download the excellent booklet "Choosing a Medigap Policy: A Guide to Health Insurance for People with Medicare." (You can also order the booklet by calling 800-633-4227.)

Select and save a bundle

Medicare allows insurance companies that offer Medicare supplement policies to somewhat limit the network of participating physicians for a significant reduction in cost. These plans are called *select plans.*

Case in point: Minnesota, where I hang my shingle, is one of many states that allow insurers to offer the select products. Blue Cross of Minnesota does just that under the Senior Gold label. The only condition is, for care in Minnesota, you must limit your choice to a Blue Cross of Minnesota provider network, which represents over 90 percent of doctors and specialists in Minnesota and all the hospitals. Even the Mayo Clinic belongs. You can see specialists at any time without a referral. Plus, if you're traveling or even move south for the winter, you can see any Blue Cross–affiliated doctor

or hospital, and claims will be paid exactly as if you were receiving care in Minnesota. All claims are paperless (meaning, you don't get stuck with the paperwork headaches). The only catch: If you get nonemergency care from a non–Blue Cross provider, that care will not be covered by the Medigap policy.

How big are the savings with the Blue Cross select plan? A whopping 40 percent to 60 percent off of Blue Cross's full-access plans. Even if you move to another state, you can keep this Medicare supplement plan. That's why, in most cases, I recommend Senior Gold for most of my clients.

There are several other quality plans in Minnesota and elsewhere that are similar. Make sure to ask your agent about the select plans she has available.

Medigap policies are available from private insurance companies, but insurance companies do not have to offer all 12 plans, so you may have to shop around to find the plan you want.

Getting prescription drug coverage

Medicare Part D prescription drug coverage is purchased from private insurers (unlike Medicare's Part A and Part B, which are purchased directly from Medicare itself). Private insurers service the Part D coverage and pay claims and then are reimbursed by Medicare behind the scenes. Because the government is picking up the majority of the prescription drug costs, the insurance company's administrative charge typically is very small.

Part D must have been created by a committee — it's confusing and illogical. You pay an annual deductible. Then Part D pays about 75 percent of the next couple of thousand dollars of the bill. Then, for some reason, you're completely out of pocket from that point on, until your total out-of-pocket expenses in the calendar year exceed $4,000. (These amounts vary over the years, but you get the idea.) This uncovered $4,000+ gap is often referred to as the "doughnut hole." When you have hit that out-of-pocket maximum, Part D pays approximately 95 percent of the balance of your prescription drugs for the rest of the calendar year. The worst part of the plan is that, by law, you can't buy insurance to cover the $4,000+ doughnut hole. (What possibly would possess them to make insuring that risk illegal? That's what I want to know.)

Here's what you need to know about your Part D decision:

- ✓ **Choose a skilled agent to help you make a good Part D choice.**

- ✓ **Put together a list of all your medications and pick a Part D plan from an insurance company with a good reputation and with a plan that covers all the meds you currently take.** Not all Part D drug plans cover exactly the same medications in the same way.

- ✓ **Even if you don't want prescription drug coverage now because you don't use prescribed drugs currently, choose some plan — the cheapest you can find.** Otherwise, when you do want the coverage later on, there's a 12 percent penalty added for each year you delayed your enrollment — and that penalty lasts *as long as you live!*

- ✓ **Don't agonize over your choice.** Even if you chose poorly, every year from November 15 through December 31, you can change plans to another plan you want, regardless of your health. The effective date of the change will be the following January 1.

Saving Money on Medicare Costs

There are two primary ways to purchase Medicare. You can buy Part A (hospital), Part B (medical), Part D (prescription drugs), and a Medicare supplement. This approach is the one I recommend to most of my clients because it gives them the broadest choice of provider care.

But suppose your budget is tight and you're willing to sacrifice some benefits in exchange for much lower costs. In this case, Medicare Part C (also known as Medicare Advantage) may be a good option for you. Part C is available in several flavors — the most common are

✔ **Health maintenance organizations (HMOs):** HMOs usually require you to choose a primary-care clinic where you'll get most of your care. You see a specialist only if your primary-care doctor will refer you to one. There usually is no out-of-network coverage except for emergencies. Because of all these limitations, I don't recommend the HMO option.

✔ **Preferred provider organizations (PPOs):** PPOs usually have a broader network that includes both primary-care doctors and specialists. You're free to see any one of them without a referral. PPOs also usually let you choose an out-of-network provider, too, subject to higher copayments. For these reasons, I recommend the PPO option for those who need to minimize insurance premium costs. However, whenever you have a reduction in premium costs, there are always some trade-offs, such as higher deductibles and copayments.

Whatever type of Part C plan you decide on can also include prescription drug coverage. Drug coverage and penalties follow the same rules as Part D.

To apply for Medicare Advantage, you must first enroll in Medicare parts A and B. As with original Medicare, I recommend applying about three months before you turn 65 or otherwise become eligible for Medicare. You must reside in the plan area to be eligible. If you move to a different geographic area outside the plan area, you'll have to change Medicare Advantage plans. Also, Medicare Advantage plans don't work well for those who travel extensively or move to a different part of the country.

Here are the advantages that Medicare Advantage (using a PPO) has over original Medicare with a good Medicare supplement:

✔ You have much lower front-end costs.

✔ You can see out-of-network providers (subject to higher copays).

✔ You have an annual out-of-pocket maximum for copayments and deductibles.

✔ You get unlimited hospitalization coverage beyond what Part A Medicare covers (90 to 150 days). Drug coverage can be added, giving you one source of care and one bill.

✔ You don't need a Medicare supplement policy, because participating providers under Medicare Advantage agree to accept whatever Medicare allows as payment in full.

✔ You can change Medicare Advantage plans once a year regardless of your health.

✔ Your plan can include medical services not covered by Medicare parts A and B (annual physicals, eye exams, dental, and so on).

And here are the disadvantages of Medicare Advantage:

✔ You pay higher deductibles and copays out of pocket.

✔ You have less choice when it comes to seeing specialists.

✔ Travel coverage is limited to only emergency care in network. Otherwise, for nonemergency care, travel coverage is considered out of network and the copayments are substantially higher.

✔ You must change plans if you ever move out of the plan service area. You will, however, automatically qualify for a new Medicare Advantage PPO plan of your choice in the new location.

✔ The plan can change its coverage dramatically or withdraw from the market altogether. You'll qualify for a new Medicare Advantage plan regardless of your health if that should happen.

For more information on Medicare Advantage plans, call 800-633-4227 or go to www.medicare.gov/Choices/Advantage.asp.

Medicare does offer financial help with the cost of Medicare parts B and D for those with limited income and assets. To see if you qualify, call Medicare at 800-633-4227. If you're already in the system prior to turning 65 (for example, because you're receiving Medicaid benefits), you'll probably be automatically enrolled.

Chapter 21

Evaluating Your Need for Long-Term-Care Insurance

In This Chapter

▶ Measuring your need for long-term-care insurance

▶ Qualifying for Medicaid assistance

▶ Understanding what makes a great long-term-care policy

▶ Buying the policy the right way

▶ Understanding how you can benefit from the new Medicaid partnership program

*P*eople are living longer than ever before. That's the good news. The bad news is that, at some point in their lives, many of the people who reach age 65 will need assistance with activities of daily living — bathing, dressing, eating, toileting, transferring from your bed to a wheelchair and back, and so on. Many will face what we all fear the most — Alzheimer's disease or some other cognitive impairment. Unless you get help from your family, you'll have to hire outside help and pay for that help by draining your investments. Or you could buy long-term-care insurance to pay some or all of your costs.

In this chapter, I show you how to determine whether you need long-term-care insurance, what to look for in a policy, and how to buy the policy that's right for you.

Determining Your Need for Long-Term-Care Insurance

Costs for long-term care vary geographically, but they're approaching six figures annually. In 20 years, they'll likely be close to $250,000 a year! One of the guiding principles of this book is: Don't risk more than you can afford to lose (see Chapter 2). Suppose you stay in a care facility six years. At $250,000 a year, that's $1.5 million you have to part with! That qualifies as a major financial risk for most people.

Another guiding principle is to consider the odds. This principle, in effect, says that if the odds are extremely unlikely (think: earthquake in Minnesota), this may be a risk worth taking without insurance. So, just what are the odds? For those who live to age 65, a whopping 50 percent will need long-term care for at least two years. Want to hear something even *more* startling? Forty-five percent of the people who are currently receiving long-term care are between the ages of 18 and 64!

Okay, so long-term-care costs can be hugely expensive and the odds of needing care are very high. This is not a risk you can ignore. In this section, I tell you who doesn't need long-term-care insurance and who does need it.

Who doesn't need long-term-care insurance

To answer the question about who does need long-term-care insurance, I think it's good to first look at who *doesn't*. There are three groups of people who do *not* need long-term care insurance:

- ✔ **People who have substantial assets:** People with a ton of money can easily pay for long-term care from liquid funds without ever depleting them, regardless of how long they need care. And they're completely comfortable using those resources for that care. What qualifies as "a ton of money"? Figure at least $3 million in *liquid assets* (such as cash, stocks, and bonds).

- ✔ **People who qualify for the federal Medicaid program:** Medicaid pays long-term care costs for those who are at or near poverty levels. To find out what those current qualifications are, call your state Medicaid office.

- ✔ **People with moderate assets who are willing to spend down those assets on long-term care to near-poverty levels at which point Medicaid will pay the balance:** If you don't have any children or heirs, you may be willing to spend down all your assets — after all, you can't take it with you, right?

Who needs long-term-care insurance

Basically, if you don't fall into one of the three categories in the preceding section, you need long-term-care insurance. Here are people who fall into the need-it category:

✔ **People with substantial assets who want to pass those assets on to their children or favorite charity and don't want their long-term care costs to deplete that inheritance.**

✔ **People with moderate assets who don't want to drain those assets:** Maybe you don't want the cost of that care to impoverish your spouse. Or you simply want to be a responsible adult and pay your own way. Or you don't want to overburden the already underfunded Medicaid program.

✔ **People who want choices as to where they can get care:** Maybe you want to be cared for at home or in a nice assisted living community. If you need to go to a nursing home for care, maybe you want to be able to choose among the nicer, better facilities. Medicaid generally only pays for nursing home care in a facility of *its* choice.

✔ **People who want to give their families permission to get professional help right away rather than forcing their family to try to coordinate and deliver care themselves.**

The bottom line is that if you fall into the group that wants or needs long-term-care insurance, long-term-care costs represent a major risk area that definitely needs to be insured. For you, there are *six* major risk areas for which you need to be well-protected:

✔ Premature death (see Chapter 23)

✔ Long-term disability (see Chapter 22)

✔ Major medical bills (see Chapters 18 to 20)

✔ Major damage or destruction to your personal residence (see Part III)

✔ Large lawsuits (see Chapters 15 and 16)

✔ Long-term-care expenses

You have to address this risk. If you don't, you have a major gap in your insurance program.

How expensive is long-term-care insurance? Very. Anytime you have a risk that has a high probability of happening and for which the costs could be substantial, the cost of insuring that risk is also high. A good example: major medical insurance. Your own cost depends on numerous variables, including your age when you buy it, the amount of coverage you'll need per month, the number of years you want the coverage, and more.

Knowing When to Buy

Make sure all the other five major risk areas — premature death, long-term disability, major medical bills, major damage to your residence, large lawsuits — are all covered adequately and in balance. Those risks are higher priority because they have a good probability of happening right now. Your long-term-care risk — although substantial and very likely — is unlikely to happen this very minute.

That said, if you're going to be buying anyway, it's less expensive to buy it when you're younger. There are three costs of delaying the purchase of long-term-care insurance:

- ✔ **If you wait and your health goes south, you may not even qualify for a policy.** I learned this lesson the hard way!

- ✔ **The cost of care is escalating faster than the consumer price index.** What costs $100,000 today may cost $250,000 in 20 years — especially with all the Baby Boomers adding to demand for care.

- ✔ **Costs increase with age.** The cost of waiting is not only expensive because you're older but also expensive because you have to buy considerably more coverage ten years from now.

Introducing the New Medicaid Partnership Program

Suppose that you're in the second group of those needing long-term care: You're not financially independent. And you don't like your choices: Either pay for expensive insurance that's tough on your budget, or begrudgingly spend down your assets to practically nothing and then become eligible for Medicaid.

Improving medical technology allowing more people to live longer, combined with a large number of people reaching retirement age, each year the number of people needing long-term care increases — and it will continue to increase greatly for years to come. The already underfunded Medicaid program is going to need some additional significant funds somewhere unless something changes. Maintaining the status quo won't be a good thing for our burgeoning deficit nor will it be a good thing for those who watch their nest egg get fully depleted by their care.

In order to reduce the drain on Medicaid, Congress passed the Deficit Reduction Act of 2005 — part of which addressed this Medicaid funding problem. The goal was to motivate consumers to buy private insurance on their own and, thus, significantly reduce Medicaid outlays for long-term care. And if the consumer's coverage ran out, they could still get their remaining care from Medicaid without having to impoverish themselves.

Here's how it works: You buy a long-term-care policy on yourself. Assume then at some later date you end up needing long-term care. Further assume that your policy pays $500,000 for your care and your coverage runs out while you still need care. At that point, you try to qualify for Medicaid benefits. The government rewards you for having a policy that has already paid $500,000 by ignoring $500,000 of your assets in the Medicaid qualification process. This is huge!

This is a win-win situation for both consumers and the government. Someone with long-term-care insurance reduces the chance that she'll need Medicaid funding — which is good for Medicaid. If that person eventually runs out of insurance, she can then preserve an amount equal to whatever her long-term-care policy has paid for her family's benefit. Her ongoing need for care won't completely drain the family's fortune and create hardship for her loved ones.

You now can protect all or a part of your estate from having to be drained as a result of your needing long-term care:

- ✔ **If you want to protect all of your current estate,** you buy a long-term-care policy for the full cost of today's care with lifetime benefits and a 5 percent compounded annual benefit increase without any corresponding premium increases. Then you'll never have to deal with Medicaid.

- ✔ **If, on the other hand, you're willing to spend some of your assets down but still preserve say $500,000 or $1 million,** buy a long-term-care policy that will pay that much in benefits (a policy paying $250 per day equals $7,500 a month, which is $90,000 a year). To shelter $500,000, you would need a five-year or six-year benefit period. To shelter $1 million, you need a ten-year benefit.

Make sure your monthly benefit is high enough to fully cover your costs. You're better off erring on the high side so you don't have to pay out of pocket. It's better to have $10,000 a month of coverage for three years ($360,000) than to have $6,000 a month for five years (also $360,000). Why? Because any shortfall in monthly coverage will drain your personal assets, whereas any excess coverage you don't need will carry forward.

My dad's tale

When my dad, who was of relatively modest means, was around 80 years old, he had a stroke that took away his speech and the use of the right side of his body, confining him to a wheelchair and creating the need for constant help with bathing, dressing, eating, toileting, and so on. He immediately went into a nursing home for that care. After we sold his home, he had about $350,000 to his name. Four years of care later, he had spent down the entire amount of his care to the point of eligibility for Medicaid — namely, $3,000. He was approved for Medicaid benefits and he was transferred to a Medicaid-approved nursing home, where he is living today. There's a good chance he'll need

care several more years. Dad didn't have long-term-care insurance, but even if he did, with his extended need for care, it probably would've run out and still drained his assets, benefiting Medicaid only and not his family.

If he'd purchased a long-term-care policy under the new long-term care partnership provisions that paid, for example, $200,000 in benefits, he, rather than Medicaid, would have reaped those benefits. His eligibility for Medicaid would now be $203,000 instead of $3,000. This new law would have allowed him to shelter an additional $200,000 from the government for the benefit of his family.

Buying the Policy

Before you buy a long-term-care insurance policy, ask your state insurance department to send you information, as well as any comparative studies it has done. Be sure to request a copy of the booklet put out by the National Association of Insurance Commissioners called "A Shopper's Guide to Long-Term Care Insurance." You can order it at `https://external-apps.naic.org/insprod/Consumer_info.jsp`. Also, research the current costs of long-term care in your geographic area, such as the cost of a semiprivate room in a nice care facility.

In this section, I walk you through buying a policy — from finding an expert to setting your coverages to choosing your company.

Working with an expert

Start by finding a skilled long-term-care insurance agent (see Chapter 4). Try to find someone with lots of expertise with long-term care. Check with your own insurance agent first. If you're fortunate, the insurance agent you're already working with is also an expert on long-term-care insurance. If your agent is not an expert with long-term-care coverage, he probably can refer you to someone who is. If not, check with other trusted professionals in your life — your financial planner, your accountant, and so on. Then meet with one or two of the agents who seem the most knowledgeable and have them determine your needs first before they quote you any prices. If they quote you prices before determining your needs, choose a different agent.

Designing coverage specifications

With the help of your agent, you're ready to design the coverage specifications you want. You only have to make a handful of decisions to buy a policy.

Step 1: Monthly benefit

Start by taking the average daily semiprivate room rate in your area. Then compare that with the cost of home care (if you're willing to pay more, if necessary, to get care at home rather than at a nursing home). Select the higher of the two numbers as your daily coverage need. Then multiply that result by 30 to calculate your monthly coverage need.

Home-care costs may be higher than nursing-home care — significantly higher if you need 24-hour round-the-clock care.

Most companies give you the option of buying a daily benefit or monthly benefit. If you have the choice, always choose the monthly benefit. If you receive some of your care at home, you may not need help every day. The monthly option gives you more flexibility for handling fluctuating daily costs.

Step 2: Waiting period

A *waiting period* (also known as an *elimination period*) is the number of months that you're willing to pay for your own care before you need the coverage to kick in. It's a lot like the deductible on car insurance. Your choices usually are 30 days, 60 days, 90 days, 180 days, and sometimes 365 days. (The waiting period options for 60 days and beyond usually have to be met only once in a lifetime and generally do not have to be consecutive. They can be cumulative over time.) Like a deductible, the longer you can wait before coverage begins, the less expensive the premium.

Choose a time frame that meets two criteria:

- ✔ You're comfortable with the length of time.
- ✔ The premium savings are large enough to justify taking extra risk.

Usually a 60-day or 90-day wait is the best value. If you're not sure which, get quotes for both options. Ask for quotes with a zero-day waiting period for home health care; the price for that option isn't too high, because, if you don't need daily care, it's usually less expensive to provide care at home than it is in a facility.

If you have a spouse who can provide some of your home health care, you may not need care every day. Some insurance companies will give you a full seven-days credit toward your facility waiting period for just one day of home health care per week!

Step 3: Where you want your care

Always choose care anywhere. Don't limit yourself to care in a facility. You have no idea what type of injury or illness will necessitate your needing care. Keep your options open. Anything else is gambling.

You have a choice of either 50 percent or 100 percent coverage at home. Choose the 100 percent option for the same reason.

Step 4: How many years you want coverage

This choice will depend on why you're buying long-term-care insurance. If you're wealthy and you're buying it to protect your children's inheritance, choose the equivalent of ten years, or lifetime if it's available.

If you're buying coverage to shelter assets from Medicaid eligibility under the new partnership program (see "Introducing the New Medicaid Partnership Program," earlier in this chapter), first determine the dollar amount of assets you want to protect and then buy enough coverage to accomplish that.

If you're married, many insurance companies offer shared-care options. Instead of buying two six-year policies, for about the same money, you can share ten years. One of you may not need care at all or you may need it for a very short time. Whatever is unused at that spouse's death is available to the other spouse.

Step 5: Your inflation option

Obviously, long-term-care costs increase every year and will continue to do so ad infinitum. So, if you buy $6,000 per month, and you don't need care for 20 years, the costs at that time may be $20,000 to $25,000 per month. Without some change in the benefit, your $6,000 wouldn't put much of a dent in the actual costs.

Here are your usual inflation options:

✔ **Option 1: No built-in inflation benefit:** If you want to increase your benefits, you'll need to physically complete an application and qualify medically. You also have to buy the additional coverage you need at the current rates and at your attained age.

✔ **Option 2: A guaranteed future purchase option:** This guarantees the right to buy additional insurance regardless of your health (15 percent every three years). The downside is that you still have to pay current rates for your current age. At some point, the additional amount becomes cost prohibitive.

✔ **Option 3: A 5 percent simple interest annual adjustment:** Here the benefits increase a flat 5 percent per year, again at no increase in premium. Not a bad option.

✔ **Option 4: An automatic increase annually tied to the Consumer Price Index (CPI):** The good news about this option is that your benefit is increasing with no increase in premium. The bad news is that the price index for long-term-care costs may be higher than the general CPI change. This is a good choice, though, if there is no cap on the percentage of increase.

✔ **Option 5: A 5 percent compound interest annual adjustment:** This is my personal favorite and the recommendation of most financial experts in the field. The good news is that the benefits are increasing on a compound basis, again with no increase in premium. The bad news is that this is the most expensive inflation option. The reason that the cost is double the price of the no-inflation option is because the premium will never increase due to this annual increase in benefit. This is really important for seniors on fixed incomes. This option is also available at a 3 percent compound rate and is correspondingly less expensive.

I recommend that you get a price for options 4 and 5. Option 4, especially for younger people, is often considerably less expensive than Option 5.

Choosing your insurance company

Because people who buy long-term-care insurance often don't need the coverage for several years, you have to be more careful about the company that you're going to do business with. Your company should have

✔ A very strong financial rating, so they'll still be around 20 years from now when you need them

✔ Several years of long-term-care insurance experience so the company is committed to the long haul

✔ A history of taking only modest rate increases on existing customers

The most well-known source of financial rating for insurance companies is A.M. Best (www.ambest.com), which has been rating insurance companies for more than a hundred years. Its highest ratings are A+ and A++ — try to deal only with companies that have one of those two ratings.

Introducing some new twists

If you're very affluent and you're buying long-term-care insurance primarily to protect your children's inheritance, there are a couple of new ideas on the market that involve the payment of one single premium.

One concept combines long-term care with permanent life insurance. You deposit a lump sum — say, $100,000 — with the insurance company. Your loved ones might receive $165,000 of life insurance whenever you die. In addition, you'll have $250,000 of long-term-care coverage if you need that first. If you decide to drop the policy before you need either one, you can generally get almost all your original $100,000 deposit back. Coverage basically costs you the interest on your money.

If you're affluent and you don't need life insurance, another possibility is a tax-sheltered annuity combined with long-term-care insurance. Again, you put a lump sum into the policy — say, $100,000. If you need long-term care, you'll receive benefits of, for example, $200,000 and if you die without needing long-term care, your heirs will get your $100,000 back. Again, the cost of long-term-care insurance is the interest on your money.

These are not real life examples, just illustrations to show how the concept works. If you fall into either one of these categories, ask your long-term-care advisor what options might be appropriate for you.

Chapter 22

Managing the Risk of Long-Term Disability

. . . .

In This Chapter

▶ Determining your need for coverage

▶ Understanding disability insurance lingo

▶ Creating your own coverage specifications

▶ Buying a disability policy

▶ Plugging the holes in group long-term disability insurance

. . . .

*W*hen you're building your insurance program, you need to deal with five possible causes of a *major* financial loss through insurance:

✔ Lawsuits

✔ Destruction of home and personal property

✔ Major medical bills

✔ Premature death with dependents

✔ Long-term disability

Most people carry protection for the first four threats, but they don't protect themselves from long-term loss of income from illness or injury unless their employer provides the insurance. Yet, before age 65, a person is three times more likely to become disabled for six months or more than to die.

Adding to the seriousness of the situation, the economic loss to disability survivors is greater than it is for families after the death of a loved one because, not only is the income lost, but the disabled person still needs a roof over her head, still has ongoing living expenses (such as groceries, utilities, and mortgage payments), and often needs additional care. Without this critical coverage in your insurance program, you're risking a major financial crisis — and it doesn't have to be this way.

In this chapter, I fill you in on how best to plug this serious gap in protection. I start by applying three of the principles from Chapter 2 to your disability insurance decision. Then I give you tips on how much disability coverage you need, guiding you through buying your own disability insurance, without leaving any gaps.

To Buy or not to Buy: That Is the Question

In Chapter 2, I introduce you to seven tried-and-true principles to help you make good insurance buying decisions. Here are three of them that you can apply to the decision as to whether you need long-term disability insurance:

✔ **Don't risk more than you can afford to lose.** Ask yourself if your paycheck stopped today, and you didn't have it for the next five or ten years, what would your life be like? How would that impact your making the mortgage payment? Putting food on the table? Your family's peace of mind and stress level? If you don't have another source to replace that lost income, you need to have long-term disability insurance.

✔ **Consider the odds.** Just how likely is a long-term disability? Pretty likely regardless of your age. Here are some stats:

   • One out of three people in the workforce today will be disabled three months or more before age 65. One out of seven will be disabled for *life*.

   • If you're disabled for as long as one year, your chances of being disabled for a long time are staggeringly high. In fact, you have a 40 percent chance of being disabled more than five years!

   • If you're 25 years old and an injury or illness knocks you out of work for just three months, you have a one in four chance of having that disability last for life. That could be 40 years or more!

Clearly, the odds of a long-term disability causing you severe financial hardship are way too high to ignore.

✔ **Don't risk a lot for a little.** If the risk is great and the insurance cost is relatively small in relation to the risk, you should buy the insurance. So, just how expensive is long-term disability insurance? On average, the cost runs 2 percent to 3 percent of your taxable income. If you don't have long-term disability insurance right now, you're definitely risking a lot for a little.

The risk of disability is real. And when it happens, it can last a long time. Protecting yourself from this huge financial risk with a good long-term disability insurance policy won't cost you much. *Remember:* The only thing worse than a long-term disability is a long-term disability with no income.

Determining How Much Insurance You Need

The goal of a good long-term disability strategy is to provide you with enough personal and insurance resources that you won't have to make major life changes (such as selling your home), if a disability occurs. Being disabled is traumatic enough without having the added pain and stress of big changes in your lifestyle.

Having the right amount of coverage is crucial. Too little coverage may mean that you still have to make major life changes in the aftermath of a disabling injury. Too much coverage and you're spending money unnecessarily.

To figure out how much disability insurance you need, you have to determine how much money you need every month to pay the bills. You have two ways to determine your monthly income need:

- ✔ **The hard way:** The hard way is to make up a budget of your monthly expenses from memory. Not only is that method extremely time consuming — leading to such evils as procrastination — but I've found, through working with scores of clients over the years, that it's also very inaccurate. People tend to underestimate their actual needs by about 20 percent.

- ✔ **The easy way:** The easy way is the approach I recommend. The computation can be accomplished in about 20 minutes and is extremely accurate. Just grab your last three months' check registers for your personal checking account(s). On the top of page one of each statement, you see a figure for the total amount of checks written for that month. Add the totals for each of the three months and divide by 3 to come up with a monthly average income need. If any particular month is extremely distorted — because you took an expensive vacation, for example, or were paying for holiday gifts — use a different month. Whatever number you come up with, add 10 percent to 20 percent (because expenses normally *increase* during a disability).

Insurance companies limit how much coverage you can buy to about 80 percent to 90 percent of your take-home pay. You may not be able to buy as much as you'd like to have. If this happens, take their maximum and make sure you have a purchase option included so that, as your income grows, your coverage can, too.

Talking the Talk: The Special Lingo of Disability Insurance

Elimination period. Own-occupation. Residual. Noncancelable. Disability insurance policies have their own unique terminology, using language you won't find in any other insurance policy. You need to understand these and other terms to make a good decision on those policy features that are important to you. In this section, I fill you in.

Total disability

A person is considered totally disabled if he is unable to perform *all* the principal duties of his job, or any other job for which he's reasonably suited, considering his income, education, and experience. The pitfall to be wary of here is that if you can work only a few hours a week, you would have zero coverage under a policy covering only total disability.

Residual disability

Residual disability usually means proportionate coverage when you're unable to work full-time (from a back injury or a heart attack, for example) and usually resulting in an income loss of at least 20 percent. Under policies that cover only total disabilities, you would not receive a dime in benefits. But with residual coverage, if you work part time and earn 40 percent of your pre-disability income, you'll receive 60 percent of your monthly benefit.

I strongly recommend this coverage for absolutely everyone! Be sure to add a residual disability coverage option to any disability policy you buy. Without it, you won't get paid a disability insurance payment if you can still work even one or two days a week.

Make sure that the residual benefit period isn't limited. If your disability coverage goes to age 65, so should the residual coverage. (Many benefits last only six months!)

Elimination period

The term *elimination period* is disability lingo for *deductible*. The elimination period or waiting period represents the number of months you're willing to wait, while disabled, before coverage begins. Usually you have a choice of 30,

60, 90, or 180 days. Your choice will depend on how much money you have in the bank as a safety net combined with how long your employer will continue your salary or provide sick leave following a disability.

The longer you can wait, the lower your premium will be. For example, waiting 60 days typically gives you about a 30 percent savings compared with a 30-day elimination period. Waiting 90 days saves you about another 10 percent. Premiums continue to go down as you increase the elimination period beyond three months, but by much smaller amounts. Your best bet is usually either a 60-day or 90-day elimination period.

Because there are always delays in getting a claim check, if you're trying to decide between two elimination periods, choose the shorter of the two. For example, if you choose a 60-day elimination period, the payment for the next 30 days of disability comes to you only after you've been disabled for 30 days. So the first claim check you receive with a 60-day wait will come to you 90 days after your disability start date.

Benefit period

Benefit period refers to the duration for which you want a disability insurance paycheck — typically two years, five years, to age 65, or for your entire lifetime. Coverage to age 65 or lifetime coverage is obviously best if you can afford the cost — it costs about 30 percent more than a five-year benefit. Because many disabled people recover within five years, the five-year option is also a reasonable choice if you couldn't otherwise afford the coverage you need.

If you have to choose the five-year plan, be prepared to make a major lifestyle change if you face a disability that continues beyond five years. The good news is that at least you'll have five years to prepare for it.

I don't recommend the two-year benefit period, because a large percentage of disabilities last beyond two years.

Noncancelable versus guaranteed renewable

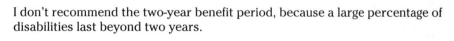

You have two options regarding the renewability of your coverage: *noncancelable* and *guaranteed renewable* contracts. Both promise to renew coverage to age 65. Noncancelable contracts also guarantee never to raise the price up to age 65. Guaranteed renewable contracts can raise their overall rates anytime, but they cannot single you out individually for an increase.

How important is a price guarantee? Disability insurance companies have experienced a worse-than-expected claims record over the past several years. Several companies have closed doors, and others have merged or been sold. The number of insurance companies offering individual disability policies has decreased dramatically. Those insurers that are still active have taken some large rate increases on their guaranteed renewable contracts.

Don't let a price guarantee be the biggest issue in your selection. Buy all the coverage and features you need first. That's the highest priority. Then, if you can afford another 20 percent or so to lock in the price, do so.

Cost of living adjustment rider

If you're disabled for several years, the monthly disability check you receive has diminishing spending power. The cost of living adjustment (COLA) option annually increases your benefit while you're disabled by some predetermined percentage (usually from 3 percent to 6 percent).

If you're buying coverage to age 65, COLA is a pretty important option to include in your coverage. However, if you're buying only a five-year benefit or if you have a spouse whose projected future income will be rising dramatically, you may not need this rider.

Future purchase option

This option guarantees, when you apply and qualify for your first policy, that, regardless of your future health, you can increase your coverage every one to three years, up to the optional limit you've purchased.

If you think that you may need more disability coverage later, with increased expenses such as a bigger house, more children, or simple cost of living increases, I strongly recommend that you pay just a little more now for the privilege of being able to increase your benefit in the future regardless of health.

A rather high percentage of people are declined for disability insurance due to back problems, diabetes, high cholesterol, and so on. You may be such a person in the future.

The future purchase option eliminates the possibility of your being turned down for additional coverage later. And it's usually quite inexpensive. Not only does the option guarantee you the opportunity to buy additional insurance regardless of your future health, but it also greatly simplifies the purchase of such additional insurance because no applications or physical exams are required.

The difference between future purchase options and COLA options is that the purchase option increases your coverage *before* you become disabled, and COLA increases your benefits *while* you're disabled. I recommend them both.

Social insurance rider

A *social insurance rider* pays you an additional monthly benefit that is reduced or eliminated when you qualify for Social Security disability benefits or workers' compensation benefits. How this rider works varies dramatically among insurance companies. Just know that it exists and what its purpose is.

Because total disability creates such a hardship on a family, in planning I like to disregard any possible Social Security benefits — that way, they can be an inflation hedge or cushion for unplanned expenses. I recommend you do the same. (For more on Social Security, see the nearby sidebar.)

Return of premium rider

The *return of premium rider* was created for people who want their cake and want to eat it, too. After a number of years — typically 20 to 25 — the policy refunds you all your premiums, less any paid claims. Sounds great, right? It is great — except for one catch: It adds 30 percent to 40 percent a year to your costs! For that reason, and because most people may buy less insurance coverage than they need, I rarely recommend it.

Catastrophic disability rider

The *catastrophic disability rider* provides additional cash benefits over and above your loss of income to help pay the costs that come with especially disabling illnesses or injuries. Coverage triggers are usually one of the following:

- ✔ Inability to do two or more activities of daily living (like bathing, dressing, eating, going to the bathroom) without help
- ✔ Cognitive impairments (such as head injuries or Alzheimer's disease)
- ✔ Loss of sight, hearing, speech, or two or more limbs

I strongly recommend including this optional benefit in your program, unless you have a long-term care policy, which essentially does the same thing. What makes this coverage particularly attractive is its relatively low cost.

Collecting disability benefits from Uncle Sam

Social Security is not just a retirement benefits program — it also offers a basic level of disability benefits. If you pay into the Social Security system, you get an annual statement from them that spells out both your estimated retirement benefits and your long-term disability benefits.

Social Security disability benefits are payable to normal retirement age. There is a five-month waiting period after you're totally disabled before benefits are payable to you. To qualify, you must have a medical condition that will disable you for at least a year or result in death. Benefits are paid for total disability only, meaning that if you can work at all, you don't qualify.

Because of the severe limitations and the fact that the majority of applicants for benefits are declined, I recommend that you ignore Social Security benefits in your planning. If you happen to receive them, that's great.

To get a current copy of your Social Security statement and an estimate of your disability benefits, go to www.socialsecurity. gov or call 800-772-1213. For a good brochure that explains the program in detail, go to www. socialsecurity.gov/pubs/10029. pdf.

If you do file a disability claim, be prepared for rather intensive scrutiny of your claim and a delay of months before you start receiving any benefits if you do qualify. If they turn down your claim, don't give up. I know several people who've finally been approved after their second or third appeal, so it can pay to be persistent.

On the bright side, after two years of collecting Social Security disability benefits, you then automatically qualify for the Medicare program, regardless of your age. If you fit this description, see Chapter 20 for what you need to know about the Medicare program.

Own-occupation protection

Own-occupation refers to the length of time you'll be paid a full benefit when you can't perform your specific occupation but could do another. In a disability policy, the period of occupation protection is found in the policy definition for *total disability*.

The most restrictive definition is probably the one the Social Security Administration uses: complete inability to engage in *any* gainful occupation. The broadest definition is probably found in the expensive, deluxe policies offered to high-income professionals such as physicians and lawyers: the inability to perform the duties of your specific occupation.

With the Social Security definition in your policy, you may not be eligible for benefits if you can sell pencils or wash dishes. With the deluxe definition of own-occupation, if you were a radiologist making $300,000 a year with a $200,000 a year disability benefit and could no longer practice your specialty of radiology but could practice family medicine or teach radiology at the university and earn $200,000, you would still be considered totally disabled. If you're that radiologist, you could take any other job other than your job as a radiologist (for example, you could teach at the university) and get your full $200,000 benefit, plus your teacher's salary. As you might guess, this coverage is expensive. I don't think it's necessary for most people.

Most disability policies use a definition of total disability that falls somewhere between the Social Security definition and the definition found in contracts that are sold to wealthy professionals. They pay full benefits if you can't perform your particular occupation for anywhere from two to five years, sometimes ten years; then, if you're still disabled after that period, your benefits are cut off only if you can't perform another occupation for which you're reasonably suited based on your education, training, and experience. The longer the period of protection for your specific occupation, the higher the premium.

Make your decision to add an own-occupation clause based on how many years you've spent mastering your craft. A brain surgeon or a lawyer would probably want the broadest definition possible. Someone with two years of college employed as a sales representative would probably be satisfied with more limited protection on the occupation.

Always buy a disability policy that, if for whatever reason you work in another occupation that pays less than your original occupation, will still pay a proportionate/residual benefit for as long as that income difference persists. So if your original salary was $100,000 per year, and you can now only do a job that pays you, say, $50,000 per year (it decreased by 50 percent), you want disability protection that will pay you one-half of your policy benefit.

Buying Disability Insurance

You've determined how much coverage you need. You've chosen the policy features that are most important to you. Your adrenaline is on high. You're primed! You're ready! The big moment you've been waiting for is finally here! Tell the truth: Is there anything more fun in life than shopping for insurance?

Knowing where to buy

If you already have a trusted insurance agent for your auto, home, or life insurance policies, she may be able to help you find the right disability insurance policy. Many — but not all — agents have disability insurance available. If your current agent does offer disability policies, make sure that she's knowledgeable about disability. If she isn't, ask for a referral to a disability insurance specialist. (For more on finding an agent, turn to Chapter 4.)

Evaluating a credit card insurance offer

If you own a credit card (in other words, if you live and breathe), you receive offers all the time to buy credit insurance that will pay off the card balance if you become disabled. Unless you're medically uninsurable, these offers are usually a rip-off. Here's just one example: I had a client who was interested in buying disability insurance from a major national credit card company solicitation. It was a "special program for business owners," the ad proclaimed. He wisely ordered a sample policy and sent it to me for an opinion. Just how "special" was it? It only had a couple of limitations:

✔ Disability must be caused by an accident only; no coverage was given for heart attacks, cancer, or any other illness.

✔ After one year of disability payments, the coverage ends unless you are (and I quote) "unable to perform FOR THE REST OF YOUR LIFE any job for which you are or *can* become qualified." Any job? Selling pencils on the street corner?

Such consumer-friendly language gets me goose-bumpy all over! Needless to say, he passed on the offer.

A small percentage of insurance agents deal principally with disability insurance products, and they're often quite knowledgeable about the subject. Unfortunately, they often tend to concentrate on the professional market (doctors, lawyers, CPAs, and so on). They also tend to deal in a more elite product that offers Cadillac coverage at a stiff price. Still, a disability specialist should be able to help you find a quality product at a price you can afford, or know someone who can.

Here are a few other sources to explore:

✔ **Your employer:** If you can get group coverage through your employer for free or at little cost, doing so is often a good idea. The major advantage of employer-based disability coverage is that you can often get the insurance even if your health is poor.

Group coverage has some pitfalls, however:

- Benefits are taxable.

- You don't get to pick the features you want (like residual or cost of living riders).

- If you change jobs, you lose the insurance.

✔ **Association plans:** Policies from associations are often attractively priced. They usually have many of the same pitfalls as employer-paid group insurance, however, and you usually have to qualify medically. You also lose it if you drop your association membership or if the plan is discontinued.

✔ **Creditors:** Often sold through lending institutions, insurance from creditors is designed to pay off loans (such as payments on a car, boat, home, or credit card balance) in the event of long-term disability.

Avoid this type of insurance unless you can't qualify for coverage anywhere else because of health problems. No inquiries are made as to your medical condition when you apply for some of these policies, so the rates tend to be two, three, or more times higher than preferred rates for healthy individuals. These policies also have the added disadvantage of covering only that part of your monthly living expenses that has a loan tied to it, and of expiring or running out when the loan is paid off. But, if your health is poor, buy all the coverage you can get your hands on.

Comparing policies

Most agents who work with disability insurance have access to more than one company. If you've taken the time to choose an agent with plenty of expertise on disability insurance, ask her to get more than one quote. Comparing policy features and optional coverages of two or more disability policies is a challenge to the best agents and next to impossible for the consumer. So it's okay to ask her to go through the policies feature by feature so that you understand their differences.

If you have an existing or past medical issue that you or your agent are concerned might affect your chances of being approved (such as an old back injury or treatment for depression), do what I recommend to my clients: Apply simultaneously to two companies. That way you won't have to answer "yes" to the question on every application "Have you ever had an application for life or disability insurance declined, rated up, or otherwise modified?" That happens more often than you might think.

Don't buy based on the lowest price. Other factors to consider include the agent's expertise, the insurance company's financial strength and reputation, or special coverage features that are really important to you.

Plugging Holes in Your Group Insurance Program

The good news about employer-paid group long-term disability insurance is that it's a no-cost benefit to you. The bad news is that every dime you receive is taxed as ordinary income. Plus, unlike privately owned disability insurance, group benefits are offset against anything you receive from Social Security or workers' compensation. Here are some other shortcomings of group coverage:

✔ **Coverage stays with the job.** You may have a right to convert the policy to an individual policy but usually with watered-down coverage and higher pricing.

✔ **Generally group policies don't have a cost-of-living adjustment, so while you're out on disability, your benefit will never increase.**

✔ **Many policies cover only total disabilities — no partial or residual benefits.**

Because group benefits are taxable, the 60 percent of salary they usually pay ends up being 40 percent to 45 percent after taxes. Unless you can live comfortably on that amount, buy an individual disability policy to cover the shortfall.

A good supplement should include all the features I recommend in this chapter plus, ideally, an option to purchase additional benefits whenever you lose your group benefits for whatever reason, regardless of the condition of your health.

Take time to select a good agent who can help you identify the holes in your group plan and how to best plug them, and who is knowledgeable about supplemental policies.

Getting group benefits tax-free

If you have a good group insurance program at work paid for by your employer, see if you can pay the premiums yourself or reimburse the employer for what they paid. Alternatively, see if your employer will add the premium for the disability insurance to your W-2 as taxable income. If you can somehow manage to pay taxes on the premiums or pay the premiums yourself, when you finally are disabled, you will receive the benefits tax-free! Definitely worth checking into.

Chapter 23

Buying Life Insurance

. . . .

. . . .

We buy life insurance because we love. We love spouses, children, and others who depend on us financially. We love them enough to face the cold reality of death. We love them enough to acknowledge the possibility that we could die young, leaving them without our income. We love them enough to plunk down our hard-earned cash for insurance, so that if we do die early, our deaths will not burden them financially — house payments will be made, groceries will be on the table, and college dreams can be realized.

In this chapter, I give you all the information you need on buying life insurance. I explain the difference between term life insurance and permanent life insurance; help you figure out whether you need insurance and, if so, how much you need; tell you where to buy it; and dispel some common myths about life insurance. With the information in this chapter, you'll be able to rest easy, knowing that your loved ones will be taken care of even after you're gone.

Assessing whether You Need Life Insurance

Life insurance isn't for everyone. If no one would be hurt financially by your death, you wouldn't buy life insurance any more than you'd buy car insurance if you don't drive and don't own a car. In this section, I give you specific guidelines on who does and who doesn't need life insurance.

Myth: Life insurance is cheaper when you're young

Life insurance really is cheaper when you're young. So are dentures, but you don't buy them until you need them, either. This myth started because the *annual* cost of life insurance is cheaper *per year* when you're young because your chances of dying are lower. But the *total* cost that you pay over the life of the policy is not cheaper! How could it be?

Suppose that you buy life insurance for $100 a year at age 25 and your friend waits until age 35 and has to pay $110 a year for the same coverage. Now you're both 35 and you pay $10 less per year — but how about the $1,000 that you paid for the ten years that you didn't need it? Plus interest? Don't buy life insurance until you need it.

Who doesn't need life insurance

Two groups of people do *not* need life insurance:

- ✔ **Those who are financially well off enough that their survivors can meet all their financial needs and obligations using existing financial resources, without the possibility of depleting those resources:** For example, if you're married, you have one teenager, and you've managed to sock away $1 million and have paid off your house, you may not need life insurance. Your existing resources can support your child through college and also provide your spouse with a cushion.

- ✔ **Those whose death won't cause a hardship to others:** For example, if you and your spouse have no children, and you each earn a high enough income to easily support yourselves if the other one dies, you don't need life insurance. If you're a single homeowner with a home mortgage and no dependents, you have enough in savings to pay for final expenses, and you're okay with the home being taken over by the mortgage company if you die, then you don't need life insurance.

Who does need life insurance

Two groups of people *do* need life insurance:

- ✔ **Those with one or more people who depend on their income:** If your family depends on your income (whether or not your spouse works) and you don't have enough savings for them to live off of, your family will need the financial help that only life insurance offers. You don't have to be married or have kids to need life insurance, though. For example, you may be single but paying the bills for your elderly mother's assisted-living apartment — if something were to happen to you, life insurance would make sure that she's taken care of. Even if you're very well off and your family would be able to survive on your savings, if you have a favorite charity that relies on your generous annual gifts, life insurance can keep those gifts coming indefinitely.

✔ **Those who provide services that would need to be hired out in the event of their death:** If you're a stay-at-home mom, and you die while your children are young, your husband will suffer a financial loss. He'll need, at the very least, money to pay for childcare. If he wants some sanity, he may want to hire household help as well. Over a ten-year span, childcare and occasional help around the house can cost $250,000 or more. Life insurance can make that outlay possible.

Plus, the surviving spouse may not want to work the same way after the death of a stay-at-home spouse. Maybe your husband would want to work fewer hours while your children are growing up. If he has the money, he can ask his employer for more flexible hours and less pay to be the present parent. Life insurance can make that possible.

Maybe you take care of your parents' home for them — cutting the lawn, painting, and doing all the handyman chores. It may cost your parents $500 per month to hire a service to do that if you die. The interest on $250,000 of life insurance can make sure that those services are provided to your parents as long as they stay in the house. And when they need additional help, the $250,000 from the insurance policy can help pay their nursing home costs.

Determining How Much Coverage You Need

If you die early, how much money will your loved ones need? How much will it take to pay off debt? How much to replace your income? Is providing funds to cover college costs for your children important, and if so, how much money will that take? How do you account for inflation?

Financial experts typically recommend that you have at least enough life insurance and liquid assets to equal a multiple of five times your annual income, ignoring inflation, or seven to eight times your income factoring in inflation.

 If you have children, be safe and err on the side of buying too much life insurance. I recommend that you buy enough life insurance to equal ten times your annual income, giving your surviving spouse and children a softer lifestyle with more time for each other. Why? Because life insurance is cheap — especially for young families, when the need for life insurance is greatest.

When buying life insurance, aim high. For the people you love who survive you, too much is far better than too little.

What if you're insuring a stay-at-home parent who doesn't have an income? My advice is to buy enough insurance to give the surviving parent the option of paying for a full-time, in-home nanny. Check the prices of an in-home nanny service, including cooking, cleaning, and so on, plus driving the kids wherever they need to go. Then multiply that cost over the number of years needed, and round up for inflation.

Here's my quick and dirty tip for insuring homemakers. Buy $500,000 of life insurance — $250,000 to replace services and another $250,000 to give the surviving spouse and children a less stressful life and some extra time for each other.

I don't recommend using retirement money to cover today's needs, even in a situation as dire as the premature death of a spouse. The survivor will still need those funds at retirement. I also don't usually recommend using home equity. Why? Because it's not very liquid, and the surviving spouse will probably want to keep the house.

Speaking the Language

Before looking at the different types of life insurance and the best places to buy them, here are a few definitions of insurance industry jargon:

- **Beneficiary:** The *beneficiary* is the person or organization to whom the life insurance proceeds are payable at the death of the person insured. It could be a spouse, children, a sibling, or a favorite charity. Every life insurance policy covering you — both those you buy and those at work — should name two beneficiaries: a primary beneficiary and a contingent beneficiary:

  - A *primary beneficiary* is the person or organization to whom the life insurance proceeds are paid if that beneficiary is alive or in existence when you die.

  - A *contingent beneficiary* is the person or organization to whom the life insurance proceeds are paid if the primary beneficiary is dead or no longer in existence. If no contingent beneficiary is named, the proceeds are paid to the estate of the primary beneficiary and possibly subject to delays and additional taxes.

- **Owner:** The *owner* of a life insurance policy may or may not be the person whose life is insured. The owner is the person or organization who controls the policy, pays the bills, chooses the beneficiary, and so on. Here are some examples of when the owner would be different from the person insured:

- A corporation owner insuring the life of a key scientist whose talents are vital to the company's survival

- A family trust owner insuring an aging parent in order to pay estate taxes due at death

- A parent insuring the life of a child to cover final expenses

✔ **Purchase options:** *Purchase options* are options available with some policies that give the person insured the right to purchase additional coverage every few years, regardless of health. Coverage is guaranteed up to a certain amount per option. The options usually cease when the person is between ages 40 and 50.

For example, a couple, both 24, are engaged to be married and are planning to buy a home and have children in two to three years. They're both in good health. They don't want to spend a lot on life insurance that they don't need right now. They would like to guarantee, while they're still healthy, that they can buy coverage later even if their health sours. They may buy starter policies for $50,000 of coverage on each and add a purchase option that every three years gives them the right to buy an additional $50,000 of coverage regardless of their health, their hobbies, or their increased size.

✔ **Waiver of premium:** *Waiver of premium* is an optional coverage that suspends your life insurance premium after you've been totally disabled for (usually) six months, until you're no longer disabled. It has two disadvantages:

- It's more expensive than personal disability coverage.

- It won't normally pay if you can work part-time.

You may not need it if you have plenty of disability coverage and you've included your life insurance premium in your estimated coverage needs.

Identifying the Types of Life Insurance

After you've determined how much coverage you need, you need to decide where to buy it and which type of policy is best suited to your needs.

There are really only two types of life insurance — permanent and term — although the two types come in many shapes, sizes, and colors. The biggest difference between them is how long the coverage lasts:

✔ **Permanent life insurance** covers you for your entire life. Your death is certain. And when you die, it pays the *death benefit* (the amount of money payable at the time of death).

> ✔ **Term life insurance** covers only a part of your lifetime. When that part, or *term,* ends, so does the coverage. It only pays a death benefit if you die within the designated term.

In the following sections, I provide a brief comparison of the two types of policies, covering their ideal use, pricing, and agent compensation. (I cover both types of insurance in much greater detail later in this chapter.)

Permanent life insurance

Permanent life insurance is ideally suited to permanent needs. For example, you may buy permanent life insurance when you're looking to supplement retirement dollars for your surviving spouse, covering estate taxes due upon your death, or paying final expenses — burial, legal costs, and so on.

Every life insurance policy has two core parts to its price:

> ✔ **Mortality cost:** This is determined by your odds of dying at that moment. The mortality charge increases each year as you age and your risk of dying increases.
>
> ✔ **Policy expense cost:** This is your share of insurance company expenses (rent, staff, and agent commissions). The expense charge stays relatively constant.

Most permanent life insurance policies have level premiums for life. How is that possible if the mortality charge increases each year? The insurance company averages the increasing mortality changes over your remaining expected life. In short, you overpay in the early years so that you can under-pay in the later years. That overpayment in the early years is set aside in a reserve for you, called *cash value.* If you cancel a permanent policy, by law you're entitled to get back much of those overpayments — that cash value. The cash value is minimal in the first couple of years because of heavy first-year costs — underwriting, medical exams, and agent commissions.

Permanent life insurance is considerably more expensive than term life insur-ance for the first several years, for the same death benefit, because perma-nent insurance has a cash value element.

Term life insurance

Term life insurance is ideally suited for covering life insurance needs that are not permanent. For example, you may buy term life insurance when you want to cover a 20-year mortgage, college costs for children, or family income needs while the kids are growing up.

Term life insurance costs, unlike permanent life insurance costs, increase regularly as you age. Sometimes the increase is annual, and sometimes it's every five or ten years or more. Term insurance costs can be averaged over 10, 20, or 30 years, so the price is level for the entire term. But term insurance doesn't have a cash value element — if you drop a term insurance policy in its early years, you get no refund of any overpayment (see the preceding section).

Because term insurance has no cash value element, premiums in the first several years are considerably lower than permanent insurance premiums for the same death benefit.

Looking At Permanent Life Insurance

All permanent policies have three components: mortality costs, expense charges, and cash value. (See "Permanent life insurance," earlier in this chapter, for more information.) Insurers offering permanent insurance compete in three ways: lowering mortality costs, lowering expense charges, and having better investment yield on the cash value.

Permanent policies vary by

✔ Whether they guarantee mortality and expense costs

✔ Whether they guarantee the yield on the cash value

Three types of permanent life insurance are on the market: whole life, universal life, and variable life. Every life insurance company offers hybrids of these three. See Table 23-1 for a quick overview of how they compare.

Table 23-1	Comparing Permanent Life Insurance Types		
	Whole Life	*Universal Life*	*Variable Life*
Mortality costs	Fixed	Variable	Fixed or variable
Expenses	Fixed	Variable	Fixed or variable
Cash value yield	Fixed	Variable	Variable
Investment risk to cash value	None	None	Yes
Option to vary the premium	No	Yes	Usually
Option to change the death benefit amount	No	Yes	Usually
Option to vary or suspend premiums	No	Yes	Yes

Life insurance dividends

Several life insurance companies that sell permanent life insurance policies offer what they call *dividends* to their policyholders.

Unlike dividends paid on common stock holdings, life insurance dividends are essentially a refund of premiums paid. Because, in most cases, you've paid your premiums with after-tax dollars, these premium refunds (the dividends) are tax-free to you.

How can some insurers pay dividends and others not? Because those that do pay dividends charge a little more on the front end — your premium. Then if they have a good year — their investments do well — they refund some or all of that overpayment to you in the form of a dividend. Note that dividends are not guaranteed, although they are very likely. If the insurance company has a worse than expected year, it can choose not to pay a dividend at all.

If you choose a permanent policy that pays dividends, you have four choices as to how they are paid to you:

✔ You can leave them on deposit to earn interest.

✔ You can have them paid in cash and returned to you.

✔ You can apply them to reduce your premium.

✔ You can buy *paid-up additions*. Paid-up additions are small increases in your life insurance coverage that are paid up for your lifetime. Your premiums don't increase, but when you die, your beneficiary will get your original death benefit, such as $100,000, plus the total of all paid-up additions paid for by the dividends, such as another $1,500 for a total of $101,500 paid to your beneficiary.

For most people with increasing life insurance needs, using dividends to buy paid-up additions is the wisest of the four dividend options. If your needs are not increasing, having the dividends applied to reduce the premium is probably best.

Whole life

People who choose whole life insurance want a lifetime policy with zero risk. They want the insurance company to guarantee, for life, the monthly cost. If an epidemic breaks out, significantly killing off a large part of the population and raising mortality costs to the insurance company, this policy cost isn't affected at all. Conversely, if science reduces heart disease rates and cures cancer, lowering deaths and mortality costs, the insurance company reaps more profits because it continues to receive the higher, guaranteed mortality charges of the whole life policy.

The same is true for expense costs. If the insurance company's expenses rise because it buys a new building or pays agents higher commissions, it can't pass on those higher costs to the whole life customers. Similarly, if it improves efficiency and cuts costs, only the insurance company reaps the benefits.

Finally, a whole life policy pays a minimal but guaranteed rate of return — usually from 2½ percent to 4 percent for life — so guaranteed, in fact, that the policy contains a page showing what the cash value will be for each year of the future. Today, 4 percent guaranteed looks good. Twenty years ago, when interest rates were in the double digits, it looked horrible.

With whole life, the insurance company takes all the risks. You take none. The insurance company bites the bullet when things sour and reaps extra profits when things improve.

If you buy a whole life policy that offers dividends, you share a little in good years and overpay in bad years. See the sidebar "Life insurance dividends" for more information.

Universal life

In the 1980s, interest rates were rising to unexpectedly high levels, approaching 20 percent. Inflation was running rampant. Not only were the fixed rates of whole life eliminating most new sales, but existing customers were dropping their old policies in droves as, one by one, insurance companies began to offer a more flexible policy called *universal life insurance,* which has flexible rather than fixed interest rates on the cash value. At that time, a 13 percent to 14 percent return was common. Universal life later proved to be both good news and bad news for consumers.

The good news is that universal life is a flexible product. Everything that's fixed and guaranteed in a whole life policy is flexible and non-guaranteed. The risks of changes in mortality costs, expense costs, and interest rates are mostly passed on to you. If costs decrease or interest rates rise, you reap the benefit. If costs rise or interest rates plummet, you're primarily the one who takes the hit. The only risk the insurer takes is that the universal life policy has a ceiling on how high the mortality charges can go and a guaranteed minimum interest rate on the cash value — usually 2½ percent to 4 percent.

What I like about a universal policy is its flexibility — not only its adaptability to changing market conditions, but also its flexibility with the death benefit. With whole life, if you want to raise your coverage, you have to take out an additional policy. With universal life, you can lower the death benefit at any time and keep the same policy. You also can raise the benefit anytime, if you can prove good health, without having to buy additional policies.

Another thing I like about a universal policy is the ability to vary premium payments: to lower them or even temporarily suspend them, such as during hard times, or to pay in additional amounts when the rate of return is attractive — especially considering that the earnings are *tax sheltered* (free of income tax until withdrawal). With universal life, you have the option at any time of dumping large additional sums into the cash value account, subject to federal maximums.

Cash value options: When you drop permanent insurance

If, for whatever reason, you decide to cancel a permanent policy that has accumulated cash value, you have three options (called *non-for-feiture values*) as to how that cash can be used to your benefit:

✔ **You can receive the cash value in cash.** Choose the cash option when your need for life insurance has ended (the kids are grown, the mortgage is paid, and you've become financially independent).

✔ **You can receive prepaid permanent insurance for life for a reduced death benefit.** Choose the reduced, prepaid permanent insurance if your life insurance needs have diminished (the kids are grown, the mortgage is paid, and so on), but you still have life insurance needs such as covering final expenses.

✔ **You can receive term insurance for a certain length of time for the full death benefit.** Choose the extended term insurance option if you still need the full death benefit and either can't afford or don't want to pay any more premiums. Extended term insurance is a great option, especially if the need you're trying to cover with the insurance is going to end (for example, college costs and living expenses for your children) before the term insurance runs out.

Some people choose the cash option during hard times. If you're having financial difficulties but you still need life insurance, you still have a couple options. If you temporarily can't make the premium payments, the cash value can pay them until you're back on your feet. Or if you just need cash, you can borrow against the cash value via a policy loan at about a 3 percent to 4 percent net interest rate.

A good way to access your cash value in a permanent insurance policy, especially when you need cash but want to continue the insurance, is to borrow against it with interest. "But it's my money," you protest. "Why can't I just pull it out? Why would I ever borrow it? And why would I have to pay interest for using my own money?"

Some permanent policies do allow you to access the cash by pulling it out. But in the first ten years or so, some surrender charges exist. If you've had the policy for a number of years, pulling out the cash value may cause some tax consequences. Borrowing from the funds has neither problem. A policy loan also has the psychological advantage of encouraging repayment, which is a good idea if you plan to keep the policy for life.

You do have to pay a modest interest charge — usually about 8 percent of the loan. But that is only done to cover the handling expenses and because, while the money is in your hands, the insurance company still credits your policy with the policy guaranteed interest rate — usually 4 ½ percent. So the true cost of the loan to you is only about 3 percent to 4 percent.

If you do take a policy loan, your death benefit will be reduced by any unpaid balance. Whether to borrow your cash value or withdraw it outright is not an easy decision. Consult with your agent for the pros and cons of both options before deciding.

Be careful not to dump in additional amounts if any penalties for withdrawal exist. If there are penalties, usually it's best not to make the additional deposit.

Now the bad news. Universal life has one pitfall to be wary of, especially when interest rates are high. The sales illustration you receive estimates the amount of annual premium needing to be paid, assuming the current (high) interest rate remains constant, to fund the policy for life. When interest rates are high, that estimated premium is low because higher interest earnings will defray some of the policy costs. But when interest rates drop significantly, as they have in recent years, the original estimated premium will be inadequate to fund the costs, and you'll be required to significantly increase your contribution or cancel the policy. A nasty surprise.

If you want to be fairly safe from unexpected premium increases happening to you when you buy a universal life policy, choose a premium payment based on a very conservative interest rate. I recommend using the minimum guaranteed rate (that is, 3 percent). If you do, you should never have to pay higher premiums later.

Variable life

When attached to life insurance, the term *variable* means that you have half a dozen or more investment options with your cash value — including investing in the stock market. The good news with variable policies is that you have the potential to outperform what you would have earned under a non-variable contract. The bad news, as with any stock market risk, is that you can lose part of your principal.

If you choose a variable policy, understand upfront that if the cash value principal declines, you'll have to make up the loss and pay increased premiums to fund the policy properly.

Considering Term Life Insurance

Term life insurance contracts are differentiated based on the length of the coverage term, whether they can be renewed, the length of the price guarantee, and whether they can be converted to permanent insurance. Here are the three most common types of term life insurance.

A reentry story

Mark's $500,000, ten-year reentry term policy renews this month. Mark, who has exercised and eaten healthy all his life, was diagnosed with cancer two years ago. Instead of the $2,000 renewal bill he would have qualified for if he were in good health, the renewal offer came in at $14,000 a year for the first year and increased about $1,000 a year thereafter.

Fortunately, Mark's policy includes a conversion option. The cost to convert to a permanent policy with cash value is only $8,500 a year. I say *only* because $8,500 is far less than $14,000, the premiums won't increase, and the permanent policy builds cash value. Mark pays $8,500 a year so that his daughter will get a $500,000 death benefit — given Mark's illness, that's a bargain. He couldn't find a new life insurance policy anywhere at any price. Even if he lives for ten more years, he'll pay $85,000 in premiums and his daughter's trust will receive $500,000. An easy decision!

Annual renewable term

Annual renewable term (ART) is pay-as-you-go life insurance. Each year, you pay for your mortality costs for that 12-month period, plus expenses. On each 12-month anniversary, you're a year older, your mortality costs have increased slightly, and your premium increases slightly as well.

You can renew ART policies every year simply by paying the premium. The ability to renew them could end, per the policy, in as few as ten years, but more typically it's guaranteed renewable until you're age 70 or even 100. Future prices are projected but normally not guaranteed for more than five or ten years. Premiums can increase, but most policies have guaranteed maximum prices. If your health deteriorates, your future rates won't be affected, and normally you can *convert* (that is, exchange) the policy to a permanent policy anytime, without medical questions being asked.

Fixed-rate level term

Instead of annual price increases, as with annual renewable term (see the preceding section), fixed-rate level term policies allow you to lock in pricing for anywhere from 5 to 30 years in 5-year increments. The most common options are 10, 20, and 30 years.

The process of setting up new life insurance policies (administering medical exams, ordering doctor reports, and so on) is expensive. The insurance company can spread these expenses over a longer period by selling level term insurance policies because people keep the policies longer than they keep annual term policies. As a result, insurers compete harder and offer more competitive prices for level term policies than they do for annual renewable term policies.

Most level term policies can be converted to permanent policies anytime, regardless of health (although some policies limit the conversion period to 15 years or so). Also, most can be renewed beyond the first term. Where level term policies differ most dramatically is how that renewal happens and what happens to the price.

Never buy term life insurance that doesn't have an option to convert to permanent insurance, regardless of your health. You never know what the future may hold, so keep your options open.

Fixed-rate level term policies are divided into two categories:

- ✔ **Traditionally renewable level term:** At the end of the first term, traditionally renewable level term policies renew for another period of the same length, without requiring you to requalify medically. The price changes on the renewal date, based on your age.

  For example, let's say that when you were 30 years old, you bought a ten-year traditional level term policy at preferred rates. On the renewal date ten years later, you receive a bill offering to renew for another ten years, only now at a preferred 40-year-old rate, without having to qualify medically.

- ✔ **Reentry renewable level term:** Reentry level term works exactly like traditional level term in all respects except one: The renewal billing at the end of the original term is for your new attained age, but at sky-high rates that climb higher each year. Only if you're still healthy and can qualify medically (in other words, if you can *reenter*) can you reapply for the lowest preferred rates for another fixed term.

  Because insurance companies aren't obligated to offer the lowest rates on renewal, reentry renewable level term policies are the lowest-priced term policies in the insurance market. The bad news is that their renewal price is the highest in the market if you're no longer in good health.

  If you decide to buy this type of policy because of its great front-end price, give yourself a cushion. Buy it for a term of five to ten years longer than you think you'll need it to protect yourself (somewhat) from possible sky-high rates. And definitely don't use the policy for a permanent need.

Life insurance from your mortgage company: Why you shouldn't bite

If you have a home mortgage, you probably receive offers in the mail for mortgage decreasing term insurance from the mortgage company. Buying the policy is tempting. You die, and the mortgage gets paid. The price looks reasonable, and they can include the insurance premium with your house payment. What could be sweeter?

Buy it. Buy all that you can. But only if your health is bad, you're obese and a chain smoker, or you've been given six months to live. And only if coverage is automatic (no medical questions asked). In short, if you can't qualify for life insurance in the open market, buy all the mortgage decreasing term insurance you can get your hands on. If you're healthy, buy your insurance elsewhere. Here's why:

✔ Insurance from the mortgage company is almost always more expensive — often considerably more — than coverage you can buy privately.

✔ The coverage ends when you sell your home, whereas the same coverage purchased privately will not end. That's important, especially if your health has soured.

✔ The beneficiary is the mortgage company, not your family. Never a good idea. Your spouse may not want to pay off the mortgage with the money. For example, maybe she could earn 4 percent in a money market account and the mortgage rate is only 5 percent. Or maybe something unexpected has happened and she desperately needs the money for something more important.

Be careful if the price from the mortgage company appears really attractive. A few years ago, one of my employees, Mary Jo, brought me an offer for mortgage insurance from her mortgage company. The rates were amazing and she was thinking of buying it. The nice brochure gave several examples of dying: car accidents, plane crashes, falling off a roof, and so on. The brochure lacked only one thing — it failed to mention that it was *accident coverage only!* No coverage for death from natural causes — which is, even for young people, the cause of the vast majority of deaths.

Decreasing term

Decreasing term policies have coverage that reduces annually, but the premium stays level for the duration — usually 15 to 30 years. Two types of decreasing term policies exist:

✔ **Level decreasing term coverage** reduces coverage a flat amount each year. For example, a 25-year level decreasing term policy reduces 4 percent a year.

✔ **Mortgage decreasing term coverage** reduces to match a mortgage payoff. Like a mortgage, coverage reduces very slowly in the first few years and picks up steam in the later years. The rate of reduction is tied to the mortgage interest rate and the length of the mortgage. So if you buy a 10-year, 7 percent mortgage decreasing term policy, like the mortgage balance, coverage declines much faster than a 30-year, 9 percent mortgage decreasing term policy. The 10-year, 7 percent policy is also far less expensive than the 30-year, 9 percent policy.

The good news about either type of decreasing term policy is that the rates usually won't change for the duration of the term you choose. The bad news is that your life insurance coverage is reducing at a time when your living expenses are rising — not a good idea. The other bad news is that your life insurance normally ends when the term ends — the policies aren't renewable. But in all likelihood, your need for life insurance hasn't ended. And the rates for this type of coverage aren't nearly as good as level reentry term rates for the same coverage period.

If you're thinking of buying a decreasing term policy, don't. Unless decreasing term life insurance coverage is court ordered (covering the mortgage of an ex-spouse and children) or mandatory as part of a loan, buy reentry level term instead of decreasing term. You get coverage that doesn't decrease and a much lower cost.

Making Your Choice

Clearly, a potpourri of different types of life insurance are out there. How do you choose among them? Here are a few pointers:

- ✔ **If you have a permanent need, buy permanent life insurance.** If you need it but can't afford it, buy cheap reentry level term that's convertible to permanent, regardless of your health. A permanent need is a need that, no matter how old you are today, will require cash for your survivors when you die — paying estate taxes, supporting an adult child with Down's syndrome in a group home, continuing to support a favorite charity after your death, or providing supplemental lifetime income to a surviving spouse.

- ✔ **If you have a nonpermanent need, buy term life insurance.** Examples of nonpermanent needs include covering living expenses while the children are growing up, paying off a mortgage, or paying for the children's college education.

- ✔ **Buy annual renewal term insurance if your need is pressing for only a year or two, but only if the price is less than that of a ten-year reentry level term policy.**

- ✔ **Buy reentry level term if your need is great and your budget is small, such as if you're a parent with young children.** However, make sure that you're clear on when the initial level term period ends. If you still need life insurance at that time, you may need to convert what you have into a much higher-priced permanent policy if you can't qualify medically for reentry. For that reason, I recommend that you buy reentry term insurance for a period of at least five to ten years longer than you think you need it. Also, because you want the company to be around when you convert, make sure that the quality of the insurance company is high. I suggest an A. M. Best rating of A or better. (See Chapter 4 for information on rating insurance companies.)

For a small charge, some reentry term products offer a guarantee that, at the end of the first level term period, you can renew for another term at the low reentry rate regardless of your health. Unless you're 100 percent sure that you won't need coverage beyond the first term, buy this option if it's available.

✔ **Buy only guaranteed renewable and convertible term products.** You never know what the future may hold.

✔ **Buy traditional non-reentry level term coverage anytime you find its pricing reasonably close to reentry term costs, or if you're willing to pay extra for the peace of mind of keeping preferred rates for another term without ever having to requalify.**

✔ **Unless the price is significantly lower, always buy privately owned term life insurance rather than the optional group life insurance through employers, associations, or creditors and banks.** Coverage from the latter sources can end (such as coverage from your employer ending when you leave your job).

✔ **Be very wary about buying decreasing term life insurance.** Prices usually aren't that competitive, and coverage is normally not renewable. Plus, people's coverage needs rarely decrease.

Evaluating Life Insurance Sources

As you get inundated with life insurance solicitations, do you ever feel that the first thing astronauts will encounter when landing on Mars will be a coin-operated machine selling accidental space-death insurance? There's certainly no shortage of places to buy life insurance out there.

After you've determined how much coverage you need and the type of policy — term or permanent — that best suits your needs, you can search out the best place to buy what you need.

Buying with an agent

Permanent insurance is available almost exclusively from insurance agents. I recommend that you buy permanent insurance only from a top agent. Keep in mind that permanent insurance, due to its complexity and cash value element, requires added expertise in choosing among different products.

Buying term insurance is a completely different issue. Unlike almost any other kind of insurance, term insurance is close to a commodity. Term policies are the least complex policies you can buy. The policy boils down to one sentence: "If you die, we pay." Because, unlike most other policies, there aren't a lot of hidden exclusions, limitations, and other dangers, buying it direct, without an agent, is less risky than buying any other policy direct.

Still, using an agent doesn't cost that much more (if anything). I recommend using one, but separate the wheat from the chaff and pick only a skilled agent. Hiring the best won't cost you a dime more, because all agents get paid about the same amount, determined by the premium you pay. (See Chapter 4 for tips on choosing an expert.)

A good agent can help you determine the right amount of coverage, determine the best type of term insurance product to use, set up the policy owner and beneficiary properly, and be an advocate for you if you're having problems with the insurance company. A top agent can also help you choose a financially solid company that will endure. And finally, if your application is rejected due to health, weight, or other problems, a good agent can help you search for a company that will insure you.

Life insurance is available from career life insurance agents whose primary occupation is the sale of life insurance, from the agent who helps you with your auto and homeowner's insurance, and from many financial planners.

Career life insurance agents

The principal advantage of career life insurance agents is that life insurance is their specialty. They tend to have a higher level of expertise, especially if they have more than five years in the business. Life insurance agents who have taken advanced classes and earned professional designations, such as the Certified Life Underwriter (CLU), are especially good bets.

Be careful of inexperienced agents, especially if you have complex needs. Many don't last. The washout rate for life insurance agents is one of the highest of any profession — close to 90 percent in the first two years! As you can guess, most new agents also have less expertise than experienced agents. (In many states, a person can legally sell life insurance with just a week of schooling!)

If you do work with a new agent and you have any concerns about what's being recommended to you, get a second opinion. If you decide to work with an agent, you may get a lot of pressure to buy permanent life insurance when you're asking for term life insurance. The dramatically higher commission that agents earn by selling permanent insurance compared to term insurance may be the reason. If the agent who's "helping" you insists that permanent insurance is your best option when your need isn't permanent, walking away from that agent may be your only option. Of course, some real pros, who care about your welfare, may also believe that permanent insurance is the only way to go. After all, permanent insurance is always going to be there for you and your loved ones, as long as you pay the premiums.

Multiple policy agents

Many agents who sell auto and home insurance also have life insurance licenses. But less than half know much about life insurance or even actively sell it. And probably only 20 percent are quite knowledgeable about the subject.

If you like your current auto and homeowner's agent's skills in those areas, but he isn't an expert on life insurance, ask for a referral to a life insurance specialist. If your agent is good at his specialty, chances are excellent that the agent he refers you to will also be good.

If your current agent is skilled with life insurance, working with him in that area, too, is to your advantage. Having one agent for everything simplifies your life. And the washout rate on these multiple policy agents is very small.

Financial planners

Two types of people licensed to sell life insurance fit the broad *financial planner* category:

- ✔ Money managers who primarily dispense investment advice but also are licensed to sell life insurance
- ✔ Career life agents who also offer investments

The primary difference between the two is that the former more often recommend buying term life insurance with your investments separate, whereas the latter often recommend permanent life insurance with its cash value as a part of your investment portfolio.

If you're considering buying life insurance from a financial planner, a pretty safe bet is that those who recommend term insurance for your nonpermanent needs are the better choice. Permanent insurance is not considered a good investment product.

Buy permanent insurance if it's the best insurance for your needs, but don't buy it solely as an investment, for three reasons:

- **Permanent life is non-portable.** If something better comes along, it's hard to move without penalty.

- **The mortality charges are usually higher than those for term insurance.** To get a true reflection of the rate of return on the cash value of a permanent policy, you need to deduct the hidden costs of those extra mortality and expense charges. How? By shopping for the lowest term life policy, requesting that the agent disclose those same charges in the permanent policy, and then subtracting the difference between the two results from the cash value gain.

- **Permanent life insurance has a heavy front-end cost due to the high sales commission, which significantly affects the cash value performances.**

I'm not in the least advising you not to buy permanent life insurance. I'm just suggesting that you not buy it as an investment.

Buying without an agent

If you're considering buying term life insurance direct from a toll-free number or on the job, first check with your favorite agent to see if she can match the price. She probably can — in which case, use an agent. If your agent can't match the quote or come close, consider paying the agent a fee (perhaps $200) to review your plans and make sure that you're not shooting yourself in the foot.

All the following sources of term life insurance allow you to buy without an agent:

- **The Internet:** Several sites are set up to comparison-shop term life insurance, but I don't recommend buying any insurance this way unless you yourself are an expert. (See Chapter 4 on buying insurance right.)

- **Creditors:** Banks, mortgage companies, and credit card companies regularly solicit their customers to buy *credit life insurance* from them to pay off any balance if the customer dies. Look at what they get! If you buy the insurance from your mortgage company, for example, it makes a nice upfront commission on the sale, and later, if you die, it gets paid your outstanding balance. What a good deal (for them)!

But how good is the deal for you? Not very. Life insurance rates from creditors are usually much higher than on the open market. And the creditor — not your survivors — is the beneficiary. Unless your health makes you uninsurable through traditional life insurance sources, avoid buying insurance from your creditors.

✔ **Associations:** Many groups and associations offer term life insurance as a membership benefit. Sometimes the price is fantastic. Most of the time, the price is mediocre. The problem is that if you leave the association or the association quits offering the coverage, you lose your life insurance.

As a general rule, don't buy life insurance from an association. However, do buy as much as you can if you're uninsurable and the insurer asks no medical questions.

✔ **Group life:** Take all the free life insurance your employer offers you. If and only if your health is poor and you can't qualify for other types of life insurance, buy all the supplemental life insurance your employer offers on a nonmedical basis. (Sometimes that can be $50,000 or more.) If you're healthy, don't buy any more than the free coverage paid for by your employer through work. Buy it privately. Why? Two reasons: You lose group insurance when you leave the job, and the rates are almost always higher than on the open market if you're in good health.

✔ **Direct mail and telemarketing phone solicitations:** Again, unless they offer guaranteed coverage and you're otherwise uninsurable, stay away from direct mail and toll-free number sources. Most have a fly-by-night feel. Plus, they rarely offer prices that can compete with those you can get in the market if you're healthy.

✔ **Slot machines:** I'm referring to those coin-operated flight insurance dispensers at airports and similar dispensers of "fear insurance." Unless you know ahead of time that the plane is going down, don't buy this stuff. (Better yet, don't take the flight!) But *do* listen to your fear. It's telling you that you feel inadequately insured. Act on that fear and raise your life insurance coverage to a high enough level that you can comfortably walk by these machines (with a smile) the next time you fly.

Avoiding Common Life Insurance Mistakes

People make all kinds of mistakes when they buy life insurance. In this section, I fill you in on the most common ones so that you can avoid falling into any traps.

Trading cash value for death protection needs

Being under-insured with permanent life insurance may be the biggest single mistake that people make in buying life insurance. They get swayed by the lure of the investment portion or cash value of the policy but can't afford to have their cake and eat it, too. In other words, they can't afford to pay for all the death protection they need plus the investment, so they buy a cash value policy with less death protection than they need in order to have some investment — something to show for it in the end when they don't (unlike the rest of us) die. However, when they do die, their family doesn't have enough money to live on, creating a serious financial problem.

The most important thing about life insurance is the protection it offers. So first things first. Determine how much life insurance you need by using a credible method. Then buy as much of that protection as you can afford, using term insurance, even lower-cost reentry products if necessary. If your budget has something left over, only then is it okay to look at permanent life products for part of your coverage. Never trade critical protection for less-important investment opportunities.

Buying your life insurance in pieces

Buying your life insurance in pieces is a lot more expensive than covering all your needs in one policy. Plus, buying in pieces leaves you vulnerable to a gap in your coverage. Examples of piecemeal buying are having mortgage insurance through your lending institution, credit card insurance through your credit card company, credit life insurance with your car loan, supplemental group life insurance at work, flight insurance at the airport, and so on. With some of these insurances, you don't have to qualify medically; therefore, if you're in poor health or near death, buy all you can. Otherwise, they're often three or four times the price of what you would pay if you're in good health.

When buying life insurance, figure out how much insurance you need to do the whole job and buy *one* policy. It's smarter — and cheaper! Only one policy fee instead of several. Plus you have the advantage of a trusted professional agent to help with determining how much coverage you need, the type of policy, the proper listing of beneficiaries, and so on.

Buying accidental death/travel accident coverage

Both accidental death and travel accident policies are varieties of Las Vegas insurance, transferring only the accidental portion of your risk. In other words, you have no coverage for death from natural causes. Buying these policies is an especially bad move if you buy them in lieu of the full life insurance you really need. My belief about travel accident coverage is that anyone who buys it at the airport or from a travel agent is really saying, "I'm not comfortable with the amount of life insurance I have." The bottom line is that if you need insurance to cover a flight you're taking, you also need it for driving down the street, potential heart attacks, and the like.

When buying life insurance, buy only coverage that pays for any death — natural or accidental.

Covering the children in lieu of the parents

When your child is born, you try to be a responsible parent. You're deluged with a lot of solicitations about life insurance because of the birth announcement in the newspaper. You have hopes and dreams for your children, so you buy a nice cash value policy on your baby. It's understandable — you're so proud. But the economic effect on the family of a child's death is minimal compared to the major impact that one of the baby's parents dying would have.

When a child is born, seriously reevaluate and raise the amount of life insurance coverage that you and your spouse have.

Being unrealistic about how much you can afford to pay for life insurance

In the 25-plus years that I've been an agent, I can't tell you how many times I've seen young people commit more money than they can actually afford to a large cash value life insurance policy and then two or three years later have to drop it and take a large financial loss — and perhaps even be exposed to the risk of a death without insurance. I recommend term insurance for young families. It provides the most coverage for the money spent. If you want a permanent policy later with more bells and whistles, you can always convert your term policy.

Part VI
The Part of Tens

The 5th Wave   By Rich Tennant

In this part . . .

1 If you're short on time, you've come to the right part, because the chapters here pack a powerful punch in a paucity of pages. Here you discover ten ingredients of a watertight insurance program, ten government insurance programs, and ten tips for saving big bucks on your car insurance bill.

Chapter 24

Ten Ingredients for a Watertight Insurance Program

I've looked at the insurance programs of over 2,000 people, and almost every one of them had at least one major gap in coverage — and most had five to ten coverage gaps. Here's the good news: Virtually all these gaps can be plugged for a minimal amount of money! In this chapter, I offer ten general tips that can go a long way toward helping you avoid major gaps in your insurance program.

Selecting the Best Insurance Agent

A good agent is the main ingredient in a watertight insurance program. In fact, if you hire an expert who is skilled in every area of personal insurance, you'll barely have to worry about the other nine ingredients for a watertight program.

An agent, expert in all types of insurance, is a great bargain in at least five significant ways:

✔ **She has the expertise and tools to help you choose adequate coverage limits in each major loss area.**

✔ **She helps you keep your coverage in those major loss areas balanced and helps you avoid inconsistent coverage.**

✔ **She takes the time to probe into your life deeply enough to identify those risks that your current insurance policies exclude.** She then applies her expertise to help you properly plug your policies with the supplemental coverages you need to fill those gaps. A really great agent also helps you change your coverages as the risks in your life change.

✔ **When you have a claim, she does more than just file a report for you.** She applies her coverage expertise to coach you on how to properly document your claim so you get paid all that you're owed with the least amount of delay or hassle.

✔ **If your claim is unjustly denied or underpaid, she cares enough (and has enough coverage expertise) to get the claims department to reverse its position and pay you everything you rightfully deserve.**

If your agent isn't as good as the agent I just described, you can and must do better. The consequences of having the wrong agent can be severe! Getting more talent generally doesn't cost you a dime. In most states, every insurance agent — from the very best to the very worst — gets paid the same commission. So spend your money wisely!

See Chapter 4 for more information on finding a top agent.

Covering All Your Natural Disaster Exposures

Floods. Earthquakes. Mudslides. Tornadoes. Hurricanes. In Minnesota, we worry about tornadoes and floods, but few of us lose sleep over a possible earthquake. Californians worry about wildfires, earthquakes, and mudslides. Floridians sweat bullets about hurricanes. Paying attention to these weather risks is an important ingredient in a great insurance program. They have the potential to destroy your home and they're often excluded from homeowner's insurance coverage.

If you live in an area where you're exposed to a weather-related risk and you haven't addressed the issue in your insurance, your insurance program has a serious leak.

You can find more information about insuring these natural disasters in Chapters 9 and 11.

Adding a Home Replacement Guarantee

One of the major losses you want to have well insured is the destruction of your home. The big risk when you buy homeowner's insurance is not buying enough structure coverage to rebuild your home if it's destroyed. You and your agent, in good faith, try to establish the replacement value of your home, but pinpointing that value is difficult at best — especially if your home is older. And you certainly don't want to grossly over-insure your home and pay too much for your insurance. So, what's the solution?

The insurance industry offers a good solution for this dilemma. It's called the *extended replacement cost guarantee* (or something similar to that, depending on the company). If your home is destroyed, this optional coverage guarantees that the policy will pay the entire cost to rebuild, even if the cost exceeds the amount for which the home was insured. The typical cost for this great coverage is only $10 to $50 a year — and, believe me, you can't afford *not* to buy it!

The coverage usually has a cap of 125 percent of your coverage limit, but some insurance companies still offer a guarantee with no cap. If your insurer offers that, grab it!

If you have an older home, avoid insurance companies that don't offer the extended replacement cost guarantee. Many insurance companies willingly make the guarantee available to owners of older homes, so you shouldn't have trouble finding a company that gives you what you need.

See Chapter 9 for the three conditions you must meet to qualify for the extended replacement cost guarantee.

Standardizing Your Liability Limits

When you buy automobile, homeowner's, boat, snowmobile, or any other liability policy, always buy the same liability insurance limit. No exceptions.

People make this mistake a lot, especially when they have their insurance coverage split between different agents and/or insurance companies. You can reduce the chances of this happening by having as much of your liability insurance as possible with the same agent.

Whenever you cause an injury or property damage, you want the same amount of money available to you for legal costs and judgments, no matter what the cause of the accident. In the same way that you wouldn't buy more liability insurance for claims that occur on Monday, Tuesday, and Wednesday than you would for claims that occur the rest of the week, it doesn't make sense to buy different liability limits for different policies.

If you have an umbrella policy, make sure that all the underlying liability insurance limits meet the minimum requirements of the umbrella policy. If they don't, you'll owe the difference.

Identifying and Plugging Liability Gaps

Plugging liability gaps is an area where having a highly skilled agent pays big dividends. You want an agent who can identify risks you're exposed to that basic auto, home, and other personal policies don't cover — an agent who, for example, knows that the following lawsuits are not automatically covered but knows how to get them covered (usually very inexpensively):

- ✔ When making a delivery to your home office, a delivery person slips and falls on your icy sidewalk and is injured (see Chapter 11).

- ✔ The roofer you hire injures his back falling off a ladder and sues you for workers' compensation benefits (see Chapter 11).

- ✔ You injure a co-worker when you drive the company car through a stop sign (see Chapter 6).

- ✔ A guest of yours is injured while vacationing with you at your timeshare condominium (see Chapter 12).

- ✔ A person is injured in the boat you rented while on vacation (see Chapter 16).

For more information and tips on plugging liability insurance gaps, see Parts II, III, and IV of this book.

Choosing the Right Umbrella Policy

If you do buy an umbrella policy (and I strongly recommend that you do), don't just automatically buy the policy that comes from the insurance company that provides your personal auto and homeowner's insurance. All umbrella policies are not created equal. For about the same money as a poor policy, you can get a top-of-the-line policy that covers most of the unique liability risks in your life.

Here are just a few examples of risks that would be covered by a good umbrella and would not be covered by a poor one:

- ✔ Renting a car outside the United States and Canada
- ✔ Renting a barn for a 50th birthday party
- ✔ Serving on the board of directors for your favorite charity
- ✔ Renting a boat on vacation

A top agent with expertise in the differences between umbrella policies can play a significant role in helping you buy the umbrella policy that best covers the unique liability exposures in your life. See Chapter 15 for general information on umbrella policies and Chapter 16 for tips on identifying those liability risks in your life that are *not* covered by your auto or homeowner's policies that *can* be covered by an umbrella policy.

Buying More Life Insurance than You Think You Need

This recommendation has two parts. The first is to buy life insurance. The second is to buy more than you think you'll need — in other words, more than you think your survivors will need. How much more? A lot — 25 percent to 50 percent more than you think your survivors will need, especially if you have a young family and/or if you're buying low-cost term life insurance. (It's cheap stuff — you can afford to be extra generous.)

For tips on how to determine how much life insurance you need, the best type of policy to meet your needs, and the best place to buy it, see Chapter 23.

Protecting Yourself from Long-Term Disability

By far, the most overlooked and undersold major-loss coverage is long-term disability insurance. Almost everyone has some life insurance, but only a small percentage of people have long-term disability insurance (unless it's provided by their employer). This is the case in spite of the fact that the odds of having a long-term disability are considerably greater than the odds of dying before the age of 65, and in spite of the fact that a family's living expenses during a disability are considerably higher than those following a death.

Unless you're one of the few people who have enough outside income to meet all your living expenses in the event of an illness or injury that would prevent you from working, buy long-term disability insurance. And don't necessarily rely on group disability insurance from your employer — it may be good, or it may not be.

For help in determining your need for disability insurance, turn to Chapter 22.

Having Major Medical Insurance with a High Lifetime Limit

Buy medical insurance with a limit of at least $3 million to $5 million. And if it contains copayment requirements, make sure that there's an annual out-of-pocket maximum on the copayments.

For a watertight insurance program, if you don't have health insurance supplied by your employer, you need to buy it yourself.

If you're age 65 or over, don't rely exclusively on Medicare. Buy a quality Medicare supplement policy.

For tips on what makes a great major medical health insurance policy and/or a great Medicare supplement policy, see Chapters 18, 19, and 20.

Choosing a Strong Insurance Company

If you're working with a top insurance agent, you won't need to spend a lot of time checking out the insurance company or companies he recommends. But if you're buying insurance direct (without an agent), if you have low confidence in your current agent, or if you simply want to be extra careful, check out insurance company ratings at www.ambest.com/ratings. A. M. Best is an independent organization that has been rating insurance companies for over 100 years; it has an excellent reputation. Stay with insurance companies rated A or better.

Chapter 25

Ten Government Programs You Should Know About

*O*ne of the functions of government is to address citizens' needs that are not being met by the private, for-profit sector. Nowhere is this more evident than the insurance industry. Insurers as a whole do a pretty good job of meeting the needs of most people with car, home, life, disability, health, and long-term-care insurance. But insurers seeking and entitled to a small profit don't have the means to provide insurance to people who either can't afford insurance or who can't qualify.

In this chapter, I introduce you to ten U.S. government and state government programs, along with tips on where you can get more information on them.

The FDIC: Insurance on Your Bank Deposits

The Federal Deposit Insurance Corporation (FDIC) protects against loss of deposits in any FDIC-insured bank or savings association — in other words, if you have money in a bank and that bank goes under, you're protected.

The insurance covers both regular and IRA funds in checking, savings, CDs and money-market accounts. The FDIC does *not* cover other financial products (like stocks, bonds, mutual funds, or insurance annuities). The FDIC insures accounts up to $250,000 per owner; $500,000 for joint accounts.

Rules on insurance limits are always subject to change, so if you have any doubt at all about which of your accounts are covered and for how much, go to www.myfdicinsurance.gov where you can find a nifty little tool, called EDIE, to estimate whether your bank funds are protected fully. For more information, go to www.fdic.gov or call 877-275-3342.

Since the FDIC was founded in 1933, no one has lost a single penny due to bank failures or other causes. Plus, the turnaround time for getting your money is only a day or two!

Insurance on Insurance: State Guaranty Funds

Most states have a guaranty fund to protect you if an insurance company fails and you lose your insurance coverage at the time of a claim. In order to pay claims after an insurer is declared insolvent, the fund assesses the other insurance companies doing business in the state. In other words, the other insurance companies have to pay to cover the claims of the company that failed.

To find out more about your particular state's guaranty fund, go to www.ncigf.org/public-guarantyfunds.asp and look up your state's contact information. Most states have two guaranty funds — one for property-casualty companies and the other for life and health companies.

Although guaranty funds are important, your best bet is to never need one in the first place. Always work with a good insurance agent who can pick quality companies for you. Check the financial rating of any insurance company you're considering doing business with by going to www.ambest.com. A. M. Best Company has been rating insurance companies for over 100 years. Whenever possible, choose a company that has received A. M. Best's highest ratings: A, A+, or A++. (For suggestions on choosing an agent or insurance company, see Chapter 4.)

COBRA: For When You Lose Your Group Medical Insurance

There are many reasons why you may be losing your group medical insurance coverage: You or your spouse may be quitting your job, you or your spouse may be retiring, you may be divorcing your spouse under whose insurance you were covered.

Regardless of the reason that you're losing your group medical insurance, employers with 20 or more employees are required by federal COBRA law to offer you the right to continue the group coverage at your expense for up to 18 months (29 months if you're disabled, 36 months if you're retiring or if you're a child forced to come off a parent's policy).

COBRA stands for the Consolidated Omnibus Budget Reconciliation Act of 1985.

For tips on whether to elect COBRA and the deadlines by which you need to make the decision, turn to Chapter 19.

Some states have extended COBRA rights to employees of companies with fewer than 20 employees. Contact your state insurance department to find out specifically how COBRA applies in your state.

HIPAA: For When COBRA Ends

The Health Insurance Portability and Accountability Act (HIPAA) was created to give people who are losing their group coverage and who have preexisting medical conditions the right to continued health coverage without preexisting-condition exclusions applying to their replacement policy. The intent of the law is to prevent "job lock," where an employee is stuck in a dead-end job in order to keep the health coverage, because he or a family member has a *preexisting medical condition* (defined by HIPAA as any condition treated by doctors or medication in the last six months). HIPAA makes it possible for an employee leave a job and take a new job with group medical coverage, with the assurance that the health issues of everyone in the family are immediately covered under the new group policy. HIPAA also makes it possible for an individual to leave the group policy and buy a private policy without preexisting-condition limitations or having to qualify medically, providing that your COBRA option, if any, has been exercised and the time frame exhausted (in other words, you've stuck with COBRA as long as it was available to you).

The federal government has left it up to each state to determine exactly what type of individual health product is made available. The only condition is that there can be no preexisting condition waiting period or exclusion — preexisting conditions have to be covered immediately, provided that everyone being covered has had consecutive coverage for the past 12 months with no lapse in coverage of more than 63 days.

For more in-depth information on how HIPAA works for you, see Chapter 19. To find out the specific HIPAA options in your state, contact your state insurance department.

Social Security Long-Term Disability

When you think Social Security, you probably think retirement program. You may think survivor benefits for children. But few people realize that Social Security also includes disability benefits that start after 5 months of total disability if that disability is expected to last 12 months or more or result in death. Benefits are payable to your normal retirement age.

If you've been paying into the Social Security system, every year you get a statement of estimated benefits. That statement includes your estimated retirement benefits, as well as your estimated long-term disability benefits.

Don't rely strictly on Social Security to meet your need for income replacement following a disability. In fact, I generally recommend that you ignore Social Security so that, if you do qualify for benefits, they'll be a little extra cushion for you.

For more information on the program and how to qualify, go to www.ssa. gov. For more information on managing your long-term disability risks, turn to Chapter 22.

State Health Insurance Pools

Whenever you apply for an individual health policy, there are four possible outcomes:

- ✔ Your application is approved.
- ✔ Your application is denied.
- ✔ Your application is approved at higher rates because of preexisting conditions (such as diabetes).
- ✔ Your application is approved, but an exclusionary rider is attached to the policy excluding coverage for a preexisting condition (such as a bad back, bad knees, and so on).

Many states have created health insurance pools that ensure people with preexisting health conditions who can't get health insurance or can't get it without surcharged pricing or exclusionary riders.

If you or a family member is facing that predicament, check with your state insurance department to see if your state has such a pool. Or go online to the National Association of State Health Insurance Plans at www.naschip.org.

National Flood Insurance

Homeowner's policies have always excluded coverage for any kind of ground or below-ground water entering the house. So, the national flood insurance program was created years ago to address this risk.

Most people think that flood insurance is only needed if you live near a river or other body of water. But, according to the Federal Emergency Management Authority (FEMA), which oversees the national flood insurance program, about one-third of all flood losses occur to homes nowhere near any body of water. Why? Because flooding from torrential rains can over-whelm an area with water. Few people realize that the flood policy covers that type of loss (in addition to loss from flooded rivers or other bodies of water). If your home is not in a high-risk flood area, you can buy a flood policy for a little more than $100 a year.

For more on the national flood insurance program, as well as my sugges-tions for managing ground water risks, turn to Chapter 11. To find out whether your home is in a low-, moderate-, or high-risk flood area, go to www. floodsmart.gov and enter your address. You can also find out what your approximate flood insurance premium will cost for different levels of cover-age. You must buy the coverage from an insurance agent — ideally your hom-eowner's agent.

The flood policy does not cover any personal property, carpeting, finished walls, and so on in any part of your home where the floor is below ground level unless one of the four outside walls has a floor at least partially at or above ground level (as in a walkout basement). Also, don't wait to buy a policy until sandbags are being filled — there's a 30-day waiting period for new poli-cies before coverage starts.

Medicaid

Backed by the federal government and administered by the states, Medicaid is a health insurance program that provides medical assistance to those in need — people at or near poverty levels. Medicaid also provides long-term care for those with little or no assets. It is of particular interest to middle-class Americans who need long-term care but don't have insurance cover-age for that. In that case, they end up spending down all their assets to near poverty levels, at which point Medicaid will pick up the costs of any ongoing care for the rest of their lives. The tragedy is that, by spending down all your assets, little (if anything) is left for your surviving spouse or children.

See Chapter 21 for more on long-term care insurance and discover how you can shelter assets from Medicaid eligibility under the new partnership program with Medicaid. For more on Medicaid eligibility, go to www.cms.hhs.gov/home/medicaid.asp.

Medicare

Otherwise known as national health insurance for seniors, Medicare provides a base level of hospital and medical benefits. In 2003, optional prescription drug coverage (known as Part D) was added. Medicare is funded by a combination of premium payments from seniors and payroll taxes from non-seniors. In addition to the three parts of Medicare — Part A (hospital), Part B (medical), and Part D (drugs) — most seniors will want a good Medicare supplement policy to pay most of what Medicare doesn't cover or disallow. Find out more about Medicare and my specific bottom-line advice for seniors in Chapter 20. For more information on Medicare, go to www.medicare.gov. For more on Part D, check out *Medicare Prescription Drug Coverage For Dummies,* by Patricia Barry (Wiley).

Hurricane Windstorm Pools

There has been a dramatic increase in recent years in coastal hurricanes — both in terms of the frequency with which they occur and in terms of the financial devastation they cause. This has led to the insurance industry no longer insuring homes located in the east and southern coastal areas for hurricane damage.

In order for insurance to work, enough homes have to not be damaged, and those homeowners' insurance premiums pay the claims of those homes that are damaged. This just isn't true with hurricanes — hence, the insurance companies' unwillingness to insure homes against hurricane damage.

So, the affected coastal states worked with insurers to allow them to still insure coastal homes while excluding storm losses. Each state created its own storm insurance pool where coastal property owners can buy storm insurance. Then when hurricanes hit, the pool pays the losses. If losses exceed the funds available, the pool is empowered to assess insurers writing property insurance in that state for the shortfall. The agent who sets up your homeowner's insurance can help you with this insurance as well.

Chapter 26

Ten Ways to Save Big Bucks on Car Insurance

*B*ecause car accidents happen so frequently and cost so much — both in injuries and property damage — the cost of car insurance is often one of the biggest insurance items in your budget. In this chapter, I offer ten tips to help keep those costs to a minimum without sacrificing coverage.

Take the Bus or Ride Your Bike to Work

If you drive more than 3 miles to work right now, you'll probably save 20 percent off your car insurance bill if you quit commuting to and from work.

If taking the bus or riding a bike aren't practical where you live, consider carpooling. Many insurance companies offer good discounts on car insurance if you carpool.

If you're the driver of the carpool, be careful. It's okay for your passengers to chip in on your gasoline and other expenses, but don't charge for the ride or your car insurance may be null and void.

Buy Cars Favored by Crash-Test Dummies

Every year, the Insurance Institute for Highway Safety conducts crash tests of new cars. There is a strong correlation between how well vehicles score on crash tests and how much they cost to insure — the better their scores, the lower their insurance costs. Buying a safe vehicle not only protects you and your passengers but also helps keep your insurance costs down — and that's a hard combination to beat!

You can find crash-test results for both new and used cars at www.iihs.org.

Choose Higher Deductibles

Large lawsuits, without enough insurance, can ruin you financially, so you don't want to try to save money by cutting your coverage. That said, the physical-damage coverage on cars typically costs 40 percent of the total insurance bill. If you just raise your collision deductible to $1,000 and raise your comprehensive deductible to $500, you can save 10 percent to 15 percent on your entire insurance bill without decreasing your major-loss coverage in any way.

If your car is older, it may be time to drop the collision and comprehensive coverage. You can find more information on how to determine the most cost-effective deductibles for you in Chapter 5.

Sell All Your Lead Shoes

Don't speed. Obey traffic laws. Drive defensively. In other words, keep your driving record clear of tickets and accidents.

Most insurance companies give people with clear driving records a *good-driver discount* of 20 percent to 25 percent. One at-fault accident or two moving violations will generally cause you to lose the discount for three years. How you choose to drive has a huge impact on how much you pay for insurance.

Put Your Teenage Driver Up for Adoption

Parents always want to know how to minimize their insurance costs when they're adding a teenage driver to their insurance. Here's my crude rule of thumb I use with my own clients:

> If the teenager will be an occasional driver in the household, the rates on the car that the teen will drive will roughly *double.* If the teen will be the principal driver of one of the cars, the rates on that car will roughly *triple.*

Hence, my recommendation to put the kid up for adoption.

Assuming you're attached to your kid, occasional bad attitude and all, here are a few things you can do to keep your costs down:

- ✔ **Make him turn off the TV and hit the books.** If your teen stays on the B honor roll, he'll earn a *good-student discount* and save about 15 percent on the cost of insurance for the car he drives.

- ✔ **Send her to college far, far away.** If she goes away to college and doesn't take a car with her, and if the college is 100 miles or more away from home, you can qualify for a *distant-student discount* and save about 75 percent off the cost of her insurance. She still can drive a car when she comes home for holidays or for summer vacation. Plus, she's covered when she drives a friend's car at school.

- ✔ **Give him an old car to drive.** Making him the driver of an older car that doesn't need collision and comprehensive coverage will save about 30 percent to 40 percent off his total insurance bill. This represents a savings of hundreds of dollars a year.

For more tips on saving money and keeping your teenagers safe, turn to Chapter 6.

Don't Drink and Drive

I hope you're obeying this law because you care about your own safety and the safety of those around you. But if you want a financial reason for always having a designated driver, note that a driving-under-the-influence (DUI) ticket leads to an automatic *cancellation* of your car insurance. Then, for about three years, your rates with a *higher-risk insurance company* (a company that specializes in insuring high-risk drivers) will be about three times *greater* than they were before your DUI; and for another two years, they'll be about twice what they were before your DUI. In other words, the price you'll pay for driving drunk (if you're lucky and don't hurt yourself or anyone else), will be five years of incredibly expensive car insurance.

If you have teenage drivers in your house, talk to them about the dangers of drinking and driving. Make a promise to your kids that you'll come pick them up, no questions asked, anyplace, anytime — and stick to your word. Students Against Destructive Decisions (SADD), formerly known as Students Against Driving Drunk, has a great Contract for Life that you and your teens can sign. You can find it at www.sadd.org/contract.htm.

Maintain a High Credit Score

In the past few years, insurance companies have begun offering large discounts of up to 40 percent for people with great credit scores. Statisticians apparently have found a strong correlation between a person's credit rating and the probability of that person having accidents: The higher the rating, the fewer the accidents.

Because your credit score has an equally huge impact on your homeowner's insurance rates, make sure you regularly check your credit reports for all three credit bureaus — Equifax, Experian, and TransUnion. You're entitled to one free credit report per year from each of the three bureaus, and you can get yours by going to the government-sponsored site www.annual creditreport.com.

Take the time to read your credit reports closely, and if you find false information on any of them, get it corrected — doing so will lower your insurance rates on both your car insurance and your homeowner's insurance. (For more information on how to get your credit reports corrected, check out *Credit Repair Kit For Dummies,* 2nd Edition, by Steve Bucci [Wiley]).

Insure Your Cars and Home with the Same Company

This strategy benefits you in two ways:

- ✔ It reduces the chance of gaps in coverage.
- ✔ You can usually save 10 percent to 20 percent on both policies, which usually means a few hundred dollars a year extra in your pocket.

Many insurance companies also give you additional discounts if you have your umbrella policy with them, too.

Don't Duplicate Your Health Insurance

Don't buy any more insurance than your state requires for reimbursement of medical bills in a car accident.

Some states call the coverage *medical payments;* other states call it *personal injury protection.* The primary difference between the two is that the personal injury protection coverage pays both medical bills and lost wages in a car accident.

Most states require some minimum level of coverage but then also require that higher limits be made available to you. Don't take the bait. This coverage just duplicates coverage you should already have anyway — health insurance and long-term disability insurance. If you do decide to buy the higher coverage anyway, make sure that your health-insurance company at least sends you a thank-you note, because they're the only one benefiting from your better coverage! (See Chapter 5 for more information on this recommendation.)

Don't Submit Small Claims for Property Damage

You don't want to automatically file claims for small property damage that you cause — whether it be to your car or to the other guy's car. Before you file a claim, talk to your agent about what kind of impact this claim will have on your rates. Do you have other tickets or accidents? If so, this additional claim might seriously jack up your premiums. An at-fault claim usually raises your rates about 20 percent for three years.

Here's an example: Suppose you back into a car in a parking lot causing $600 of damage to the other car and nothing to yours. Also suppose that you're currently paying $2,000 a year to insure two cars for full coverage. If turning in this accident will raise your rates 20 percent a year for three years, that's a $1,200 total increase ($2,000 × 0.20 = $400 × 3 years = $1,200). You're far better off paying the other guy $600 out of your own pocket than you are submitting a claim.

Do, however, submit all claims for injuries, no matter how small. Otherwise, if that apparent minor injury ends up being more substantial than first thought, and you end up getting sued later, your insurance company has grounds for denying your claim because you violated one of your policy conditions of prompt reporting of accidents.

Index

• *I* •

• S •

BUSINESS, CAREERS & PERSONAL FINANCE

Accounting For Dummies, 4th Edition*
978-0-470-24600-9

Bookkeeping Workbook For Dummies†
978-0-470-16983-4

Commodities For Dummies
978-0-470-04928-0

Doing Business in China For Dummies
978-0-470-04929-7

E-Mail Marketing For Dummies
978-0-470-19087-6

Job Interviews For Dummies, 3rd Edition*†
978-0-470-17748-8

Personal Finance Workbook For Dummies*†
978-0-470-09933-9

Real Estate License Exams For Dummies
978-0-7645-7623-2

Six Sigma For Dummies
978-0-7645-6798-8

Small Business Kit For Dummies, 2nd Edition*†
978-0-7645-5984-6

Telephone Sales For Dummies
978-0-470-16836-3

BUSINESS PRODUCTIVITY & MICROSOFT OFFICE

Access 2007 For Dummies
978-0-470-03649-5

Excel 2007 For Dummies
978-0-470-03737-9

Office 2007 For Dummies
978-0-470-00923-9

Outlook 2007 For Dummies
978-0-470-03830-7

PowerPoint 2007 For Dummies
978-0-470-04059-1

Project 2007 For Dummies
978-0-470-03651-8

QuickBooks 2008 For Dummies
978-0-470-18470-7

Quicken 2008 For Dummies
978-0-470-17473-9

Salesforce.com For Dummies, 2nd Edition
978-0-470-04893-1

Word 2007 For Dummies
978-0-470-03658-7

EDUCATION, HISTORY, REFERENCE & TEST PREPARATION

African American History For Dummies
978-0-7645-5469-8

Algebra For Dummies
978-0-7645-5325-7

Algebra Workbook For Dummies
978-0-7645-8467-1

Art History For Dummies
978-0-470-09910-0

ASVAB For Dummies, 2nd Edition
978-0-470-10671-6

British Military History For Dummies
978-0-470-03213-8

Calculus For Dummies
978-0-7645-2498-1

Canadian History For Dummies, 2nd Edition
978-0-470-83656-9

Geometry Workbook For Dummies
978-0-471-79940-5

The SAT I For Dummies, 6th Edition
978-0-7645-7193-0

Series 7 Exam For Dummies
978-0-470-09932-2

World History For Dummies
978-0-7645-5242-7

FOOD, GARDEN, HOBBIES & HOME

Bridge For Dummies, 2nd Edition
978-0-471-92426-5

Coin Collecting For Dummies, 2nd Edition
978-0-470-22275-1

Cooking Basics For Dummies, 3rd Edition
978-0-7645-7206-7

Drawing For Dummies
978-0-7645-5476-6

Etiquette For Dummies, 2nd Edition
978-0-470-10672-3

Gardening Basics For Dummies*†
978-0-470-03749-2

Knitting Patterns For Dummies
978-0-470-04556-5

Living Gluten-Free For Dummies†
978-0-471-77383-2

Painting Do-It-Yourself For Dummies
978-0-470-17533-0

HEALTH, SELF HELP, PARENTING & PETS

Anger Management For Dummies
978-0-470-03715-7

Anxiety & Depression Workbook For Dummies
978-0-7645-9793-0

Dieting For Dummies, 2nd Edition
978-0-7645-4149-0

Dog Training For Dummies, 2nd Edition
978-0-7645-8418-3

Horseback Riding For Dummies
978-0-470-09719-9

Infertility For Dummies†
978-0-470-11518-3

Meditation For Dummies with CD-ROM, 2nd Edition
978-0-471-77774-8

Post-Traumatic Stress Disorder For Dummies
978-0-470-04922-8

Puppies For Dummies, 2nd Edition
978-0-470-03717-1

Thyroid For Dummies, 2nd Edition†
978-0-471-78755-6

Type 1 Diabetes For Dummies*†
978-0-470-17811-9

* Separate Canadian edition also available
† Separate U.K. edition also available

 **WILEY**

INTERNET & DIGITAL MEDIA

AdWords For Dummies
978-0-470-15252-2

Blogging For Dummies, 2nd Edition
978-0-470-23017-6

Digital Photography All-in-One Desk Reference For Dummies, 3rd Edition
978-0-470-03743-0

Digital Photography For Dummies, 5th Edition
978-0-7645-9802-9

Digital SLR Cameras & Photography For Dummies, 2nd Edition
978-0-470-14927-0

eBay Business All-in-One Desk Reference For Dummies
978-0-7645-8438-1

eBay For Dummies, 5th Edition*
978-0-470-04529-9

eBay Listings That Sell For Dummies
978-0-471-78912-3

Facebook For Dummies
978-0-470-26273-3

The Internet For Dummies, 11th Edition
978-0-470-12174-0

Investing Online For Dummies, 5th Edition
978-0-7645-8456-5

iPod & iTunes For Dummies, 5th Edition
978-0-470-17474-6

MySpace For Dummies
978-0-470-09529-4

Podcasting For Dummies
978-0-471-74898-4

Search Engine Optimization For Dummies, 2nd Edition
978-0-471-97998-2

Second Life For Dummies
978-0-470-18025-9

Starting an eBay Business For Dummies, 3rd Edition†
978-0-470-14924-9

GRAPHICS, DESIGN & WEB DEVELOPMENT

Adobe Creative Suite 3 Design Premium All-in-One Desk Reference For Dummies
978-0-470-11724-8

Adobe Web Suite CS3 All-in-One Desk Reference For Dummies
978-0-470-12099-6

AutoCAD 2008 For Dummies
978-0-470-11650-0

Building a Web Site For Dummies, 3rd Edition
978-0-470-14928-7

Creating Web Pages All-in-One Desk Reference For Dummies, 3rd Edition
978-0-470-09629-1

Creating Web Pages For Dummies, 8th Edition
978-0-470-08030-6

Dreamweaver CS3 For Dummies
978-0-470-11490-2

Flash CS3 For Dummies
978-0-470-12100-9

Google SketchUp For Dummies
978-0-470-13744-4

InDesign CS3 For Dummies
978-0-470-11865-8

Photoshop CS3 All-in-One Desk Reference For Dummies
978-0-470-11195-6

Photoshop CS3 For Dummies
978-0-470-11193-2

Photoshop Elements 5 For Dummies
978-0-470-09810-3

SolidWorks For Dummies
978-0-7645-9555-4

Visio 2007 For Dummies
978-0-470-08983-5

Web Design For Dummies, 2nd Edition
978-0-471-78117-2

Web Sites Do-It-Yourself For Dummies
978-0-470-16903-2

Web Stores Do-It-Yourself For Dummies
978-0-470-17443-2

LANGUAGES, RELIGION & SPIRITUALITY

Arabic For Dummies
978-0-471-77270-5

Chinese For Dummies, Audio Set
978-0-470-12766-7

French For Dummies
978-0-7645-5193-2

German For Dummies
978-0-7645-5195-6

Hebrew For Dummies
978-0-7645-5489-6

Ingles Para Dummies
978-0-7645-5427-8

Italian For Dummies, Audio Set
978-0-470-09586-7

Italian Verbs For Dummies
978-0-471-77389-4

Japanese For Dummies
978-0-7645-5429-2

Latin For Dummies
978-0-7645-5431-5

Portuguese For Dummies
978-0-471-78738-9

Russian For Dummies
978-0-471-78001-4

Spanish Phrases For Dummies
978-0-7645-7204-3

Spanish For Dummies
978-0-7645-5194-9

Spanish For Dummies, Audio Set
978-0-470-09585-0

The Bible For Dummies
978-0-7645-5296-0

Catholicism For Dummies
978-0-7645-5391-2

The Historical Jesus For Dummies
978-0-470-16785-4

Islam For Dummies
978-0-7645-5503-9

Spirituality For Dummies, 2nd Edition
978-0-470-19142-2

NETWORKING AND PROGRAMMING

ASP.NET 3.5 For Dummies
978-0-470-19592-5

C# 2008 For Dummies
978-0-470-19109-5

Hacking For Dummies, 2nd Edition
978-0-470-05235-8

Home Networking For Dummies, 4th Edition
978-0-470-11806-1

Java For Dummies, 4th Edition
978-0-470-08716-9

Microsoft® SQL Server™ 2008 All-in-One Desk Reference For Dummies
978-0-470-17954-3

Networking All-in-One Desk Reference For Dummies, 2nd Edition
978-0-7645-9939-2

Networking For Dummies, 8th Edition
978-0-470-05620-2

SharePoint 2007 For Dummies
978-0-470-09941-4

Wireless Home Networking For Dummies, 2nd Edition
978-0-471-74940-0